MASTER QUILTER'S WO

Illustrated Guide to Scrap Miniature Magic™

By Christine Carlson

HOUSE of WHITE BIRCHES
PUBLISHERS SINCE 1947

Table of Contents

Illustrated Guide to Scrap Miniature Magic

- 5 About This Book
- 6 Getting Started
- 14 Choosing Fabric
- 20 Working With Fabric
- 22 Construction Techniques
- 32 Finishing Your Quilt
- 38 Special Techniques
- 41 Illustrated Guide to Bias Squares

Projects

- 45 Country Star
- 49 Old-Fashioned Scrappy
- 52 Scrappy Hole in the Barn Door
- 56 Homecoming
- 60 Whirling Crowns
- 64 Dainty Basket
- 67 Spools Variation
- 70 Swedish Chain
- 74 Fiery Baskets
- 78 Radiant Bear Paw
- 83 Churn Dash Delight
- 86 Crown of Thorns
- 90 Clothing
- 94 Country Folk
- 98 Fanciful Daisies
- 102 Fans
- 106 3-D Sunbonnet Sue
- 110 Nine-Patch Floral Garden
- 115 Kaleidoscope
- 118 Sunbonnet Sue & Sam
- 122 Log Cabin Pine Trees
- 125 Log Cabin Baby Dolls

Editors: Jeanne Stauffer, Sandra L. Hatch; **Associate Editor:** Dianne Schmidt; **Technical Artist:** Connie Rand; **Copy Editors:** Michelle Beck, Sue Harvey, Nicki Lehman, Mary Martin; **Graphic Design:** Jessi Butler; **Graphic Artist:** Ronda Bechinski; **Photography:** Kelly Heydinger; **Photography Stylist:** Tammy Nussbaum

ILLUSTRATED GUIDE TO SCRAP MINIATURE MAGIC is published by House of White Birches, 306 East Parr Road, Berne, IN 46711, telephone (260) 589-4000. Printed in USA. Copyright © 2003 House of White Birches. RETAILERS: If you would like to carry this pattern book or any other House of White Birches publications, call the Wholesale Department at Annie's Attic to set up a direct account: (903) 636-4303. Also, request a complete listing of publications available from House of White Birches. Every effort has been made to ensure that the instructions in this pattern book are complete and accurate. We cannot, however, take responsibility for human error, typographical mistakes or variations in individual work.

E-mail: Customer_Service@whitebirches.com

Library of Congress Number: 2003100521
ISBN: 1-59217-020-X   1 2 3 4 5 6 7 8 9

About This Book

*M*iniature quiltmaking has opened up a whole new avenue of exploration for many quilters. Techniques and tools previously reserved for full-size projects have been refined and scaled down to help make miniature quilting available for all quilters.

Miniature quiltmaking provides the perfect opportunity to enjoy the creative options of different block settings. Patterns and color may be explored on a small scale, which helps to encourage originality. The skills you use carry over to benefit other aspects of your quiltmaking, so making miniatures is a good place for a beginner to start.

Even if you have never sewn a miniature quilt before, the subject matter in the pre-assembly section includes many helpful hints to help make your sewing a pleasurable, informative and stress-free experience. It is recommended this section be read entirely before starting a project.

Miniature quiltmaking satisfies the need to complete a quilt quickly. These little quilts do not require as much time or fabric as larger quilts. Many quilts in this book use a variety of scrap fabrics while others use stash pieces small enough to be considered a scrap. In addition, the pieces are small so they are very portable, making them the perfect take-along project. An added bonus is that everyone who sees the results thinks you are so talented. Friends, family and colleagues are always thrilled to receive a small quilt because, even if they do not quilt themselves, they realize they have received a special gift from the heart.

If you are new to miniature quiltmaking, you are in for a pleasurable learning experience—one that might change your quilting habits forever.

MEET THE DESIGNER

Christine Carlson, born and raised in the Chicago area, brought up her two children in Florida before moving to the Atlanta area and starting her miniature quilting career.

As her love of quilting became a passion she saw that she would never be able to make all the quilts she desired in her lifetime, so she focused on miniature quiltmaking as a way of satisfying her designing and sewing skills. Over time this lead to authoring, teaching and lecturing regionally and nationally.

Her first book, *Bias Square Miniatures,* published in 1995 by That Patchwork Place, laid the groundwork for her working exclusively with a miniature bias square ruler technique. Taking writing and designing a step further, this *Scrap Miniature Magic* book is a compilation of many diverse techniques applicable for miniature quiltmaking.

To date, Christine has completed over 325 miniature quilts, many representing near and dear patterns to quilters as well as a large collection of her own original designs. In her collection are also many miniatures she's made using authentic 1930s and 1940s fabrics; her favorite era is easily seen in her miniatures. Although mostly self-taught, Christine attended many American Quilter's Society classes and lectures, and often refers to her large book collection featuring current and antique quilts for design ideas and authenticity as well as viewing many quilt shows.

Aside from collecting antique fabric, antique quilts and antique quilt tops, Christine salvages old quilt tops in need of repair or restoration. When too fragile to quilt, she backs them with comparable fabric for easy display, or uses the pieces to sew pillows or miniature quilts, many with fabric from the 1800s.

For evening relaxation, Christine enjoys counted cross-stitch sampler handiwork, as well as making numerous miniature rugs with counted cross-stitch patterns from around the world. Another side interest is making and teaching loom-made rag rugs as a perfect way to use up leftover memento fabric. Christine also enjoys designing original cloth dolls and of course, dresses them in antique fabric finery.

Christine's one wish is that her only grandchild, Cortney, being surrounded with quilts and fabric, will one day follow in her footsteps and keep the family quilting legacy alive.

Getting Started

WHAT IS A MINIATURE QUILT?

The expressions miniature quilts, small quilts and doll quilts are all synonymous. For the sake of simplicity, in many quilt books and magazines small quilts are considered miniature, although there are some whose block size does not fit the miniature description.

According to many quilt show guidelines, measurements for a miniature quilt cannot exceed 24" on any one side with blocks no larger than 3" x 3". However, these measurements need further clarification.

Block size is only relevant when based on complexity. For example, a 3" Nine-Patch block will not appear miniature when placed next to another 3" block having many seams and block pieces. But a 1½" Nine-Patch block is considered miniature since each square in the block is only ½".

Quilt size is also only relevant when based on complexity. It is judged, for example, by the number of blocks, their difficulty, arrangement and size and how the border is handled in relation to the quilt size.

A miniature quilt has many of the same elements as a full-size quilt, such as value, proportion, contrast and balance, and is, in many respects, a replica of a full-size quilt. However, one difference between the two is that the small intricacies of a miniature quilt encourages the viewer to come closer, while many full-size quilts are best viewed from a distance.

COLOR & FABRIC

Scrap miniature quilts are exciting to make because the full impact of combining so many different fabrics will not be seen until all blocks are sewn together.

Needing special consideration, scrap miniature quilts differ from full-size scrap quilts because they require a planned color study due to their small size. Discrepant colors will stand out like a sore thumb. As a rule, I handpick scrap fabrics in a controlled color combination.

If uncertain, think of putting a quilt together in terms of light, medium and dark fabric values so that you can still differentiate between the pieces. Then sort your scrap collection accordingly. To help achieve that scrappy look, search for prints in a variety of scales and designs and from different eras.

Stick to a theme because this provides cohesion or a focus that will bind everything together. This is readily seen with the *Kaleidoscope* quilt in which vivid colors coordinate with a border that is equally outstanding in color.

A coordinating color and fabric theme is found in the *Fanciful Daisies* quilt in which antique fabrics all having the same look are used for both flowers and borders.

To augment your scrap collection, ask fellow quilters to save their scraps for you. Send away for precut fabric squares advertised in quilt magazines and, of course, save scraps from your own larger-size projects.

ASSEMBLY & SEAMS

During the block assembly process, the measurements specified include dimensions for accurate piecing. Seam pressing is indicated by little seams and directional arrows on the drawings for guess-free pressing. The quilt size given for each project includes the binding. All quilt pieces are identified with a letter to match assembly directions, including border pieces. The Materials list specifies items needed for all aspects of sewing including thread and supplies.

The use of a sewing machine and rotary-cutting equipment make for faster and more accurate piecing, and sewing with a ¼"-wide seam allowance allows for easy piecing.

Kaleidoscope quilt

SUPPLY LIST

If any special notions are needed for any quilt, they will be listed with each project. All projects require some basic sewing supplies and tools as follows:

1. Sewing machine with an accurate $1/4$"-wide seam allowance
2. No. 65 or No. 70 machine needle
3. A good-quality thread, such as Mettler Metrosene Polyester Plus thread, which may be found in any quilt shop
4. 100 percent cotton fabric
5. Small, sharp-tip fabric scissors
6. Long, straight-head silk pins
7. Magnetic pin holder—do not use with computerized sewing machine
8. Fine-point seam ripper
9. Stiletto—found at quilt shop
10. Steam/dry iron and ironing board
11. Light body fabric spray sizing—found at grocery store, sometimes called spray starch
12. Small brass pins or white basting thread for layering
13. 1" x 12" C-Thru No. W25 ruler found at office supply store
14. $1/4$"-gridded plastic template product and marker
15. Paper-cutting scissors

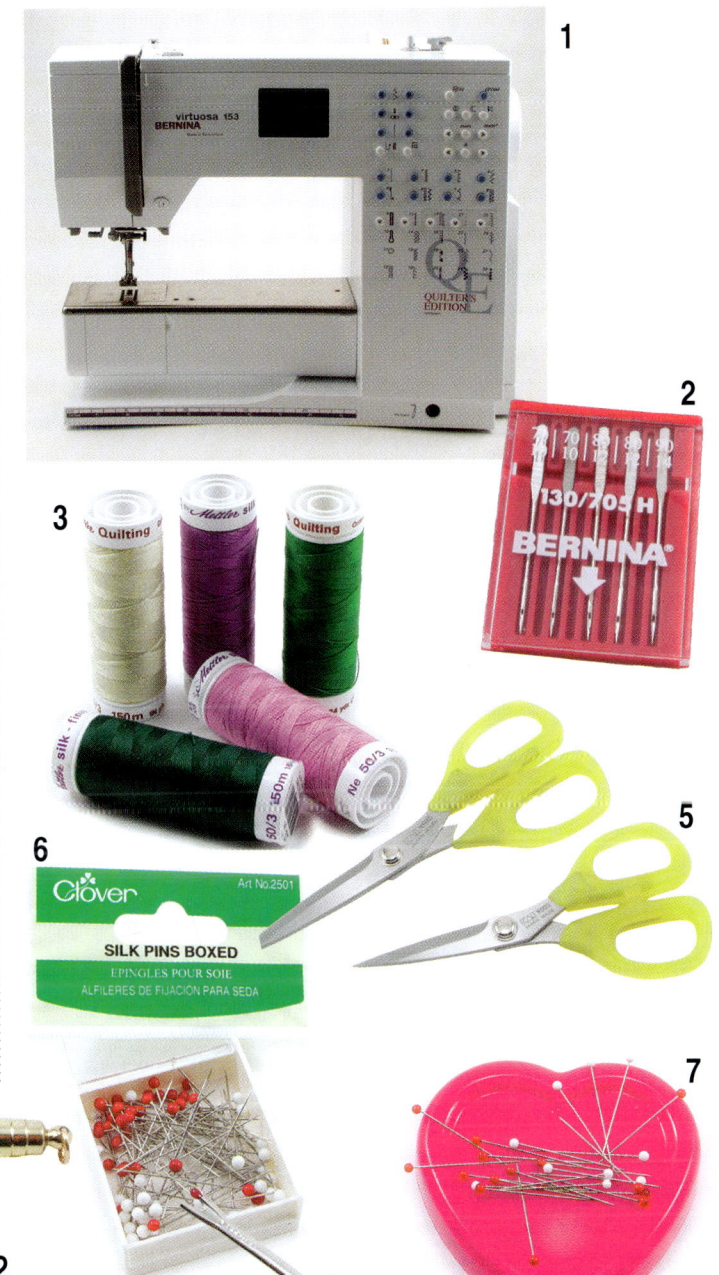
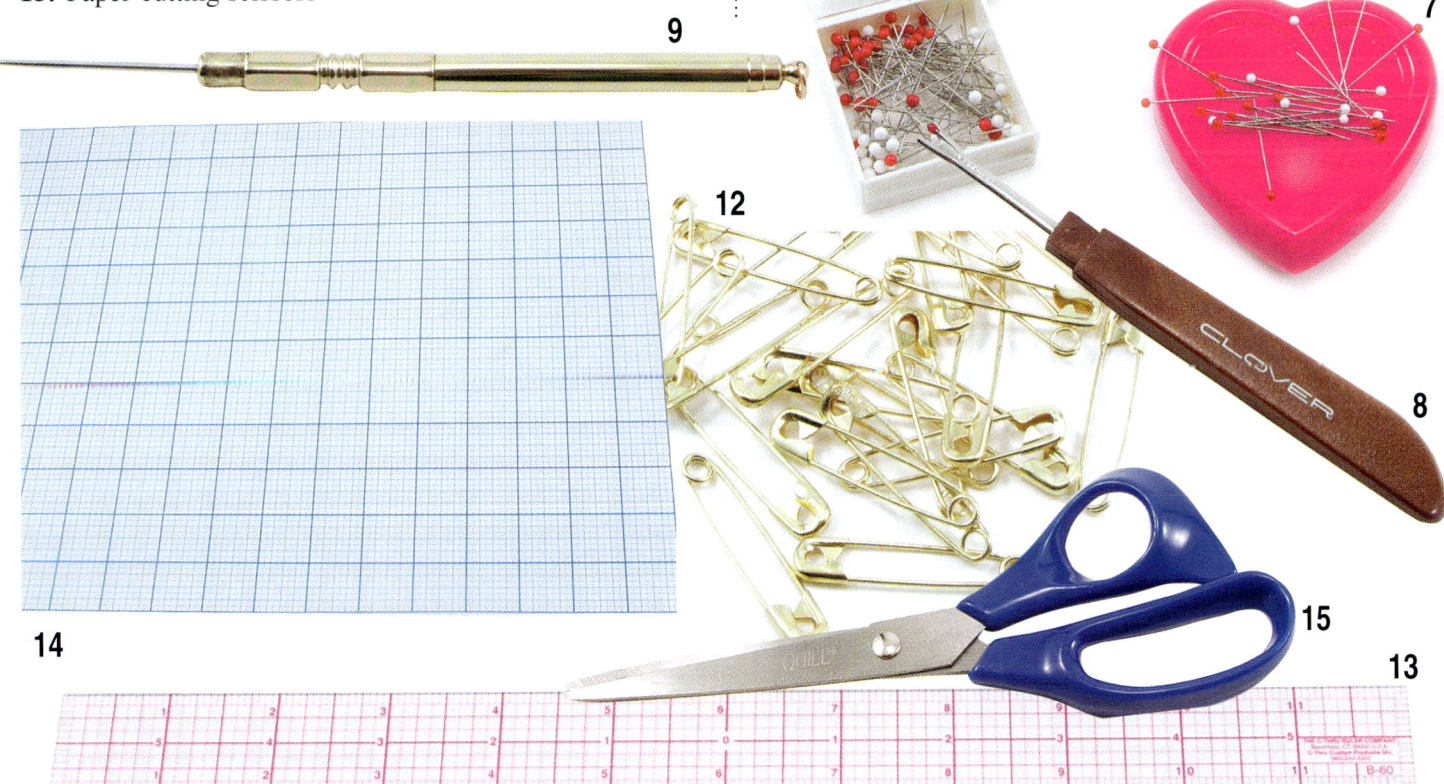

Illustrated Guide to Scrap Miniature Magic 7

PLANNING

To save a lot of headaches, start by planning your quilt project. Here are some practical suggestions:

- Every quilt plan in this book is classified with a sewing-skill level. Even though you may have already made many large-size projects, this may be your first miniature quilt, so consider beginning with an easy quilt plan having larger-size blocks. As your skills progress, proceed to a more complicated pattern.

- If you can sew with an accurate 1/4"-wide seam allowance, know quilting terminology, have little trouble following a pattern and have a grip on using rotary-cutting equipment, any skill-level pattern is suitable.

- After choosing fabric, the next step is figuring if there is enough to cut your pieces, unless large pieces are available. If uncertain, or if it is a different size than listed with the quilt plan, measure and draft fabric to scale on 1/4"-gridded graph paper, with each grid square equaling one square inch of fabric. Measure and pencil in the required fabric pieces and make note of grain lines.

- If using the same block fabric for borders and binding, set aside enough fabric to accommodate cutting these pieces before cutting smaller block pieces. Wait until the quilt top is finished to cut these long pieces as the quilt top must be measured first.

- Cut just enough fabric to make a sample block for previewing fabric choices and checking sewing accuracy. Be flexible here again as you may have to swap out fabrics or make a sewing adjustment. If fabric is limited, make a sample block with different scrap fabrics.

WHICH COMES FIRST—FABRIC OR PATTERN?

The question of which comes first, the fabric or the pattern, often depends on whether you have some particular fabric in mind before you begin. This could be a floral or novelty print that you want to accentuate or harmonize with other fabrics as seen in the *Fanciful Daisies* quilt. You might have a great collection of country prints and want an uncomplicated pattern that will complement them. *Whirling Crowns* is a good example of this situation.

Whirling Crowns

On the other hand, it may not matter at all, as almost any pattern can lend itself to a variety of impressions from 1930–1940 reproduction prints to something brilliantly hand-dyed. It all depends on the look you want to convey, and the color and print you use will determine this.

DRAFTING THE BLOCKS

To draft a block, you need some specific supplies:

- Draftsman's quality 1/8"- or 1/4"-gridded graph paper
- .2–.3mm hard-lead mechanical pencil
- 1" x 12" C-Thru No. W25 plastic ruler
- Eraser

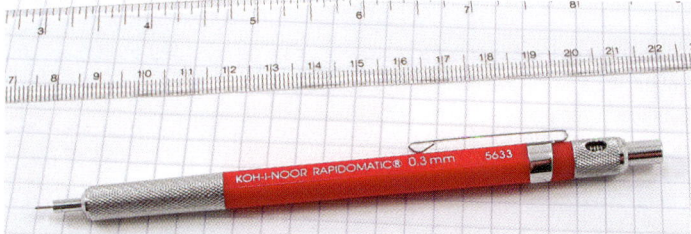

Fanciful Daisies

8 Master Quilter's Workshop

An accurate way of either reducing or scaling down a large block, or increasing or scaling up a small block for usable miniature quiltmaking is easy to accomplish with simple drafting.

Keep in mind that the simpler the block, such as a Nine-Patch, the easier it is to scale it down in size. However, it will lose its miniature block appearance if scaled up too large. A complicated block having many seams is best when drafted to a not-too-small, workable size.

Blocks either have equal-size units, such as the Nine-Patch block in the *Swedish Chain* quilt, or unequal-size units, as in the *Scrappy Hole in the Barn Door* quilt as shown in Figures 1 and 2. The goal is to draft a block with units kept in the same proportion as the original block.

 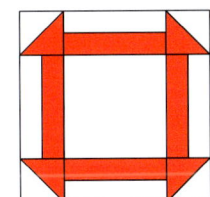

Figure 1
The Nine-Patch block has equal-size units.

Figure 2
The Hole in the Barn Door block has unequal-size units.

To get started, count the number of units in a block and determine the size they are and the size you want them to be when finished. Draw a new finished-size block on graph paper, using the number of units and their new size as a guide. For example, a finished 9" Nine-Patch block can be readily drafted down to a 3" block if using a 1" unit measurement, or a $1^1/2$" block if using a $1/2$" unit as shown in Figure 3.

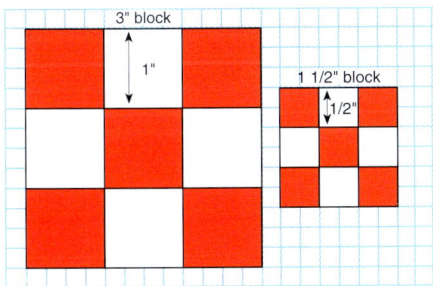

Figure 3
A Nine-Patch block can be easily drafted down from 3" to 1 1/2" by changing the size of each unit.

After drawing a finished block, label each piece. Next, draw each piece individually, adding a $1/4$" seam allowance all around, and record the dimensions. Use these for making templates or figuring cutting measurements as shown in Figure 4.

The unit method is problematic with any odd-size block, such as one measuring $2^3/16$", because this number cannot be divided evenly by any other number. It helps to always try to stay with an even unit measurement, such as $1/2$" or $3/4$", and not an odd size, such as $3/16$" or $7/8$", for easier math computation.

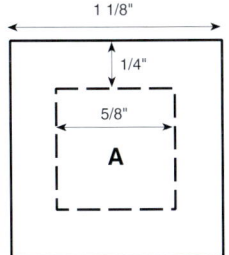

Figure 4
Draw the template finished size and add a 1/4" seam allowance; add template label.

Use a $1/8$"-gridded graph paper if the finished block ends with a $1/8$" measurement such as a $2^1/8$" x $2^1/8$" block size.

BLOCK SETTINGS

Quilt blocks may be set several different ways—straight, or side by side, or on point, or on the diagonal.

Side-by-side blocks can either be sewn together, or a sashing can be used to separate them. This is especially useful if there are a lot of seams to match. Adding sashing will automatically expand the quilt size as shown in Figures 5 and 6.

Figure 5
Blocks may be set side by side as shown.

Figure 6
Adding sashing strips enlarges the size of the quilt.

Illustrated Guide to Scrap Miniature Magic **9**

An example of a quilt with blocks set side by side is *Spools Variation*. An example of a quilt with blocks set side by side (or in vertical rows) with sashing is *Log Cabin Pine Trees*.

A little different example is the *Churn Dash Delight*. The pieced blocks in this quilt are set off using plaid squares to add a little interest to the background.

Churn Dash Delight

Setting blocks on the diagonal expands the quilt size and requires setting triangles. The blocks and triangles may be sewn together in diagonal rows or separated by sashing strips, which expands the quilt size even further as shown in Figures 7 and 8.

Figure 7
Blocks may be set on point, or on the diagonal, using setting squares and triangles.

Spools Variation and *Log Cabin Pine Trees*

Figure 8
On-point blocks combine with sashing strips to expand the size of the quilt.

Diagonally set blocks also add visual interest. Look at the *Flaming Baskets* quilt whose points peak upward. Turned on their sides, these blocks would lack visual interest and appear quite ordinary.

Flaming Baskets

Other examples of quilts with blocks set on the diagonal are the *Log Cabin Baby Dolls* and *Swedish Chain*.

The way a block is set can also change its appearance. Take the Scrappy Hole in the Barn Door block. When set side by side or straight, it has one look. When set on point, it takes on a completely different look as shown in Figure 9.

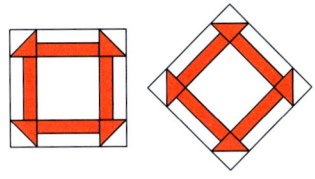

Figure 9
The Hole in the Barn Door block takes on a different look when set straight or on point.

Log Cabin Baby Dolls

If undecided about how to set blocks, set up a viewing area that allows you to step back and look at each setting choice from a distance.

FIGURING SIZE OF DIAGONAL BLOCK SETTING TRIANGLES

When quilt blocks are set on point or on the diagonal, outside triangular-shaped empty spaces will appear on all corners and sides as shown in Figure 10. To fill these side and corner spaces, triangles are cut from squares and their resulting outside edges will be on the straight of the grain. The square sizes and how they are cut depend on the placement of the triangles. The following examples are figured for use with a 2" finished-size block.

Figure 10
Half-square triangles are used on the corners and quarter-square triangles are used on the side, top and bottom edges.

The corner triangles are called half-square triangles because a square is cut once on the diagonal to result in

Illustrated Guide to Scrap Miniature Magic **11**

two triangles. Draw a 2"-long straight line. Draw a line at each end at a 45-degree angle to the first line to make a right-angle triangle as shown in Figure 11. Add a ¼"-wide seam allowance all around the edges. Measure the length of one of the shorter triangle sides referring to Figure 12, which is 2¼". Therefore, the cut size of the square is 2¼" x 2¼", which, when cut once on the diagonal, results in two half-square triangles for the quilt corners.

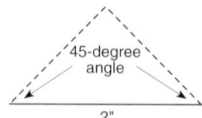

Figure 11
Draw a 2" line; draw a line at each end at a 45-degree angle to the first line to make a right-angle triangle.

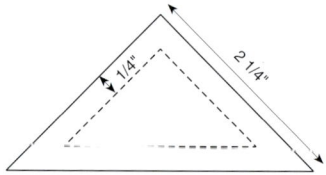

Figure 12
Add a 1/4" seam allowance all around; measure 1 side to determine the size to cut the squares.

Swedish Chain

Side triangles are called quarter-square triangles because a larger square is cut on both diagonals to result in four triangles as shown in Figure 13. In this case, the longest side of the triangle should be on the straight of grain of the fabric.

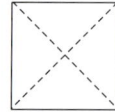

Figure 13
A quarter-square triangle results from cutting a square on both diagonals.

To figure the size to cut the square for a quarter-square triangle, draw a line from corner to corner on a 2" square. Measure the length, which is 2⅞". Add 1¼" to this measurement to include a seam allowance for each of the four triangles; the cut size of the square would be 4⅛" x 4⅛" or 2⅞" + 1¼" = 4⅛". The number of squares needed depends on the number of blocks in a quilt plan. The one shown in Figure 10 needs six quarter-square triangles, which means you would need to cut two squares; two triangles would be wasted.

The reason for cutting the squares this way is straight-of-grain consistency. The half-square triangle is used when the straight of grain has to be on the short sides of the triangle as shown in Figure 14. The quarter-square triangle is used when the straight of grain has to be on the longest side of the triangle, again referring to Figure 14. The

general rule of thumb concerning grain is that if a piece will be on the outside edge of a block or quilt, that edge should be cut on the straight of grain.

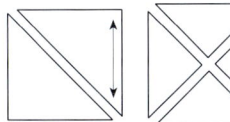

Figure 14
Straight-of-grain lines are shown on the half-square and quarter-square triangles.

FLOATING BLOCKS

A quick-and-easy way to impart visual interest to diagonally set quilt blocks is to float them against the quilt background by using oversized setting triangles as shown in Figure 15. When the border is sewn on, there will be a measurable space between a block corner and border seam. This technique also easily expands the quilt size. Either a solid or a print fabric may be used.

Figure 15
The side and corner triangles provide a space between the blocks and the borders so that the pieced blocks appear to float on the background.

Cut squares for setting triangles at least 3/4" larger than required, even bigger if undecided. The bigger the triangle, the wider the space. The extra triangle fabric can always be trimmed down if the space is too wide.

The *Swedish Chain* quilt has a space of 3/8" between the points of each outside block and the border seam. A dramatic violet solid fabric is used for the setting triangles, giving a good visual separation between the blocks and borders. See photos on the bottom of page 12.

3-D Sunbonnet Sue

Another good example of floating blocks is the *3-D Sunbonnet Sue* quilt. Here the extra space is covered up by the narrow pink sashing. With this quilt, a white solid fabric is used effectively for both the quilt block background and the setting triangles. ❖

Tip

It is helpful to cut squares for corner triangles about 1/4" larger than required. The extra fabric makes it easier to square the quilt top corners before layering. Rounding-up any odd-size measurements resulting in over-sized squares and triangles works in the same way.

Choosing Fabric

Due to their small size, the most important and outstanding component of a successful miniature quilt is the effective use of color. The presence or lack of a winning coloration is the first thing that will be noticed instead of imperfect piecing or quilting stitches.

If stumped when choosing colors, overcome this by following a few general guidelines regarding value, contrast and proportion. Value and contrast go hand in hand—both are used to differentiate small quilt pieces and add visual interest.

ELEMENTS OF COLOR

Value: Value refers to the significance or merit of a color. A fabric's value is determined by other fabrics it is with. For example, place a medium-value color next to a light color, and the medium color will appear dark. Place this same color next to a dark color, and it will appear light. (Photo 1)

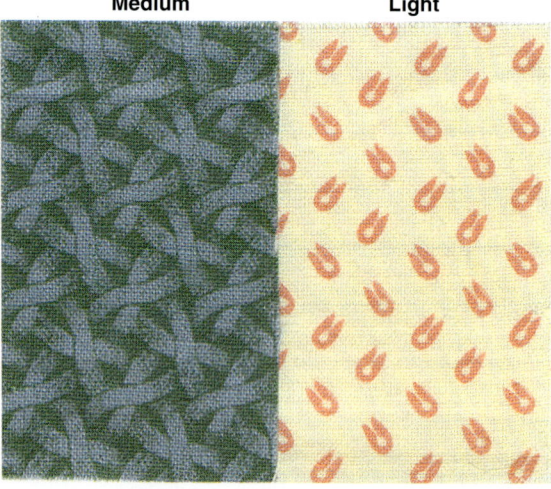

1. The blue/green fabric looks dark when placed with a light fabric but looks light in value next to the dark fabric.

Value is designated into categories of light, medium and dark as shown in Photo 2. There are degrees of value within each category, such as medium-light and medium-dark.

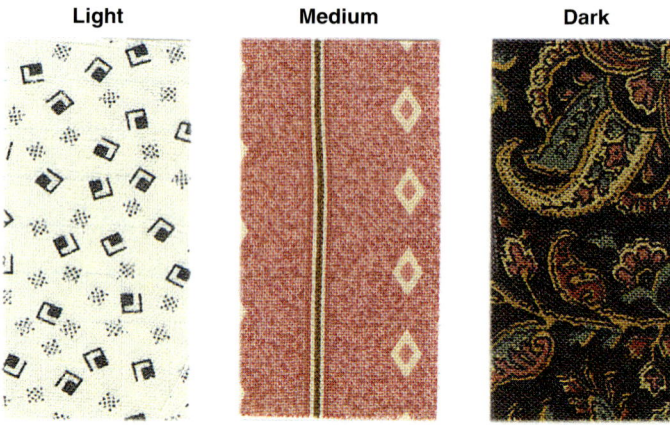

2. The first step in deciding value is to separate your fabric into light, medium and dark categories.

A quilt having all the same values, such as just light pastels, will not be as eye-catching as one in which the value is more dramatically defined. A poor use of color value can be seen in the *Fans* (page 102) quilt in which the setting triangles and squares are a medium value. The blocks would stand out more if a lighter value had been used for the setting pieces.

Contrast: To achieve contrast, use appropriate block background and/or quilt background fabric. The more contrast, the greater the differentiation. A good example of this is the *Log Cabin Baby Dolls* quilt with a light background, which makes the blocks stand out.

Contrast is also achieved by varying or heightening the intensity of saturation of a color. For example, change from light to bright, such as pale yellow to golden yellow, or dark to deep, such as dark blue to midnight blue. This is especially applicable when working with only a few colors.

The decision about how much color to use should be based on the proportion or balance to the quilt plan and surrounding colors. For example, no one color should overwhelm others in piece size or intensity. A good example of this is the *Homecoming* quilt (page 56) in which the use of solid white does not overpower the total quilt plan and, in fact, picks up the white in the prints. *The Country Folk* quilt (page 94) is another good example showing distinct colors that are not overwhelming.

EFFECTIVE USE OF COLOR

To use color effectively, work with a specific color family

3. Color schemes, such as these pastel prints, combine to give a spring look.

4. The earth tones in this collection range in value from light (gold) to dark (blue).

5. The glowing, hot prints in this collection share geometric qualities.

or scheme to enhance a quilt's theme, such as all Easter pastels, subdued earth tones or glowing, hot prints as shown in Photos 3–5.

Use color to convey a certain feeling or mood. Red, white and blue colors convey a patriotic message, dark colors convey a masculine or somber mood. Integrate a color recipe, such as country colors of cranberry, tan, navy blue and dark green. Look for the smallest pieces in a quilt plan and make them the most outstanding. Using all subdued solids brings to mind Amish-style quilts.

Draw on red, yellow and black colors to create movement as they cause the eye to move over a quilt to find its match.

Colors also impart temperature to a quilt. Pale green is soothing and tranquil, while a brilliant red appears hot and unsettling. If feeling lost, refer to a color wheel and choose colors in an uncomplicated format.

Illustrated Guide to Scrap Miniature Magic **15**

If uncertain of color placement, draw a block or quilt design on graph paper. Place lightweight tracing paper over it and start filling in spaces with coloring pens or crayons. When finished with one color family, replace the tracing paper and color again with a different color combination.

Hang up the various colorings, stand back, and choose the most engaging and eye-appealing drawing on which to base your quilt.

WORKING WITH FABRIC

Buying Fabric: Choose only top-quality, 100 percent cotton fabric, which can always be found at your local quilt shop. A good fabric has a high (200) thread count, does not stretch much when pulled on the crosswise grain and shows good color value.

Amount to Purchase: One-half fat quarter cuts (11" x 18") and fat quarter cuts (18" x 22") are always good choices for miniature quilts. They are easy to work with and perfect for long border pieces. Coordinating bundles are readily found at quilt shops, making shopping easy and guess-free with no decisions.

Do not be dismayed if that stack of handpicked fabrics does not all work together when you begin your quilt. Quilts are known to have a life of their own, so be flexible and willing to swap out fabrics. This is the reason all quilters need to continually add to their fabric stashes.

Scale: Select prints in a variety of scale, from small to medium-small to keep them in proportion to the small scale of miniature quiltmaking (Photos 6 and 7). A medium-size print is useful for border or backing as shown in Photo 8. A medium-large print may also be used for borders and backing if many of the print elements are small in scale as shown in Photo 9.

6. Small-scale prints are perfect for miniatures.

7. Medium-small-scale prints will also work well in miniatures.

8. Medium-size prints, such as those shown, may work in miniatures for borders or setting squares and triangles but not in tiny pieces required in blocks.

9. This medium-large print will work for borders on a miniature quilt.

10. Use a variety of fabrics to create texture.

11. Directional fabrics add movement to a quilt and are perfect choices for borders.

12. Movement is created by using boldly patterned border prints.

13. Choose a centerpiece fabric with no more than three colors. Then choose fabrics to coordinate with the centerpiece fabric.

Texture: Add visual texture by incorporating a good variety and range of prints. This includes checks, plaids, stripes, florals, polka dots, calicos, pin dots, paisleys and geometrics as shown in Photo 10.

Movement: Create movement by using fabrics that accentuate direction such as directional prints, plaids, stripes or whirly prints. These add excitement to a miniature quilt. The *Scrappy Hole in the Barn Door* quilt (page 52) uses several border prints that add movement to the quilt.

Borders: Boldly patterned directional prints are excellent fabric choices for borders. However, remember that you are creating a miniature quilt and keep the scale of the print small (Photos 11 and 12).

Centerpiece Print: Start fabric choices with a centerpiece print having no more than three colors. Use this fabric as a coordinating tool for remaining fabric choices. A fabric with an even or allover design is preferable to one containing scattered designs as shown in Photos 13–15.

Illustrated Guide to Scrap Miniature Magic **17**

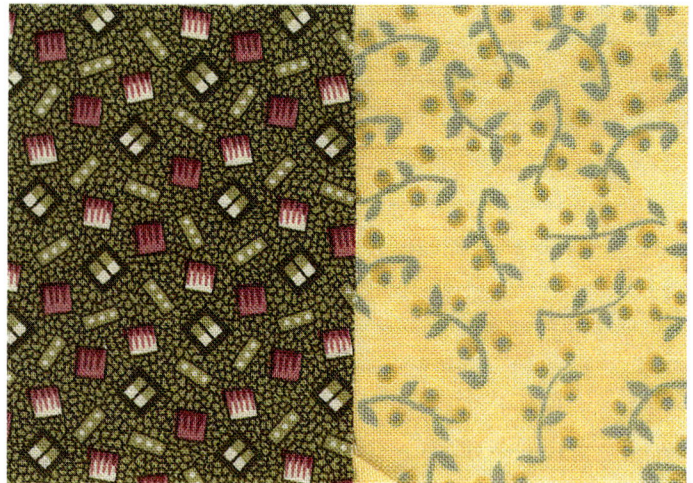 

14. *These fabrics are examples of even, allover prints.*   15. *These fabrics are examples of widely scattered prints.*

Choosing Setting Fabrics: Use care when choosing fabrics for setting blocks and triangles. This fabric should complement, not compete with, the pieced or appliquéd blocks. Avoid a small, dense print as it can appear as a blur or a solid when viewed from a distance (Photo 16).

Using Solids: When a quilt is made with just solid fabrics, it is important to integrate colors that fit into a color category, such as all subdued country colors, all pastels or all intense colors. Use the brightest, lightest or darkest colors for small block pieces to make them stand out (Photos 17 and 18).

Hand-dyed solids add distinctive color and intensity when used in any quilt. Hand dyeing is very easy and can be done at home. Quilt shops carry a line of white solid fabric already primed for hand dyeing. They also often carry a line of hand-dyed fabrics; avoid any of these fabrics that have a washed-out or dull look.

Vintage and Reproduction Prints: Vintage fabrics work up very nicely in miniature quilts due to their irresistible and irreplaceable prints (Photo 19). They have gained popularity, sometimes making them

Overall Random Print   **Densely Packed Print**

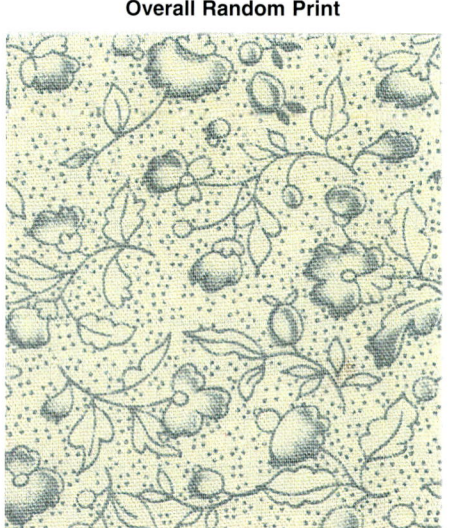 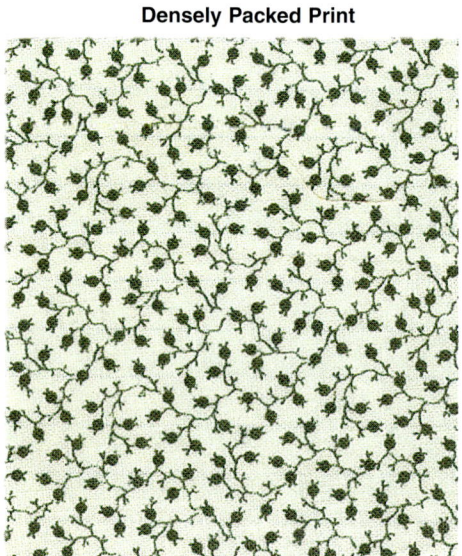

16. *These prints do not make good setting blocks.*

17. *Subdued country-color solids in a range of darks and lights provide contrast.*

18 Master Quilter's Workshop

18. Bright, hand-dyed solids make a cheery statement.

difficult to find and expensive. The hunt is worth the effort. Look for them at quilt shows, antique shops and garage sales. Be sure these fabrics are in excellent condition; worn-out fabrics won't last in a quilt.

Reproduction prints (photo 20) from the 1930s and earlier have been on the quilting scene for some time. Their large range of small-scale prints and pleasing colors make them very desirable and popular for use in miniature quiltmaking. The *Sunbonnet Sue and Sam* (page 118), *Old-Fashioned Scrappy* (page 49) and *Homecoming* (page 56) quilts all use reproduction fabrics.

Using Wool and Flannel: Wool and flannel are difficult to use in miniature quiltmaking. They tend to move around a lot and are difficult to quilt through. They will work in machine paper-foundation piecing.

Felt is compatible with miniature quiltmaking when small, cutout pattern pieces are appliquéd on the quilt top with a blanket stitch. Paper can add unusual and eye-appealing texture to a quilt. Felt can be seen on the *Sunbonnet Sue and Sam* (page 118) and *Log Cabin Baby Dolls* (page 125) quilts.

Auditioning the Fabric: If stumped when making fabric choices, try auditioning the fabric. Cut out small geometric shapes, such as a triangle or square, from white paper and place the paper over the fabric to isolate the print. Start with a border print and work toward the center of the quilt for fabric and color coordination. Set up an audition area where fabric can be seen from a squinting distance.

Remember that the fabric choice is the first thing that will be noticed on a quilt. If it does not pass this first test, the viewer won't bother to take a closer look. Although there are no hard-and-fast rules, and a quilter can choose any color combination and any fabric she likes, it may or may not work to make a successful quilt. ❖

19. Vintage prints create a special look in miniature quilts.

20. Reproduction prints make successful substitutes for real vintage fabrics.

Illustrated Guide to Scrap Miniature Magic **19**

Working With Fabric

Preparing fabric for use requires a few steps. Skipping these steps might create problems in construction steps later.

FABRIC PREPARATION

Once the fabrics have been chosen, they require some work to prepare them for use.

Quilters have a difference of opinion about prewashing fabric. The main reasons a new fabric is washed and dried before use is to check for colorfastness and to shrink it. It is my opinion that fabrics do not need to be prewashed when used in miniature quilts unless they are soiled or tired looking. Miniature quilts are not used the same way larger quilts are and probably won't require cleaning on a regular basis.

New fabrics sometimes have a stiffer feeling from the sizing used during the manufacturing process. This stiffness is an advantage when cutting and sewing pieces for miniature quilts. In fact, I recommend using a spray sizing or starch product if the fabrics are not stiff enough.

Exceptions to my no-prewashing rule are some dark fabrics, especially red, navy blue and dark green. Fabrics with these colors often contain excess dye that might run if using steam heat when pressing, rub off on fingertips during quilting or be transferred to lighter fabrics. If this happens, immediately immerse the quilt in cold water to stop the running action.

To test for colorfastness, place a small piece of fabric in a jar with hot water, cover and shake and let set. If dye runs, place the fabric in hot water and keep changing the water when it cools until the water is clear. Other remedies include the use of salt or vinegar with water to set the dyes.

Another exception to the no-wash rule is any loosely woven fabric such as muslin. This fabric should be washed and placed in a dryer to help shrink and stabilize the weave.

Always pretreat soiled or stained fabrics before ironing as heat will permanently set the stains. Either spot-clean or immerse and soak the fabric in a stain removal agent such as Biz™. Remove cleaning agent by rinsing fabric thoroughly in cold water.

To remove wrinkles or fold lines, liberally spray fabric with light body spray sizing. This not only makes the fabric lie flat, but adds a nice crispness and body back to the fabric, making it easier to cut and sew.

Tip

If washing more than several pieces of fabric, place them in a securely closed nylon net laundry bag to prevent them from becoming tangled.

When treating several pieces that run, place only same-color fabrics together.

Pretreat questionable fabric as soon as it is bought and before storing to prevent guesswork later when needed for a project.

FINDING GRAIN LINES

The selvage or woven edge along the lengthwise edge is useful in helping to find grain lines. If missing, pulling on the fabric in different directions will help you determine the grain. Every fabric has four grain lines, and they are easy to find.

The straight of grain is the true grain line where the horizontal and vertical threads are woven at right angles as shown in Figure 1.

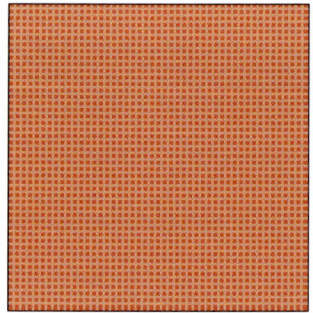

Figure 1
Horizontal and vertical threads are woven at right angles on the fabric's straight of grain.

The lengthwise grain of the fabric runs parallel to the selvage edge as shown in Figure 2. When pulled the fabric has little or no give along the lengthwise grain. Placement of pieces on the straight of grain is a consideration before cutting. It is important the pieces at the outside edges of a block or quilt center be placed on the lengthwise grain of the fabric.

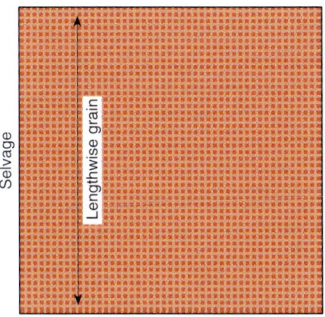

Figure 2
The lengthwise grain of the fabric runs parallel to the selvage edge.

The crosswise grain of fabric runs across the width of the fabric and is perpendicular to the selvage edge as shown in Figure 3. The width is anywhere from 40"–44" on newer fabric but can be as narrow as 36" on vintage yardage. When pulled, the crosswise grain has some stretch.

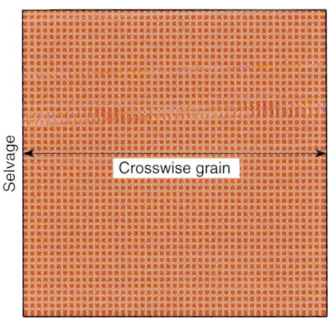

Figure 3
The crosswise grain of fabric runs across the width and is perpendicular to the selvage edge.

The bias grain of fabric refers to a true 45-degree angle across the straight of grain as shown in Figure 4. When pulled, the bias grain will stretch. Folding a square piece of fabric in half on the diagonal will yield a true bias grain line. The true bias grain line is used as a reference when cutting bias strips.

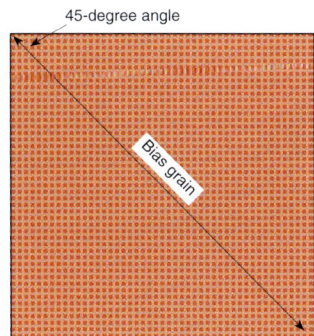

Figure 4
The bias grain of fabric refers to a true 45-degree angle across the straight of grain.

Tip

Square up an odd-size piece of fabric, find the straight of grain and make a square corner at the same time by tearing a strip off one edge and then repeat on an adjacent edge as shown in Figures 5 and 6.

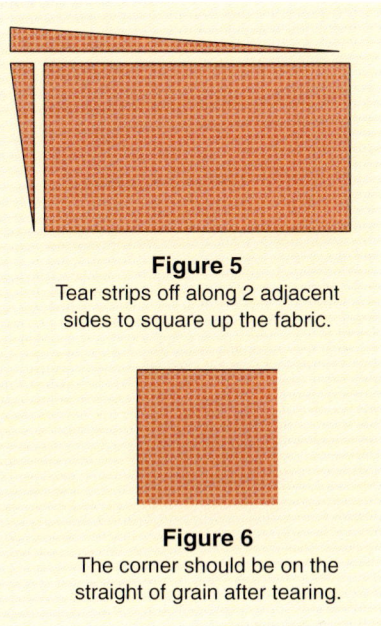

Figure 5
Tear strips off along 2 adjacent sides to square up the fabric.

Figure 6
The corner should be on the straight of grain after tearing.

SQUARING UP FABRIC

When a length of fabric is torn rather than cut off a fabric bolt, one end is often slanted when the fabric is folded in half along the length as shown in Figure 7. This happens when, during the factory winding process, the fabric near the beginning of the bolt gets pulled or skewed unevenly to one side and continues to do so as the entire bolt is wound.

Figure 7
When folded along the length, the ends don't match.

To correct this skewing, wet the fabric and pull on it along the diagonal as shown in Figure 8 to bring its slanted end back to a square shape in order to find an accurate straight of grain. Iron until dry. Or, sometimes a fabric piece can be pulled and steam-pressed into shape. Some fabrics are impossible to square up and may be best used for small pieces.

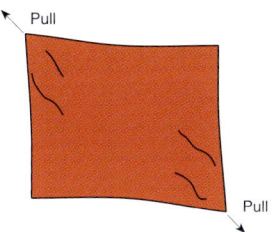

Figure 8
Pull the fabric on the bias to pull the threads back in place.

If fabric has been cut at the quilt shop, it is a good idea to tear a strip off the cut end to see if the fabric is square. ❖

Construction Techniques

Miniature quilts require a few different construction techniques than those used on projects with larger pieces. This section will help you adapt your sewing skills for working the smaller pieces.

YOUR SEWING MACHINE

Many miniature quiltmakers like to hand-stitch their projects. I prefer to use my sewing machine and use quick-cutting and quick-piecing methods. Some adjustments should be made for sewing on tiny pieces. The following methods/techniques work best when working with the tiny units needed to complete a miniature quilt.

For years I have preferred using my vintage Singer Featherweight sewing machine because, aside from producing fine, even stitches, the two feed dogs are closer together and the presser foot is smaller than those on larger machines. This aids in sewing small pieces. The straight-stitch throat plate has a small round hole rather than an oval one, which prevents the machine from chewing up the ends of pieces when starting to stitch.

If you plan to use a larger sewing machine, look for one with a round hole in the throat plate and a clear plastic presser foot.

Tip

Stay with the same sewing machine for the entire project. Switching machines mid project can cause a slight difference in seam allowances resulting in different block sizes.

Before starting a new project, oil and clean the machine, especially the bobbin case.

IRONING & PRESSING

Unlike pressing, ironing involves a sizeable and quick sweeping motion, often with a heavy hand, to remove wrinkles and fold lines.

The rest of the time, use a gentle, slow and light-handed pressing technique, usually with the iron tip. When pressing a seam, sewn block or a quilt top, avoid using a distorting side-to-side motion.

Whether one uses a steam or dry iron is of personal preference. While I do both, I prefer to steam-press seams for a flatter affect. One of my favorite irons is a travel-size one that's perfect for pressing small areas.

The ironing board needs only minimum padding. The flatter the ironing surface, the more accurate the pressing.

As you sew, it is important to press each seam precisely for more accurate piecing and measuring. Finger pressing, or using a wooden pressing stick, does not provide adequate flattening for miniature quiltmaking, except when foundation piecing.

Seams can be pressed either open or together flat to one side. Flat seams are pressed toward the darker fabric. Figure drawings given with each pattern show the direction to press by providing tiny little seams pointing toward the pressing direction. If a drawing is not provided, the instructions provide pressing direction (see Figure 1).

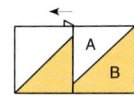

Figure 1
Figure drawings show the direction to press seams.

Be very careful when pressing bias edges to avoid distortion or stretching.

ROTARY CUTTING

All rotary cutting for projects in this book used Omnigrid rotary-cutting rulers—6" x 6" square and 6" x 12" and 3" x 18".

"Measure twice, cut once" is probably the most commonly skipped part of cutting fabric. This is especially important to remember when the only fabric piece available is small, no longer available or perhaps vintage and must be cut right the first time.

Accurate cutting is an important stepping stone to a successful miniature quilt, and using rotary-cutting equipment will help ensure this. Because there is a great variety of rulers, cutters and mats on the market, take a trip to your local quilt shop and ask to sample their cutting equipment to see what you like best.

Use a scaled-down mat size and ruler. Equipment needed for a larger-size project will prove to be unmanageable and may not have the necessary markings needed for miniature quiltmaking. Keep the mat away from extreme cold or heat as they can permanently warp the mat. Omingrid makes scaled-down rulers marked for both left- and right-handed cutters.

Stay with the same ruler(s) for an entire project for more consistent cutting. When cutting larger pieces into smaller ones, do not pick them up for repositioning. Rather, turn the cutting mat around into its new cutting position.

While many quilters like to quick-cut fabric stacked up to four layers, stack only two layers for truly accurate cutting of very small pieces.

Be aware of the very sharp rotary blade and always use the safety shield when laying it down. Never cut over a pin as it will nick the blade, thereby causing skipped or missed threads. Save a dull or nicked blade for cutting paper or other objects and mark the blade as such.

Tip

Stand up for more accurate cutting.

Cut during daylight hours, especially when cutting dark fabrics.

For an odd strip measurement, rotary-cut a strip of 1/8"-gridded graph paper the width of the cut strip and affix to underside of ruler with clear tape. The paper template is now your cutting guide. Use this same technique for cutting odd-shaped pieces.

To keep track of small pieces, place them on paper plates and then stack them. Or, store them in plastic zipper bags for future sewing.

Occasionally, take rotary cutter apart and clean out any accumulated debris.

Hold rotary cutter with one hand and place fingertips of other hand on ruler surface. Place the blade perpendicular to the ruler and always cut in a forward motion and away from your body—never cut toward it. When cutting long strips for borders or binding, walk fingertips up the length of ruler to prevent ruler slippage.

If unfamiliar with rotary-cutting equipment, practice first on scrap pieces until you feel comfortable enough to cut your quilt fabric. Or, often quilt shops will offer a rotary-cutting class.

Fight the temptation to cut all the fabric for a project at one time. A misread or changed quilt plan, figures added up wrong when drafting or a repeated simple mis-cut can add up to unnecessary and discouraging hours of recutting, ripping or resewing.

MACHINE SEWING

You must be able to stitch an accurate 1/4" seam allowance with your sewing machine. Adjust your machine as necessary. Make an accurate seam guide by placing a rotary-cut strip of adhesive moleskin 1/4" away from the machine needle on the throat plate of your machine. Use a small, square rotary ruler to help line it up. Replace or trim when guide edge gets fuzzy from use.

To check for 1/4" sewing accuracy, cut three different fabrics each 1 1/2" x 10"; sew the strips together along the length. Press the seams away from the center strip. Place a 1" x 12" C-Thru ruler down on the center strip; it should measure 1" wide. Next, measure several times across the sewn strips. This measurement should be 3 1/2" wide. If your measurements do not match these, your sewing machine is not stitching an accurate 1/4" seam.

Before starting to sew, run some stitching lines down a fabric scrap to check for even thread tension on both sides of fabric.

Use same thread when threading the machine and in the bobbin, and wind several bobbins ahead of time to save time. Sew the entire length of seam without backstitching.

To begin sewing, hold the two threads back and away from seam, take several stitches to help lock them, then begin sewing. When ending a seam, again take several stitches to help lock them and leave a short tail when cutting off threads.

If a seam needs resewing, rip first then resew. Double seams will only add bulk and interfere with accurate pressing.

Sewing over a pin can bend or break the needle or cause a wave in the seam.

Illustrated Guide to Scrap Miniature Magic

Sit parallel to the sewing machine to avoid shoulder, neck and back stress. Be sure you have adequate light and a comfortable chair with a backrest.

Tip

Avoid large, glass-head pins.

Save sewing small, dark pieces for daylight.

Do not use magnetic seam guide on the throat plate as it can be unknowingly moved out of position.

MATCHING SEAMS

The usual practice of pinning matched seams and then directly sewing the entire seam length is not practical or efficient in miniature quiltmaking. It often results in much ripping and resewing especially with closely spaced seams. However, the "pin and baste" method is ideally suited and results in perfectly matched seams. It is especially helpful when matching more than two seams that meet in one spot.

For seams pressed open, position the two pieces right sides together. From one wrong side, place a pin perpendicularly through both seams and 1/4" down from top raw edges as shown in Figure 2. Align seams, place a pin on either side of them and remove the first pin. With about 4 or 5 basting stitches per inch, sew across matched seams with 1/4"-wide seam allowance. Remove pins and gently open basted area to check for perfect seam alignment as shown in Figure 3. If not, remove basting and start over. Do this for every seam that needs matching along a raw edge.

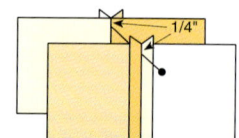

Figure 2
Place a pin perpendicularly through both seams and 1/4" down from top raw edge.

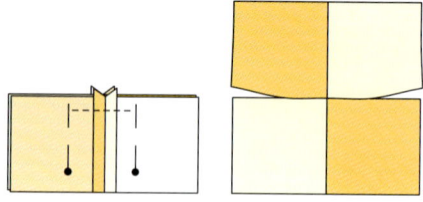

Figure 3
Remove pins and gently open basted area to check for perfect seam alignment.

If seams match, pin and sew entire seam length with about 12–14 stitches per inch as shown in Figure 4. Gently remove basting thread.

For seams pressed flat to one side, place pieces with right sides together and butt or slide opposing seam allowances together for a tight fit as shown in Figure 5. Repeat the above steps of pin and baste for seams being pressed open as shown in Figure 6.

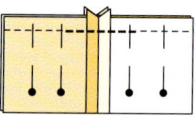

Figure 4
If seams match, pin and sew entire seam length with about 12–14 stitches per inch.

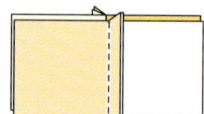

Figure 5
Place pieces with right sides together and butt or slide opposing seam allowances together for a tight fit.

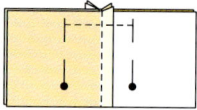

Figure 6
Baste together, matching seams in opposite directions.

A block having all seams pressed open will be more accurate in size than one having seams pressed to one side. In the latter process, a thread or two are taken up in the seam line, and this adds up quickly in a miniature block.

TRIMMING SEAMS

To trim or not is a personal choice, but trimming during assembly does help make a block lie flatter, be more accurate in size and enable easier quilting. However, once a seam or area has been trimmed, it cannot be undone. Therefore, make trimming decisions when making a sample block. Always press first, then trim.

There are two ways to trim. A seam can be trimmed or graded to 1/8"-wide along a seam line to reduce bulk or thickness. For example, if sewing a sashing strip to a pieced block, trim the bulkier block raw edge.

You may want to trim seams to reduce bulk at matching or intersecting seams by trimming off a small triangle across the top of the fabric corners as shown in Figure 7.

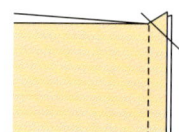

Figure 7
Trim off triangles at ends of seams.

24 *Master Quilter's Workshop*

MEASURING A BLOCK ACCURATELY

Pattern measurements are perfect dimensions and are not always easy to achieve, especially for very small blocks with many pieces.

Block size can be affected by slight variations in sewing machines, needle and thread size, how precisely fabric was cut and sewn, how seams were pressed open or flat and the fabric itself. Any inaccuracy will compound itself, resulting in odd-size blocks that do not match. A block that is a wee bit off-size can be fudged into place. However, if one is way off, it is faster and more accurate to cut and sew a new block.

For accuracy as you sew and press, constantly measure with a 1" x 12" C-Thru ruler to check size. Be prepared to rip, if necessary.

To measure a sewn block accurately, measure the finished-block size in both directions, from inside seam allowance to inside seam allowance as shown in Figure 8. Next, measure the outside block size, which should equal the finished block size plus $1/2$" seam allowance all around as shown in Figure 9.

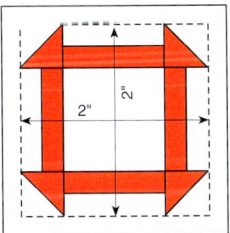

Figure 8
Measure the finished-block size in both directions, from inside seam allowance to inside seam allowance.

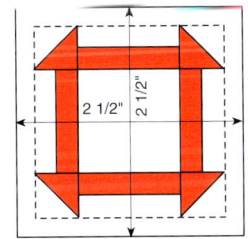

Figure 9
Measure the outside block size, which should equal the finished-block size plus 1/2" seam allowance.

Another way to keep on track is to make a full-size copy of the pattern on a piece of $1/4$"-gridded plastic template material. Next, make a sample block and position the marked template over the block facing right side up to check for sewing accuracy and help pinpoint trouble spots referring to Figure 10.

An identical finished-block size helps assure that everything will fit together, especially if setting blocks side-by-side and matching their seams. It is okay if the blocks are either all larger or all smaller than the quilt plan, as long as their measurements are consistent. However, you must then make some corresponding mathematical adjustments when cutting other pattern pieces, such as sashings and borders.

RIPPING STITCHES

Even the best of quilters have to rip stitches. To remove a line of stitches, use a small-size seam ripper to break every third stitch or so. Remaining stitches can now be easily removed with the seam ripper. Remove all broken threads before resewing.

Be careful when ripping stitches along a bias edge to avoid stretching it, and take care not to snare and break threads in the fabric patches.

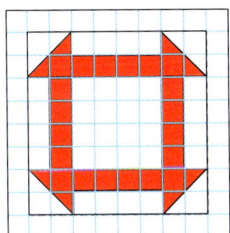

Figure 10
Position the marked template over the block facing right side up to check for sewing accuracy and help pinpoint trouble spots.

ASSEMBLY-LINE PIECING

Assembly-line piecing is a quick-and-easy way to sew up blocks, whether identical or scrap. Place like block pieces in piles next to the sewing machine according to their correct color order and position. After sewing, press them all at once and continue on with more like block pieces in the same fashion until blocks are complete.

Before putting machine needle in fabric, lock threads by making several stitches. After stitching seam, again lock several stitches; then position next piece to be sewn. Repeat locking threads when finished as shown in Figure 11. With this method, block pieces are not butted next to one another and when locked stitches are cut, the stitched ends of each piece will not come unstitched.

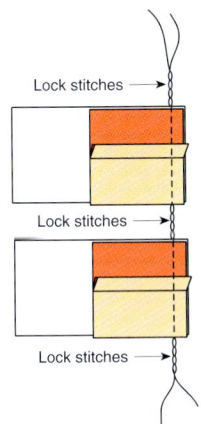

Figure 11
Lock stitches between segments as shown.

STRIP PIECING

Many block patterns are ideally suited for strip piecing. The Nine-Patch is a perfect example; instead of cutting small individual squares, the quick and accurate strip-piecing method is used (Figures 12 and 13).

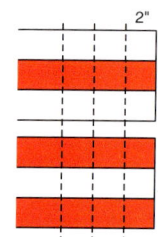

Figure 12
Join strips in 2 color combinations; subcut into specified size.

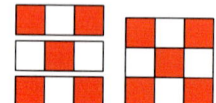

Figure 13
Join segments to complete a Nine-Patch block.

Strip piecing is the method by which two or more rotary-cut fabric strips are sewn with right sides together along the length to make a strip set. The strips can be of either equal or unequal widths. After pressing seams, cut pieced segments, which are re-assembled into a block, or use the strips for sashing or border.

There are some basic rules of thumb when strip piecing. Find both the lengthwise and crosswise grains of fabric.

When cutting multiple strips, it will occasionally be necessary to square up the long cutting edge of the fabric to keep it on the straight of grain. Tear off a fabric strip along this edge, trim torn edge with rotary equipment, press edge flat and resume cutting. Also, when cutting many pieced segments from a strip set, it will be necessary to occasionally square up the cutting edge of the strip set with rotary equipment.

Sew strip sets with about 16–18 stitches per inch to avoid stitches coming undone at the edges when pieced segments are cut from a strip set.

To avoid strip-set bowing, reverse the direction in which strips are sewn. That is, sew first seam from top to bottom, the next from bottom to top and so on. After strips are sewn into a strip set, press seams on both sides, starting with the wrong side, in order to set stitches into the seams. Or, if strips are narrow, press each seam after stitching.

Take multiple measurements across the width of the strip set to check for accurate sewing as shown in Figure 14. If any area is not sewn accurately, either rip and resew or cut it out from the strip set as shown in Figure 15. Trim seams afterward. The strip sets are now ready to be cut into pieced segments for block assembly.

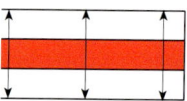

Figure 14
Take multiple measurements across the width of the strip set to check for accurate sewing.

Figure 15
Remove inaccurately sewn sections from a strip set.

Some examples of strip-pieced quilts are *Old-Fashioned Scrappy,* where each colorful block consists of four strip-pieced units, *Log Cabin Baby Doll,* with its strip-pieced heads and arms, and *Nine-Patch Floral Garden,* which contains strip-pieced sashing and two Nine-Patch sashing blocks.

Old-Fashioned Scrappy

Log Cabin Baby Doll

Nine-Patch Floral Garden

BIAS SQUARES

Bias squares are triangle-square units or half-square triangle units that are cut from stitched bias squares to result in straight-grain edges. When stitching triangle-square units for miniature quiltmaking, the bias-square method results in accurate-size squares no matter the size.

A bias square is made up of two equal-size, right-angle triangles as shown in Figure 16. When cutting the fabric bias strips to be used to make bias squares, it is easiest to work with fabric pieces no larger than 11" x 18" or half of a fat quarter.

Figure 16
A bias square is made up of 2 equal-size, right-angle triangles.

Start by making sure that the two fabric pieces required are on the straight of grain. Layer them right sides together, matching one short edge and one long edge of each fabric at a corner. Spray them with fabric spray sizing and iron flat.

Place a 3" x 18" ruler with a 45-degree diagonal line on the matched long fabric edges and make the first cut from the corner as shown in Figure 17. Move the ruler and make a second cut the desired bias strip width, resulting in two matching bias strips as shown in Figure 17.

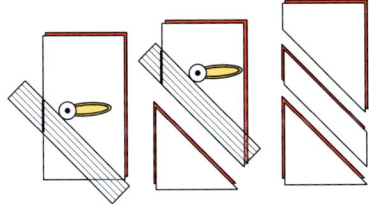

Figure 17
Place a 3" x 18" ruler with a 45-degree diagonal line on the matched long fabric edges and make the first cut from the corner.

Some of the bias strips may be of different lengths; these may be treated like all other strip sets as shown in Figure 18.

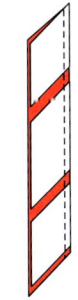

Figure 18
Use bias strips of different lengths.

Sew bias strips together with 16–18 stitches per inch on one long edge to make a bias set. Gently steam-press seam open, first on wrong side, then on right side, again referring to Figure 19.

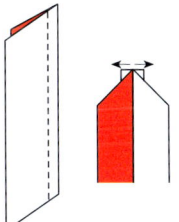

Figure 19
Press seam open.

Place the prepared template on the strip with diagonal line on the square template on the stitched lines of the bias strip as shown in Figure 20; cut out shapes.

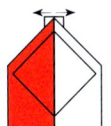

Figure 20
Place template on strip as shown.

Use a ruler to cut the bias squares. Place the ruler on the strip with the correct-size square at bottom point and cut along edge as shown in Figure 21. The resulting unit will need to be trimmed one more time using the ruler to

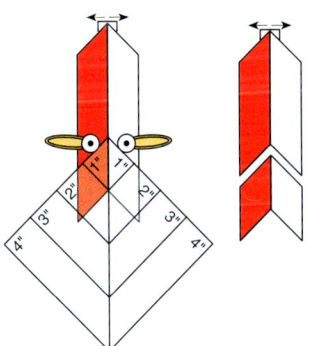

Figure 21
Use a ruler to cut units the desired size from the bias strip.

Tip

If using a ruler to make bias squares is new to you, make a sample bias set and practice cutting bias squares before using on actual project.

Be sure to have good contrast between the two colors used to make the bias strips.

Cut extra bias strips from leftover fabric and set aside for future projects.

Save any extra bias squares for future miniature scrap quilts.

complete the bias square as shown in Figure 22. Repeat cutting and trimming with the ruler to cut multiple bias squares from one strip.

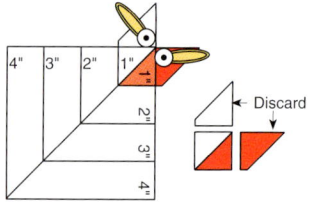

Figure 22
Trim off angled ends to make bias squares using the ruler as shown.

ADDING SASHING

Sashing, sometimes called lattice, are narrow strips of fabric used to separate either small blocks or blocks having many seams to match. It also expands the size of a quilt and adds visual interest, especially if there is good color separation between sashing and blocks.

Sometimes it is difficult to differentiate between a sashing and a border in a quilt plan, especially when there is more than one sashing. Sashing tends to be narrower than the border and is found in the inner part of the quilt.

After blocks have been sewn together, it can be sewn

Sunbonnet Sue and Sam

Country Star

just around the outside edges. In the *Sunbonnet Sue and Sam* quilt, a coordinating reproduction gold print sashing frames the four blocks to help separate them from the border print.

Sashing can be sewn on either horizontally or vertically but is usually a combination of both. Combined sashing is shown in the *Country Star* quilt.

Multiple sashings are more complicated. The *Radiant Bear Paw* quilt becomes a rectangle instead of a simple square. Due to multiple sashings, its size is expanded, and the sashing provides a repeat of a striking color strip elsewhere on the quilt.

A strip-pieced sashing is also a bit more complicated. The *Nine-Patch Floral Garden* is the perfect example of this type of sashing.

For something a bit different, simple folded sashing strips may be stitched between the border and the quilt center as shown on the *3-D Sunbonnet Sue* quilt.

Instead of strips, sashing can be pieced as seen in the purple-and-gold bias squares surrounding the inner portion of the *Radiant Star Bear Paw* quilt.

Sashing width is usually cut in mathematical propor-tion to a finished-block size. For example, a $1/2$"-wide finished sashing would be appropriate for a $2^{1}/_{2}$" x $2^{1}/_{2}$" finished block. If in doubt, cut sashing wider than needed, preview it with the blocks and trim down, if necessary.

Radiant Bear Paw

Sashing strips should be cut on the lengthwise grain of the fabric unless using a print and the fabric design runs along the width.

After sewing, press seams toward the sashing. Seams may be trimmed or graded to reduce bulk.

SQUARING UP THE QUILT TOP

It is always a good idea to measure and square a quilt before adding a border. Start by measuring down both sides of the quilt. These measurements should be identical. Repeat with top and bottom measurements, which should also be identical. If any of the measurements are off more than $1/8$", now is the time to examine the quilt for sewing discrepancies and repair, if possible.

If oversized setting triangles are used, it may be necessary to even up the raw edges and square corners. Corners that are not square are very common with diagonally set blocks, and can be made square again by using the corner of a square ruler as a trimming guide.

If a raw edge is uneven, position the top right side up and trim any excess fabric while trying to maintain a $1/4$"-wide seam allowance and not cut off block points. Next, using a ruler and marking tool, mark on the wrong side of the quilt where the seam allowance should be to serve as a sewing guide.

BORDERS

Borders frame your quilt. They can be simple fabric strips, pieced designs or appliqué motifs. For miniature quilts, they should not compete with the quilt center.

Some quilters put off choosing border fabric as the last item on their sewing agenda, while others start with a border fabric and build their quilt around it.

Borders can have either butted or straight ends or have angled, mitered corners. Mitered borders take more time and patience, but add a professional finish, especially if there are lines that must be matched in the fabric used.

To cut side borders, first measure straight down the center of the quilt. If using mitered corners, add twice the border-strip width plus an extra 2". Next, measure the width straight across the center of the quilt for top and bottom border measurements, again adding twice the border-strip width plus an extra 2" if mitering corners.

Cut border fabric on the lengthwise grain of fabric for less stretching. Its width is usually cut in mathematical proportion to the block size. For example, a quilt made with $3^{1}/_{2}$" x $3^{1}/_{2}$" blocks would look good with a border $3^{1}/_{2}$" wide or two borders that combine to $3^{1}/_{2}$". An exception is when one would not want to interrupt or cut into a directional print in order to maintain the fabric design in one piece.

Nine-Patch Floral Garden

Illustrated Guide to Scrap Miniature Magic

For butted or straight ends, the sewing is simple. Sew sides first, press seams toward borders. Sew top and bottom edges and repeat pressing.

For sewing mitered corner seams, sew a side strip first, stopping stitching on the seam line of the quilt center as shown in Figure 23. Repeat with strip on the opposite side and then the top and bottom as shown in Figure 24.

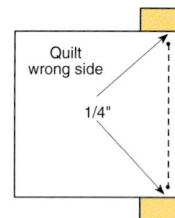

Figure 23
Sew a side strip first, stopping stitching on the seam line of the quilt center.

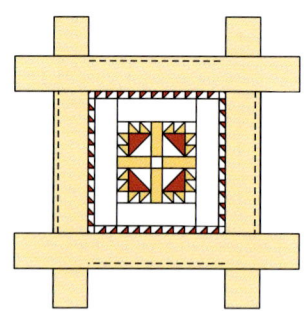

Figure 24
Strips are sewn to sides and top and bottom.

Fold and press the strips at a 45-degree angle to the corner as shown in Figure 25. Turn the quilt over; pin strips, matching edges, and stitch along the pressed line from the outside point to the point where stitching border strips ends as shown in Figure 26. Trim seam to ¼" referring to Figure 27; press seam open.

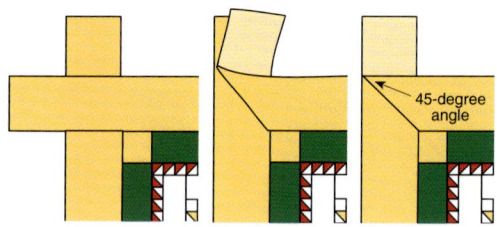

Figure 25
Fold and press the strips at a 45-degree angle to the corner.

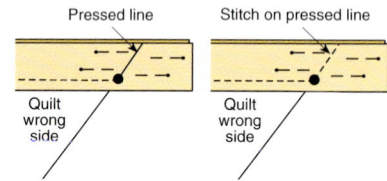

Figure 26
Stitch along pressed line to the center stitching point.

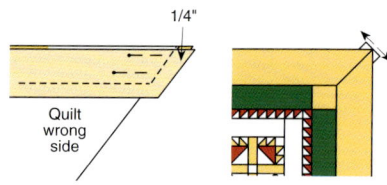

Figure 27
Trim seam to ¼"; press open.

After pressing, turn the quilt to the right side and check each corner to be sure it lies flat. If it does not, rip stitches out carefully and start over.

If mitering a sashing and a border, first join the strips and then sew to the quilt as one edge piece, mitering corners as one and matching seams of strips when sewing corner seams.

Repeating a quilt fabric in the border or border cornerstone is an easy way to tie everything together as shown on the *3-D Sunbonnet Sue* quilt.

For a very busy quilt, a simple border helps to contain the excitement. The *Kaleidoscope* quilt is a perfect example of a busy quilt with a simple border.

3-D Sunbonnet Sue

Tip

Sew with 14–16 stitches per inch.

Use stiletto tip to help guide pieces under the presser foot.

Use a pair of small embroidery scissors, as the short points can be easily inserted into small areas.

A too-hot iron can leave a shiny surface on fabric.

Press while standing for more accurate results.

A directional border print similar to the one used on the *Log Cabin Pine Trees* quilt, can give life to a common block setting.

Multiple borders can change the dimensions of a quilt making it square or rectangular. This technique is put to good use in the *Scrappy Hole in the Barn Door*.

Multiple borders and sashings are also an effective way to surround and accentuate a quilt center. The *Crown of Thorns* quilt shows how this works. The borders on this quilt provide the perfect place to show off hand-quilting skills.

The right border print can help to continue the theme of the quilt center as is seen on the *Fanciful Flowers* quilt. Here

Scrappy Hole in the Barn Door

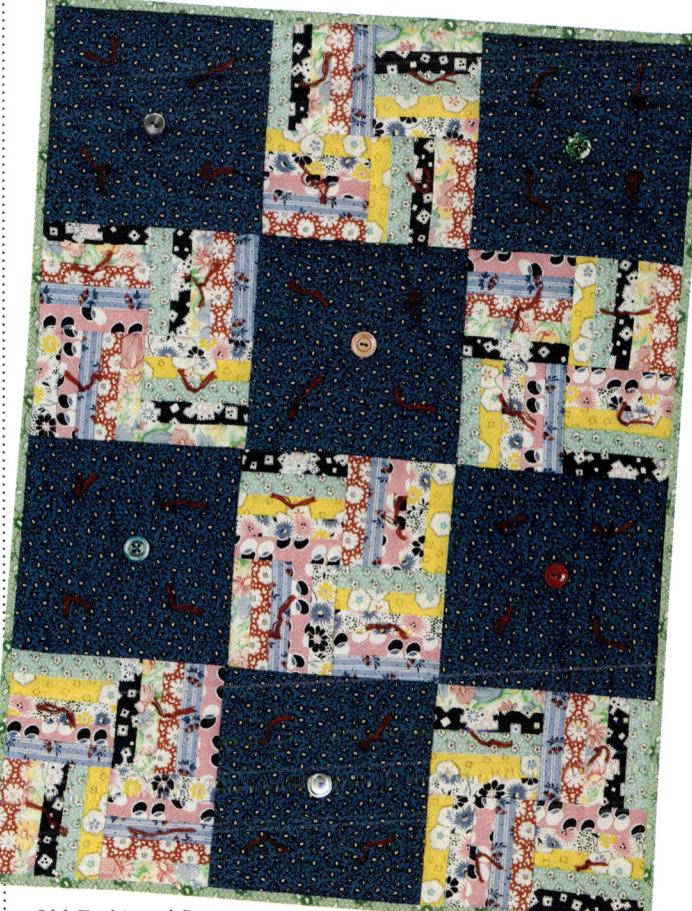

Old-Fashioned Scrappy

the flower theme of the blocks is repeated with a floral print in the border. The same is true in the *Sunbonnet Sue and Sam* quilt, which uses a reproduction vintage fabric in the borders to continue the vintage look of the center.

Multiple borders and multiple cornerstones lend a certain penâche to an otherwise ordinary-looking quilt as demonstrated in the *Whirling Crowns* quilt. Pieced cornerstones can also add flair to the borders as seen on the *Flaming Baskets* quilt.

In my opinion, not every miniature quilt needs a border to make it complete. The *Nine-Patch Floral Garden* and *Old-Fashioned Scrappy* quilts would seem too busy with added borders.

FINISHING DETAILS

When you have finished sewing the quilt top, steam-press on both sides. Check for proper seam pressing and trim loose threads before preparing to quilt. ❖

Finishing Your Quilt

For some quilters, finishing the quilt top is the fun part; for others finishing is the dreaded part. Larger projects require much more time during the finishing process. Miniature quilts are easy to manipulate because of their small size, making the finishing process less tedious and more fun.

MARKING TOP FOR HAND QUILTING

Several basic sewing supplies and tools are required for marking the quilt top for hand quilting.

The proper tool for marking is important. The goal is to mark the top with a design so it is easy to see during the quilting process, but is not visible once the quilt is complete. You may use any of the following marking tools:

- A fine .2mm, hard-lead pencil (soft lead leaves a blurry line)

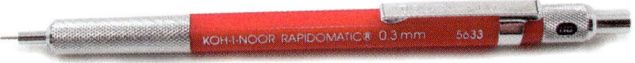

- Ultimate Marking Pencil for Quilters

- .5mm colored pencils (except red)

- Blue or white fine-point, water-soluble pens

- Quilter's Choice silver or white pencils

- Fabric-pencil eraser

- Marking-Pencil Removal
- Other supplies include: 1/4"-wide quilter's tape, plastic templates, light box and medium-fine sandpaper.

Before you begin, test a scrap of quilt fabric to check for easy marking and complete removal. In most cases, the top should be marked before the layering process. However, some markers do rub off easily during quilting so it may be necessary to mark as you quilt. The use of a thin, lightweight batting makes marking easy even after layering.

Always use a light hand when marking with a pencil. Be sure to remove the marks completely after quilting. If you wait, the marks can become permanent with time.

If using a water-soluble marking pen, soak the finished quilt in cold water since the marking substance could migrate to the batting with simple wiping or spraying.

Quilter's tape is useful when quilting straight lines. Do not leave tape on the quilt surface for long periods of time, especially in a warm climate.

If the fabric is a light color, tape the quilting design to a window and tape the quilt top over the design to mark. A light box works even better than a window, and many inexpensive options are available at your local quilt shop.

32   Master Quilter's Workshop

If marking the quilt top on a tabletop, place a piece of medium-fine sandpaper under it to prevent slippage.

Many appealing small plastic template designs can be purchased at a quilt shop or through mail-order sources. Be sure they are laser-cut and are clear plastic. You may reduce larger-size patterns to fit these small quilts and make your own plastic templates to add to your quilting-design choices.

If you are quilting in the ditch of seams or echo quilting (repeating a design's shape a certain distance from its edge either inside or outside) you don't need to mark the top. Some fabrics are hard to mark so these quilting options work best with those types of fabrics.

CHOOSING BATTING

There are several batting options that work perfectly for miniature quilts. The following is a list of those I have used successfully:

- Quilter's Dream Cotton Batting Select 100 percent cotton

- Hobb's Heirloom Premium cotton batting (80 percent cotton, 20 percent polyester)

- Mountain Mist Blue Ribbon All Cotton batting

- Low-loft polyester batting

Unlike a full-size quilt, batting requirements for a miniature quilt are quite simple—batting is used for quilting purposes and appearance only, not for warmth. The type of batting chosen is a matter of personal taste and should be appropriate for a particular project. The following are some guidelines to help you choose the right batting for your quilt.

A 100 percent cotton, or 80 percent cotton/20 percent polyester batting, can produce eye-catching results. They are easy to quilt through and they do not slide around during the quilting process. They work similar to a flannel board used to hold illustrations. The layers stick together naturally. There are many different brands of these battings. Through trial and error you will find your preference. There is a difference between different battings in the way they feel, the thickness and pliability.

Using a low-loft polyester batting will result in a quilt with a puffier appearance. It is more difficult to quilt due to slippage, so it must be well secured during layering. It is easier to make stitches through polyester batting than cotton. Some polyester battings beard, leaving little white lint pieces on the quilt top. These show up more on darker fabrics.

A high-loft polyester batting is not suitable for use in a miniature quilt. It produces too much loft. You may split this type of batting by peeling off a thin layer, but it results in a very flat and unappealing appearance.

Any cotton batting will produce a quilt with a more traditional look, while a polyester batting conveys a fuller, more contemporary look.

Use a light-color batting, such as natural or white, when making a light quilt, as a dark batting will shadow through. A light-color batting may be used in a dark-color quilt. Dark-color battings are rare, but are available.

Cut batting at least 1" wider all around than the finished

Tip

Do not use flannel for batting as it is difficult to quilt through and results in a flat look.

Take care when pressing any type of polyester batting after layering as it might melt.

Silk batting, although expensive, is easy to quilt through but does result in a somewhat flat look.

A longer quilting needle is required for quilting through polyester batting.

If planning to machine-quilt, experiment first with scrap fabric and different battings to find your comfort zone and perfect results for this type of quilting.

Illustrated Guide to Scrap Miniature Magic **33**

quilt-top measurements. This allows for some shrinkage during the quilting process. The extra batting will be trimmed away later when binding is added.

CHOOSING & PREPARING BACKING

There are several decisions to make when choosing a fabric for the quilt backing. A fabric print that coordinates with or matches the quilt top adds a pleasant and often overlooked finishing touch. This fabric may or may not be used in the quilt top. A matching solid may also be used, but, unlike a print, every quilting stitch will be highly visible. A medium-to-large scale or overall print is appropriate. Muslin may be used, but is rather dull.

Cut the backing fabric at least 1½" larger all around than the measurement of the finished quilt top. This allows for some shrinkage during quilting. Larger quilt tops require more backing exposed around outside edges for use when attaching the quilt to a frame and to protect the batting and top edges during the quilting process. These tiny quilts don't require frames so this excess is not necessary.

> **Tip**
> For a rectangular-shaped quilt, cut backing fabric with its lengthwise straight of grain parallel to the quilt's longer side edges.

LAYERING THE QUILT

The process of layering the batting between the quilt top and backing is often called sandwiching. When the quilt is finished with a bound edge, the layering process requires the batting to be secured between the top and bottom layers.

To layer, place the backing fabric wrong side up and tape to a flat surface along the raw edges. Center the batting on top; center the finished quilt top on the batting layer. *Note: You might want to iron the layers together if they do not lie flat. If the quilt top has been marked for quilting, do not iron. Do not iron on a cutting mat.*

There are two ways to secure the layers—pinning or basting. When pinning, use small brass safety pins and start in the quilt center and work out to the edges. The pins may be removed as the areas around them are quilted.

> **Tip**
> Do not pin or baste in the way of future quilting.
> Tape backing fabric to a cutting mat that cannot be damaged either by pinning or basting.
> Avoid using a colored thread for hand basting, such as red; it can leave a color trail when being pulled out, especially on a light fabric.

To hand-baste the layers together, use white basting thread, knotting end tails on the quilt top for easy removal. Begin basting at the quilt center and work to outside edges as shown in Figure 1.

Figure 1
Baste through all layers starting in the center and working to the outside edges.

The goal when securing the quilt layers is to keep them from shifting during the quilting process. The shifting could cause lumps, wrinkles and a skewed finished quilt.

HAND QUILTING

Hand quilting is a way of adding your personal touch to a miniature quilt and gives an air of authenticity. Machine quilting is not only harder to do, but it flattens the quilt in a way that is unappealing to me. But that is a personal choice.

Needle size and brand are a personal choice. It is a good idea to try several different ones to see how they work for you. The higher the number the finer the needle. I prefer No. 10 large-eye needles.

Using a thimble to prevent sore fingers is also a personal choice. A large variety of thimble tools are available from leather to metal. I prefer to use rubber finger cots, found in an office-supply store.

A quilt frame is not necessary for quilting miniature quilts. If the layers are secure, they will not wrinkle or buckle.

The color and kind of thread to use is also a personal choice. Avoid using one that will be totally lost in the quilt unless you are worried that your stitches are not even or consistent in length. Sink both beginning and ending knots in a seam as you quilt as shown in Figure 2.

Hand-quilting threads are available in a variety of colors. I prefer using Mettler Metrosene Polyester Thread found at most quilt shops. This is not sold as quilting thread, but it does not break easily, and the wide range of colors makes it a practical choice.

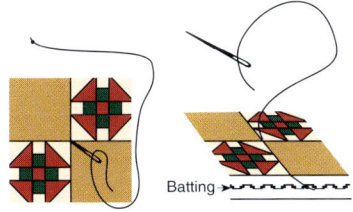

Figure 2
Sink both beginning and ending knots in a seam as you quilt.

Begin quilting in the center of the quilt and work out to the outer edges. Some quilters like to start at the top and work down. Whatever method you choose, it is best not to add too much quilting. Quilt minimally at first and return to quilt more later, if desired.

As you quilt, turn the work to the backside and check for evenly spaced and sized stitches free of tangles. If a quilt has a border, quilt the inside of blocks first and the borders last.

If you are new to hand quilting, it is more important to strive for evenly sized and spaced stitches than small stitches, which will come with time and practice.

There are basically two ways to hand-quilt. The first is a running stitch where several stitches are loaded onto the needle at one time, and then the thread is pulled through. Some quilters prefer to keep the needle stationary and manipulate the fabric, while others do just the opposite.

The second method is the stab-and-jab stitch in which just one stitch is made at a time and is most commonly mastered with a hoop or frame. The needle is stabbed into the fabric perpendicular to the quilt top and pulled downward to the backside of the quilt. Next, the needle is moved a short distance and brought straight up or jabbed up to the quilt top where it is moved again for the next stitch.

Beginning quilters with hand-sewing experience have a difficult time adjusting to the smaller needle and using a thimble. Practice makes these changes easy to handle with time.

If you like the quilt-in-the-ditch quilting pattern, place small stitches in the seam line between pieces. This is the best type of quilting to use inside very small pieces as shown in Photo 1.

Outline quilting is done $1/8"–1/4"$ away from a seam line or appliqué design. If repeated several times, it is called echo quilting. The quilting stitches follow the outline of the pieces as shown in Figure 3.

Figure 3
Outline quilting is 1/8"–1/4" away from shape or seams and following the design of the shape.

Background quilting fills in large, plain spaces. A common quilting design for this purpose is a crosshatch design in squares or diamonds as shown in Figure 4.

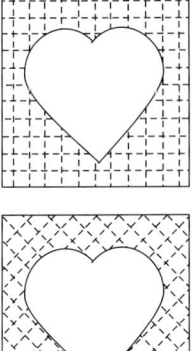

Figure 4
Crosshatch quilting can form squares or diamonds.

1. This photo shows quilting in the ditch of seams inside a small piece.

Illustrated Guide to Scrap Miniature Magic **35**

Design quilting includes a variety of designs that add detail to open spaces. Common examples include feather wreaths, clamshells or a braided design as shown in Figure 5.

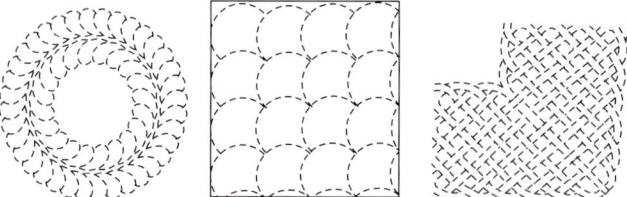

Figure 5
A feather wreath, clamshell or braided quilting design is perfect for showing off your quilting stitches.

The last quilting design is one that you make yourself from 1/4"-gridded template material. These designs include practically any shape that you can trace around. Hearts and stars are common quilting shapes you can make yourself.

Tip
Thread and knot a number of needles ahead of time to speed up quilting time.

If choosing to start quilting in the center of your quilt, cut an extra-long thread and do not knot. Thread needle and use half of the thread from the center to one outside edge; thread needle again with the remaining half of the thread and stitch to the opposite side outside edge. This prevents extra knots in the center of your quilt.

BINDING YOUR QUILT
When the quilting is complete, the edge of the quilt needs to be finished. Begin by trimming the backing and batting edges even and square with the quilted top; remove pins or basting if any still remain. Remove any quilting marks.

Choose binding fabric to match the fabrics used in the quilt to tie the quilt together. This may be a fabric used in blocks or background. To keep it in proportion, the finished binding is 1/4" wide on both the front and backside of the quilt. Larger quilts have a wider binding.

To make binding, cut 1"-wide binding strips on the lengthwise fabric grain, 1 1/8" wide if the fabric is loosely woven. Turn under one long raw edge 1/4"; press.

If binding each side with a separate strip, each strip should be cut 1" longer than the measurement of the side to be stitched. Sew a strip to opposite sides of the quilt top with the right side of the strip against the right side of the quilt, matching raw edges as shown in Figure 6.

When stitching is complete, turn the binding strips to the backside of the quilt to enclose the quilt edge as shown in Figure 7; hand-stitch in place. Trim ends even with quilt. Repeat with top and bottom strips, leaving 1/2" excess at each end as shown in Figure 8.

Figure 6
Sew a strip to opposite sides of the quilt top with the right side of the strip against the right side of the quilt, matching raw edges.

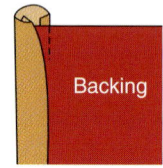

Figure 7
Turn the binding strips to the backside of the quilt to enclose the quilt edge.

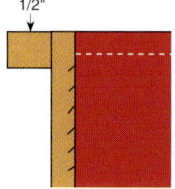

Figure 8
Leave 1/2" excess at each end.

Press strip up and fold in each end as shown in Figure 9; fold to the backside to enclose seam and hand-stitch in place as before. Blind-stitch open ends of seam closed.

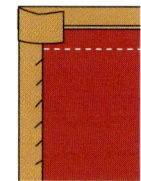

Figure 9
Press strip up and fold in each end.

If binding all sides with one continuous piece of binding, measure to find total distance around the quilt top edge. Add 6"–8" to the measurement for mitering corners and overlapping beginning and ends.

Cut strips to equal this measurement along the length of the fabric. Cut ends of each strip at a 45-degree angle as shown in Figure 10; join strips to make one long strip. Press seams open and trim to 1/8".

36 *Master Quilter's Workshop*

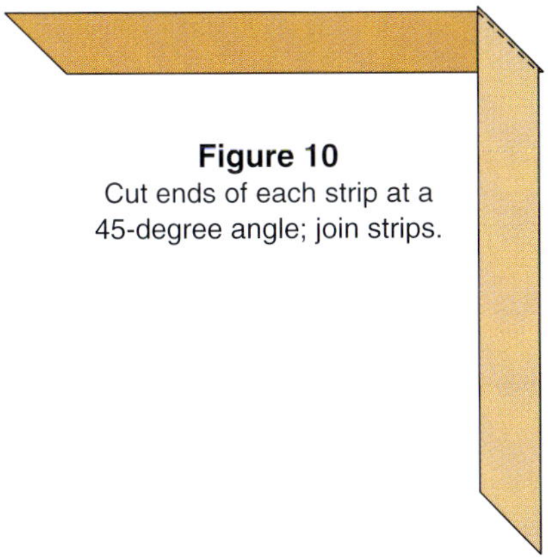

Figure 10
Cut ends of each strip at a 45-degree angle; join strips.

Press under one long edge ¼". Pin strip to quilt with right sides together, starting at least 2" from a corner. Stitch to ¼" from a corner and stop stitching; leave the needle in the quilt, turn and sew diagonally to the corner as shown in Figure 11.

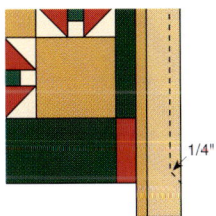

Figure 11
Sew to within 1/4" of corner; leave needle in quilt, turn and stitch diagonally off the corner of the quilt.

Fold the binding at a 45-degree angle up and away from the quilt as shown in Figure 12 and back down flush with the raw edges. Starting at the top raw edge of the quilt, begin sewing the next side as shown in Figure 13. Repeat at the next three corners.

 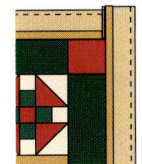

Figure 12
Fold binding at a 45-degree angle up and away from quilt as shown.

Figure 13
Fold the binding strips back down, flush with the raw edge, and begin sewing.

As you approach the beginning of the binding strip, stop stitching and overlap the binding ½" from the edge; trim. Join the two ends with a ¼" seam allowance and press the seam open. Reposition the joined binding along the edge of the quilt and resume stitching to the beginning.

To finish, bring the folded edge of the binding over the raw edges and blind-stitch the binding in place over the machine-stitching line on the backside. Hand-miter the corners on the back as shown in Figure 14.

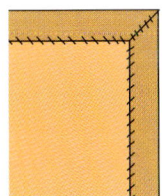

Figure 14
Miter and stitch the corners as shown.

A pieced binding requires a bit more planning. An example of a pieced binding is used on the *Fiery Baskets* (page 74) quilt.

The method of attaching the binding is the same for a pieced binding, but measuring the sides and piecing in the exact right location is essential. In this method you cannot use the continuous method of binding, but rather you must bind each side one section at a time.

WASHING & PRESERVING YOUR MINIATURE QUILTS

Unless a miniature quilt is being handled a lot, it is not necessary to wash it often. If it does require washing, soak it in a cold-water wash containing Orvus paste found in quilt shops, referring to the manufacturer's directions. Rinse thoroughly in cold water, place it on a towel. Gently roll the towel up to remove excess water. Let it dry flat on a clean, dry towel.

If your fabrics were not prewashed, there is a chance that the fabric dyes could run. In this case, it is best to have the quilt dry-cleaned.

If desired, the surface may be protected with Scotchgard. This will help keep the surface from attracting dust and dirt.

To preserve your miniature quilt, keep it out of direct sunlight. It is nearly impossible to avoid dust. When not in use, store flat, not folded.

If your miniature quilt is being framed, use acid-free mounting and provide space between the quilt and glass; do not use plastic.

By taking good care of your little quilts, they should last for generations to come. ❖

Special Techniques

Several of the miniature quilts in this book use special techniques. The following instructions will help you when using the techniques.

MAKING YO-YOS

Using the yo-yo circle pattern given with the quilt project, prepare a plastic template. Cut out as directed for the project.

Turn under ¼" around the outside edge of the circle. Knot a single thread and sew short running stitches around the turned-under edge as shown in Figure 1.

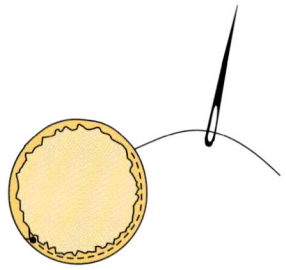

Figure 1
Turn under 1/4" around the outside edge of the circle. Knot a single thread and sew short running stitches around the turned-under edge.

When finished stitching, gently pull the thread to draw the circle into a small pouch as shown in Figure 2; knot the thread.

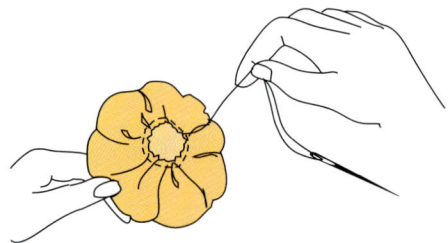

Figure 2
Gently pull the thread to draw the circle into a small pouch.

Flatten the pouch into a circle to create a yo-yo as shown in Figure 3.

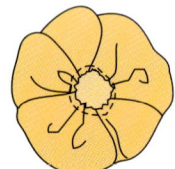

Figure 3
Flatten the pouch into a circle to create a yo-yo.

Yo-yos are commonly used to simulate flowers. They may have uncovered centers or buttons sewn in the centers. These 3-D circles are fun to stitch. Use small fabric scraps and add color and dimension to any quilt, large or small.

MACHINE PAPER-FOUNDATION PIECING

Commonly called the flip-and-sew method, machine-paper-foundation piecing is done with numbered fabric pieces. However, for a change, in this book, the seam lines are numbered and the first fabric piece is identified with an X as shown in Figure 4. This will avoid confusion in fabric placement and order of stitching.

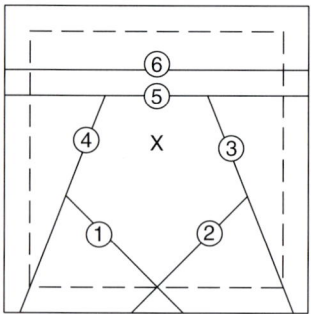

Figure 4
The seam lines are numbered and the first fabric piece is identified with an X.

This flip-and-sew method is easy to understand once several fabric pieces are sewn in place. Each block is made with a paper foundation marked with pattern sewing lines that are stitched in numerical order. Although time-consuming, this method results in precise sewing of tiny fabric pieces that can be cut freehand ahead of time. Some finished blocks require mirror-image or reversed parts as shown on Figure 5. Others might require several

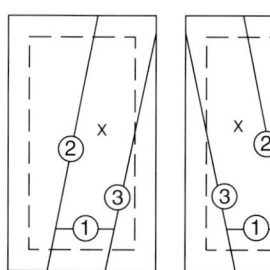

Figure 5
Mirror-image or reversed parts may be needed to complete a block.

38   *Master Quilter's Workshop*

foundation-pieced units, which are then joined to create the block as shown in Figure 6.

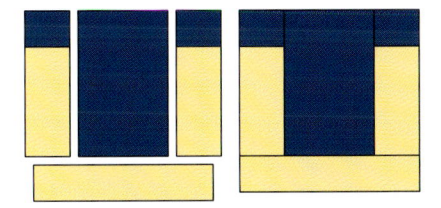

Figure 6
Several foundation-pieced units must be stitched and joined to create a block.

Place tracing paper over the foundation pattern given. Transfer the X, numbered sewing lines and outside 1/4"-wide seam allowance using a dark pen or marker keeping traced copy precise. Duplicate the number of copies required to finish the project. Leave a space between blocks for ease of handling. Cut out patterns leaving a margin around each one.

Choose small-scale prints with good color contrast and close design. Solids work in well. Decide fabric placement before sewing. Repeat fabrics throughout blocks to help tie the blocks together. Highlight smallest block pieces with the brightest or darkest fabrics to make them stand out. If they blend in, they will be lost.

Fabric scraps should be the same size as the pattern piece plus an extra 1/4"-wide seam allowance all around, which will be trimmed after sewing. Wrinkled scraps do not need to be ironed in advance. Place directional prints as necessary to create the proper placement in the finished quilt.

Cut triangles from oversized squares. For a more professional look, cut fabric pieces so their grain lines all run in the same direction and on the straight of grain, especially in those pieces on block outside raw edges.

Sew with 16–18 stitches per inch unless thread pulls up on the machine while sewing. Use a neutral color thread for scrap quilts or matching thread for coordinated color quilts.

Begin and end each seam with 3–4 extra stitches beyond the seam lines as shown in Figure 7. For identical blocks, sew fabric pieces assembly-line fashion. Before trimming seams, flip fabric pieces right side up to be sure they were sewn in the correct numerical order.

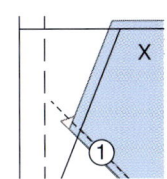

Figure 7
Begin and end each seam with 3–4 extra stitches beyond the seam lines.

The X or first fabric piece is the only one placed right side up and not flipped over after stitching. To start, hold the paper foundation up to the light for fabric placement, if necessary. Pin or spot-glue fabric piece X in place right side up on unmarked side of the foundation paper as shown in Figure 8.

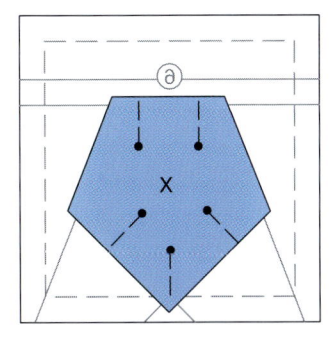

Figure 8
Pin or spot-glue fabric piece X in place right side up on unmarked side of the foundation paper.

With right sides together, place fabric piece 1 over piece X as shown in Figure 9; match and trim raw edges 1/4" wide along seam 1 line. Sew on seam 1 line; trim raw edges 1/8" wide and flip fabric piece 1 right side up and flat as shown in Figure 10. Finger press seam and fabric flat.

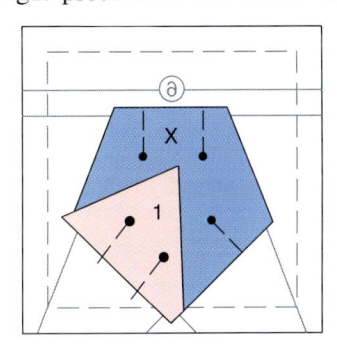

Figure 9
With right sides together, place fabric piece 1 over piece X.

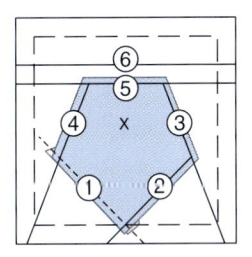

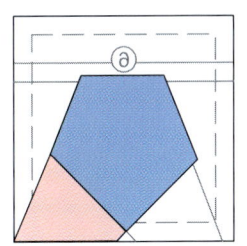

Figure 10
Sew on seam 1 line; trim raw edges 1/8" wide and flip fabric piece 1 right side up and flat.

Illustrated Guide to Scrap Miniature Magic **39**

With right sides together, place fabric piece 2 over piece 1; match and trim raw edges ¼" wide along seam 2 line. Sew on seam 2 line; trim raw edges ⅛" wide and flip fabric piece 2 right side up and press flat.

Continue sewing, trimming, flipping and finger pressing in this manner until all lines are sewn on and the block or unit is complete. Be sure to leave a ¼"-wide seam allowance on block outside raw edge.

If necessary, trim block edges square with rotary equipment. Do not sew outside raw edges flat. Finish quilt top according to instructions. Carefully remove paper foundations with seam ripper tip. Avoid ripping stitches.

Tip

To help find the seam line, place pins through the line from the marked side of the pattern; position fabric raw edge accordingly on the unmarked side.

Place fabric glue only on fabric edges.

For larger pieces, flipped raw edges may need spot gluing or pinning to keep everything taut.

Trim loose threads after every seam.

Repair torn paper with tape.

EMBROIDERY STITCHES

Several projects use embroidery stitches to highlight or add detail to the projects. The stitches are usually done with 2 or 3 strands of 6-strand embroidery floss. To use, separate the floss into single strands and then use the required number for stitching. Two strands make a lighter-weight stitch than 3 strands.

BLANKET STITCH OR BUTTONHOLE STITCH

A blanket stitch or buttonhole stitch is a good stitch to use to attach appliqué pieces to a background, especially when you want the stitches to show. Aim for evenly spaced stitches.

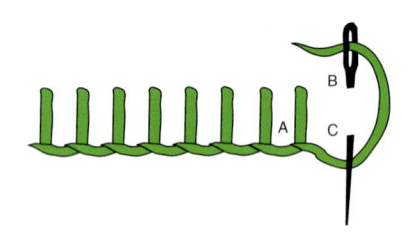

CHAIN STITCH

The chain stitch is used when a line is needed to connect designs.

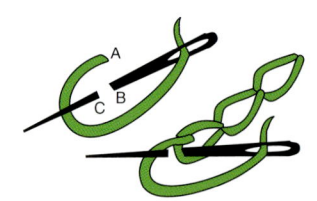

FRENCH KNOT

A French knot is often used to fill in centers of flowers. If you want a larger knot, use more strands of floss.

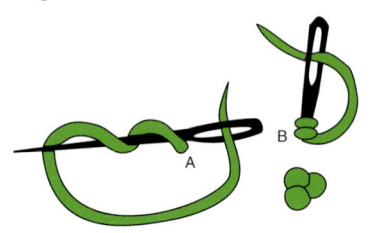

LAZY-DAISY STITCH

The lazy-daisy stitch is used to make flower petals.

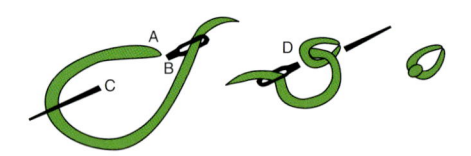

OUTLINE OR STEM STITCH

The outline or stem stitch is used to outline shapes or to make stems for flowers. It is a good stitch to use for straight or curved lines.

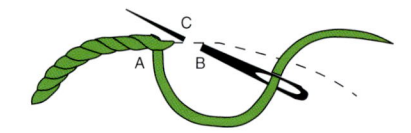

RUNNING STITCH

A running stitch is a simple stitch that is used for many purposes. Aim for same-size stitches with consistent spacing between stitches. ❖

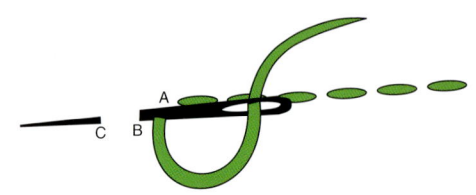

Illustrated Guide to Bias Squares

Bias squares are triangle-square units or half-square triangle units that are cut from stitched bias squares to result in straight-grain edges. When stitching triangle-square units for miniature quiltmaking, the bias-square method results in accurate-size squares no matter the size.

1

CUTTING BIAS STRIPS

1A. Place a 3" x 18" ruler with a 45-degree diagonal line on the matched long fabric edges. Make the first cut from the corner.

1B. Move the ruler and make a second cut the desired bias strip width, resulting in two matching bias strips.

Illustrated Guide to Scrap Miniature Magic **41**

2

SEWING BIAS STRIPS TOGETHER

2A. Sew bias strips together with 16–18 stitches per inch on one long edge to make a bias set.

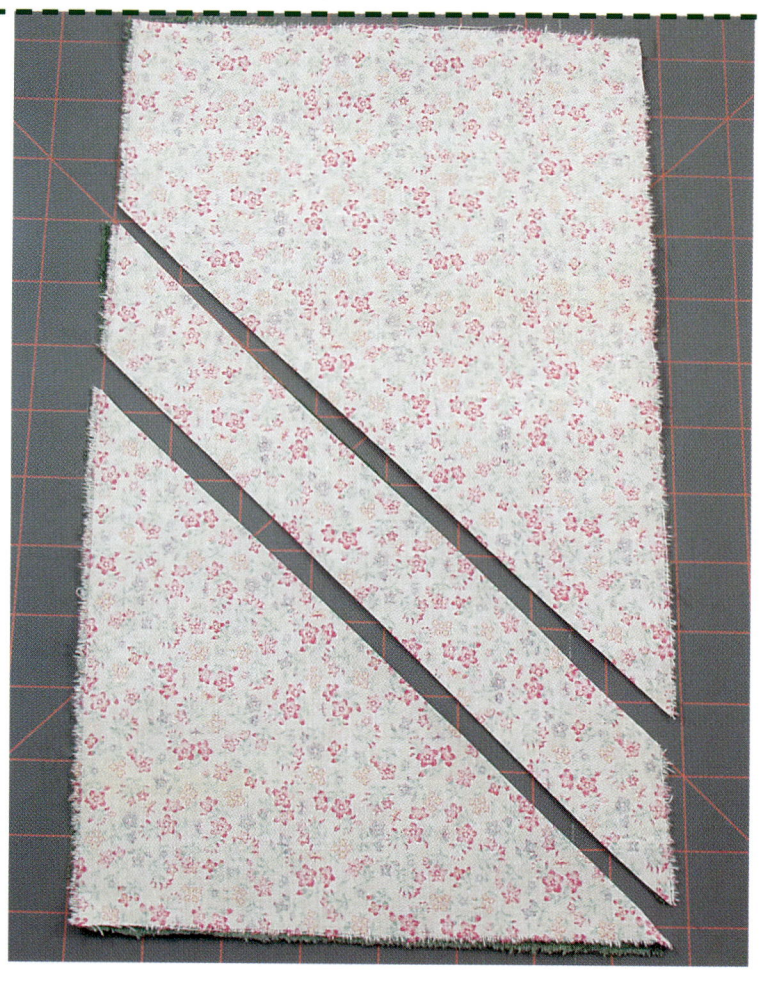

¼" seam →

2B. Some of the bias strips may be of different lengths; these may be treated like all other strip sets.

2C. Gently steam-press seam open, first on wrong side, then on right side again; trim to ⅛".

42   *Master Quilter's Workshop*

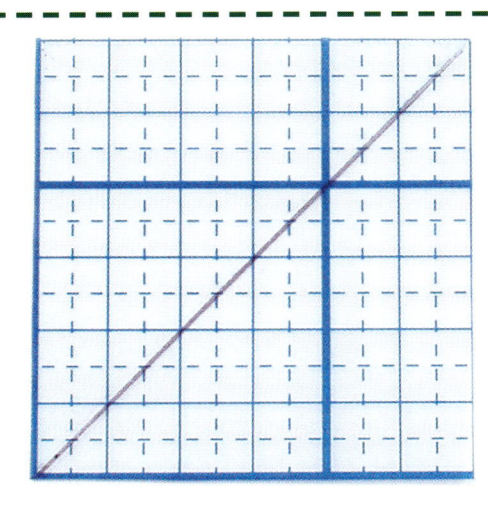

METHOD 1: PREPARING BIAS SQUARES WITH TEMPLATE

3A. Prepare template on gridded plastic. Draw diagonal line on template.

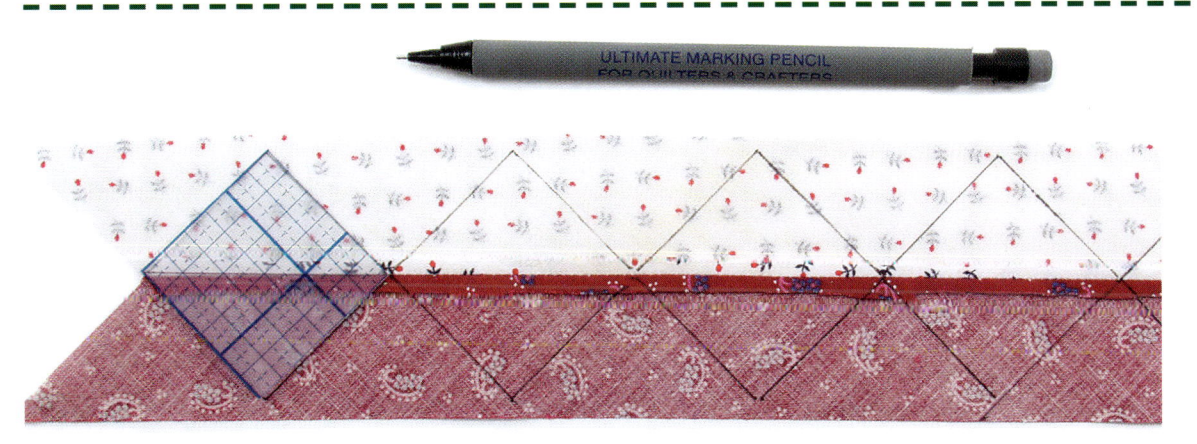

3B. Place the prepared template on the strip with diagonal line of the square template on the stitched lines of the bias strip. Trace around template; move and continue process.

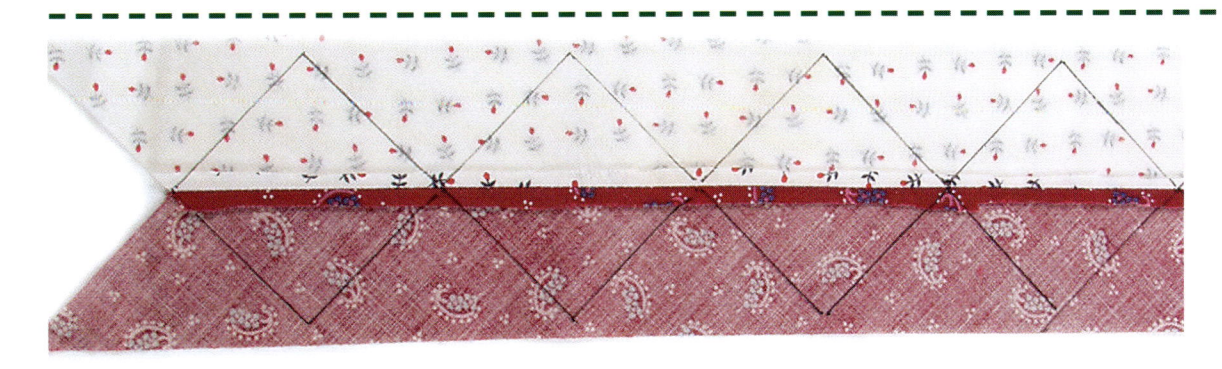

3C. Cut out squares.

Illustrated Guide to Scrap Miniature Magic

4

METHOD 2: PREPARING BIAS SQUARES WITH RULER

4A. Place the ruler on the strip with the correct-size square at bottom point and cut along edge.

4B. The resulting unit will need to be trimmed one more time using the ruler to complete the bias square.

44 *Master Quilter's Workshop*

Country Star

Easy to make and easy on the eye, this simple quilt can be made over a weekend, and is perfectly suited for a beginner. Any color combination would be suitable, especially red, white and green for Christmas.

PROJECT SPECIFICATIONS
Skill Level: Beginner
Quilt Size: 16" x 16"
Block Size: 3" x 3"
Number of Blocks: 4
Techniques: Bias square, strip piecing and 3 straight borders

Country Star
3" x 3" Block

MATERIALS
- 5" x 8" strip brown print
- 1½" x 1½" square pink print (F)
- ½ fat quarter navy print
- 1 strip each 4 different blue prints 7" x 11"
- ½ fat quarter muslin
- ½ fat quarter red print
- ½ fat quarter green-and-cream floral stripe
- 1 fat quarter dark blue-and-cream floral
- 18" x 18" lightweight batting
- 19" x 19" backing
- Neutral color all-purpose thread
- Cream and green quilting thread
- Basic sewing tools and supplies, 3" x 18" ruler and 4" Baby Bias Square ruler

CUTTING
Note: Use the 3" x 18" ruler to cut 45-degree bias strips; reverse cutting direction if left-handed.

Step 1. Referring to Figure 1, place each 7" x 11" blue strip wrong side up on a flat surface and cut one 1½" x 10" bias strip from each fabric for A.

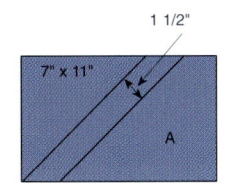

Figure 1
Cut one 1 1/2" x 10" bias strip for A.

Step 2. Cut a 7" x 15" muslin rectangle and place right side up on a flat surface; cut four 1½" x 10" bias strips for B referring to Figure 2.

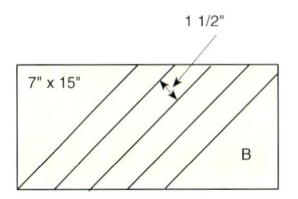

Figure 2
Cut four 1 1/2" x 10" bias strips for B.

Step 3. Cut sixteen 1½" x 1½" squares muslin for C.

Step 4. Cut four 1½" x 1½" D squares, two 1¼" x 7½" G strips and two 1¼" x 9" H strips red print.

Step 5. Cut four 1½" x 3½" E strips brown print.

Step 6. Cut two 2" x 9" I strips and two 2" x 12" J strips green-and-cream floral stripe.

Step 7. Cut two 2½" x 12" K strips and two 2½" x 16" L strips blue-and-cream floral.

Illustrated Guide to Scrap Miniature Magic

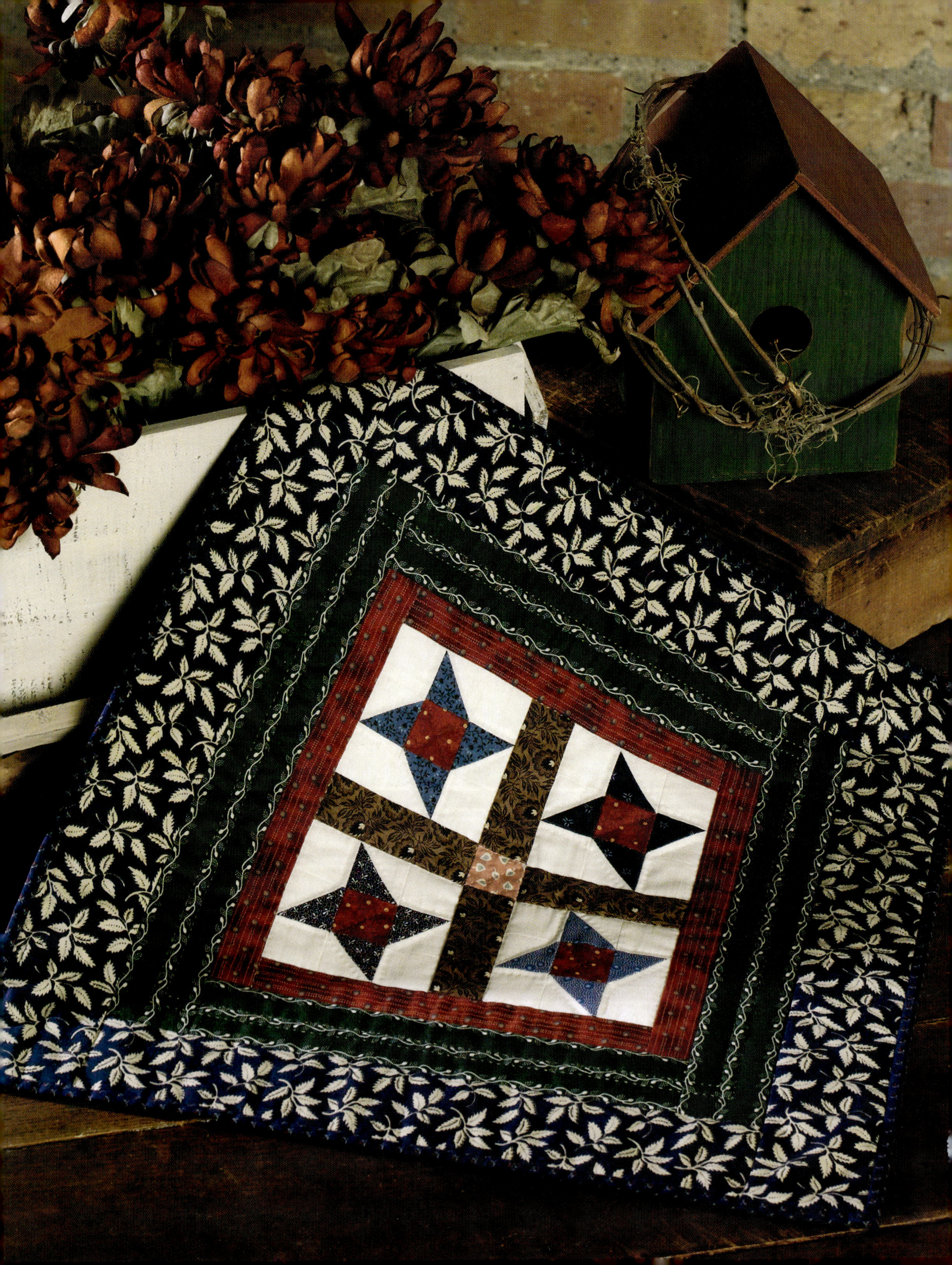

Step 8. Cut 1"-wide strips navy print and join to create a 72" binding strip referring to Binding Your Quilt on page 36.

PIECING BLOCKS

Note: Use Baby Bias Square ruler to cut bias squares or prepare template A/B using pattern given. Press seams before trimming. Press all seams in the direction of small arrows shown on figure drawings.

Step 1. Sew one A bias strip to one B bias strip with right sides together along length to make an A/B strip set; repeat for four strip sets. Press seams open.

Step 2. Cut four 1½" x 1½" A/B bias squares from each strip set using bias ruler or template A/B, matching line on template to seam between strips as shown in Figure 3. Keep bias squares together in matching color sets.

Figure 3
Cut 4 A/B bias squares, matching line on template to seam between strips.

Step 3. Sew a C square to opposite sides of one A/B unit referring to Figure 4; repeat for two matching sets.

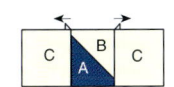

Figure 4
Sew a C square to opposite sides of 1 A/B unit.

Step 4. Sew two matching A/B units to opposite sides of D as shown in Figure 5.

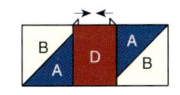

Figure 5
Sew matching A/B units to opposite sides of D.

Step 5. Sew an A/B/C unit to opposite sides of the A/B/D unit to complete one block; press seams toward the A/B/C units. Repeat for four blocks.

PIECING THE TOP

Step 1. Join two blocks with E to make a row as shown in Figure 6; repeat for two rows.

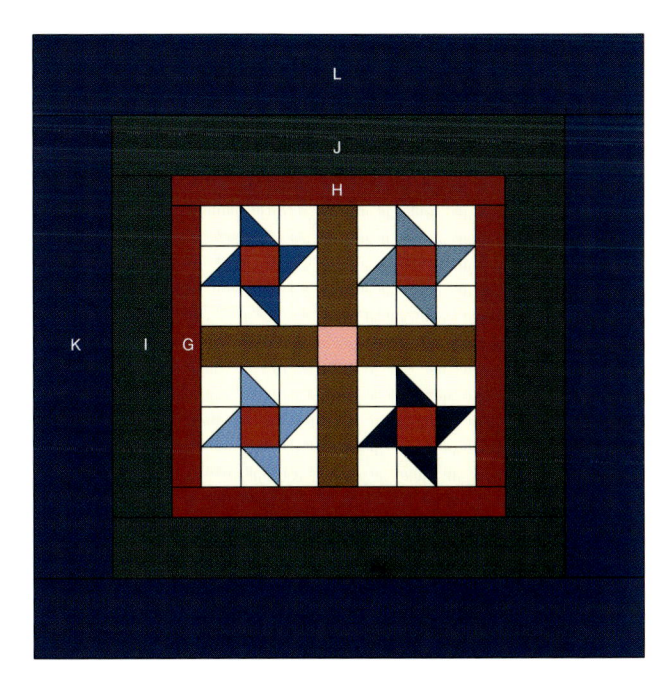

Country Star
Placement Diagrm
16" x 16"

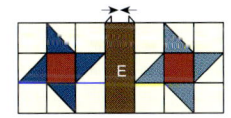

Figure 6
Join 2 blocks with E to make a row.

Step 2. Sew E to opposite sides of F as shown in Figure 7.

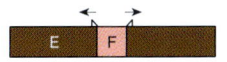

Figure 7
Sew E to opposite sides of F.

Step 3. Join the block rows with the E/F row as shown in Figure 8 to complete the pieced center.

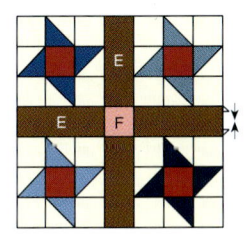

Figure 8
Join the block rows with the E/F row.

Step 4. Sew G to opposite sides and H to the top and bottom of the pieced center; press seams toward strips.

Step 5. Sew I to opposite sides and J to the top and bottom of the pieced center; press seams toward strips.

Step 6. Sew K to opposite sides and L to the top and bottom of the pieced center; press seams toward strips.

Illustrated Guide to Scrap Miniature Magic

FINISHING

Step 1. Press quilt top on both sides; check for proper seam pressing and trim all loose threads.

Step 2. Mark top for quilting. *Note: The quilt shown was hand-quilted 1/8" from dark star shapes, with an X through F, in the ditch of quilt center seams, and on stripes of the K and L border strips using cream quilting thread and in the ditch of seams of I and J, and K and L border strips using green quilting thread.*

Step 3. Sandwich batting between the stitched top and the backing piece; pin or baste layers together to hold. Quilt as desired by hand or machine.

Step 4. When quilting is complete, trim batting and backing fabric even with raw edges of quilt top.

Step 5. Bind edges with 1"-wide navy print prepared binding strips referring to Binding Your Quilt on page 36. ❖

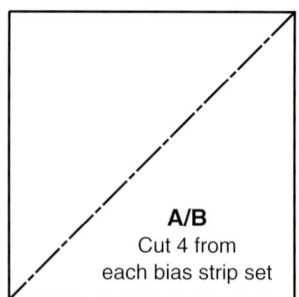

A/B
Cut 4 from each bias strip set

Old-Fashioned Scrappy

Combine hand quilting and tying, and add buttons to the plain blocks to hold the layers of this simple scrappy quilt together.

PROJECT SPECIFICATIONS
Skill Level: Beginner
Quilt Size: 15½" x 20½"
Block Size: 5" x 5"
Number of Blocks: 6
Techniques: Strip piecing, straight block setting and tied blocks

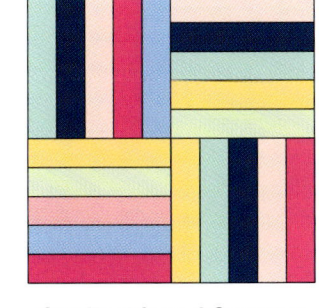

Old-Fashioned Scrappy
5" x 5" Block

MATERIALS
- 7" x 11" rectangle each of 8 assorted prints
- ½ fat quarter medium blue print
- ⅛ yard green print for binding
- 17" x 22" lightweight batting
- 18" x 23" backing
- Neutral color all-purpose thread
- Blue quilting thread
- Red 6-strand embroidery floss
- 6 (⅝") assorted buttons
- Basic sewing tools and supplies and large-eye, sharp needle

CUTTING
Step 1. Cut five 1" x 11" strips from each of the eight assorted prints. Label fabrics A–H; stack strips in separate piles.

Step 2. Cut six 5½" x 5½" squares medium blue print for I.

Step 3. Cut 1"-wide strips green print to create a 72" binding strip referring to Binding Your Quilt on page 36.

PIECING BLOCKS
Note: Use a ¼" seam allowance; press seams before trimming. Press all seams in the direction of small arrows shown on figure drawings.

Step 1. Join the A–H strips with right sides together along length in different color order to make eight strip sets referring to Figure 1.

Step 2. Subcut each strip set into three 3" segments, again referring to Figure 1.

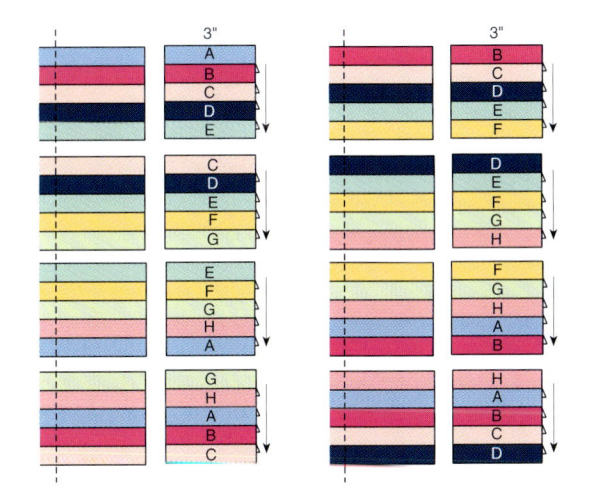

Figure 1
Join A–H strips; subcut into 3" segments as shown.

Illustrated Guide to Scrap Miniature Magic 49

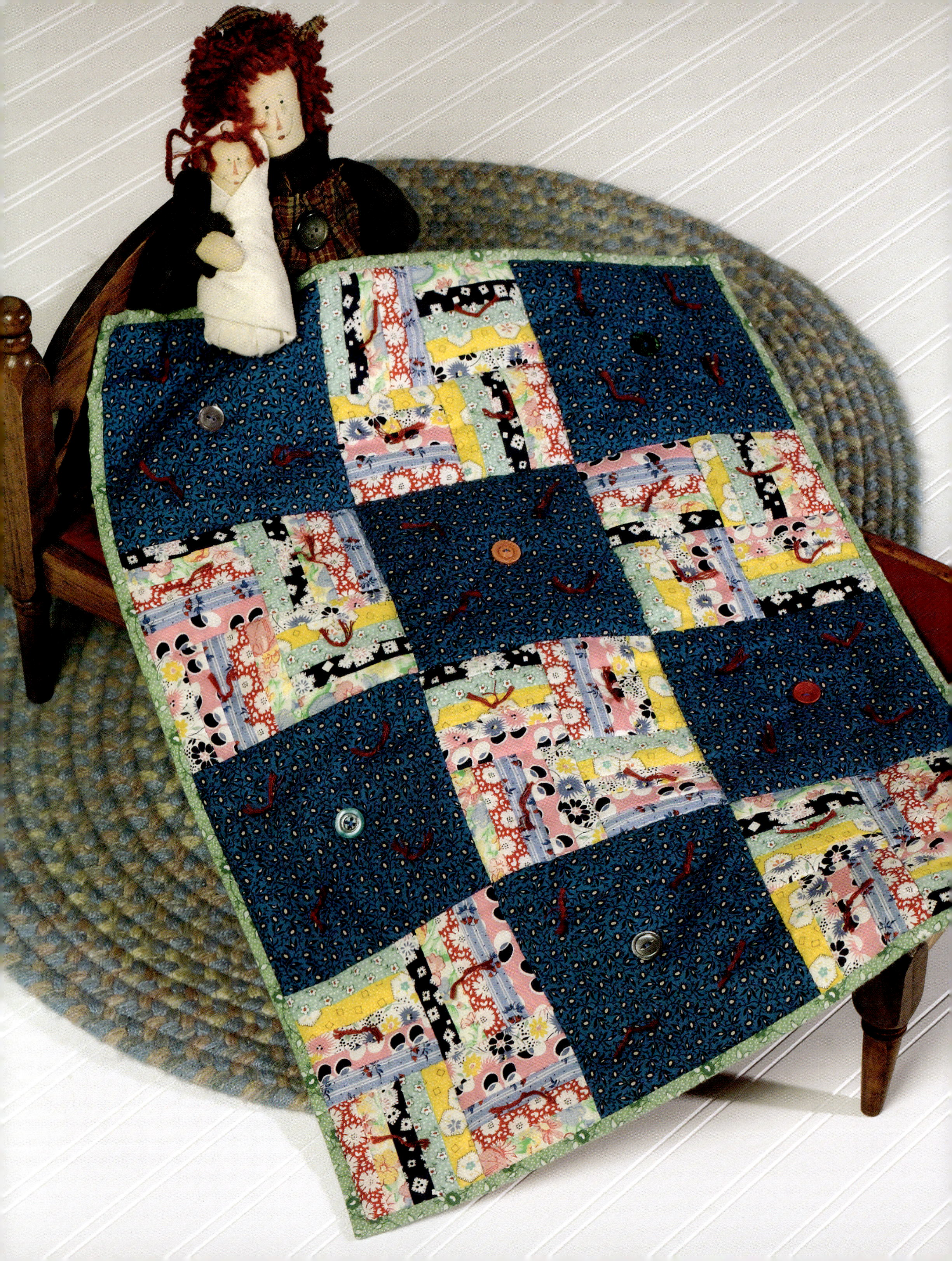

Step 3. Join two different segments as shown in Figure 2; repeat.

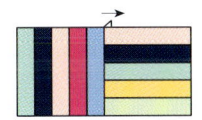

Figure 2
Join 2 different segments.

Step 4. Join two stitched segment units to complete one block as shown in Figure 3; repeat for six blocks.

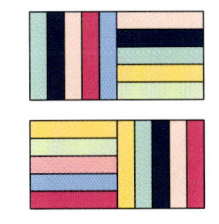

Figure 3
Join 2 stitched segment units to complete 1 block.

PIECING THE TOP
Step 1. Join two I squares with one pieced block to complete one X row referring to Figure 4; repeat for two X rows.

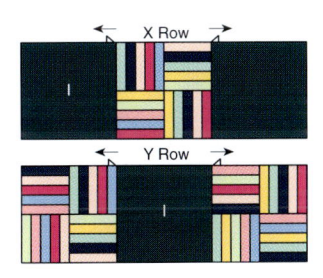

Figure 4
Join blocks with I to make rows as shown.

Step 2. Join one I square with two pieced blocks to complete one Y row, again referring to Figure 4; repeat for two Y rows.

Step 3. Join the X and Y rows referring to the Placement Diagram for positioning of rows; press seams in one direction.

FINISHING
Step 1. Press quilt top on both sides; check for proper seam pressing and trim all loose threads.

Step 2. Mark top for quilting. *Note: The quilt shown was tied in the center of each strip segment and in each quarter of the I squares using a square knot as shown in*

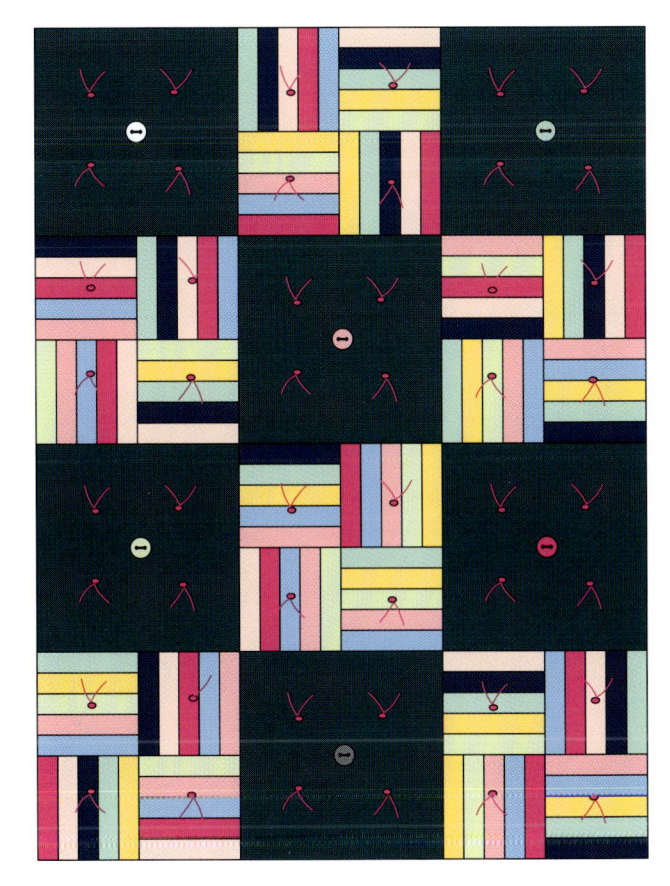

Old-Fashioned Scrappy
Placement Diagram
15 1/2" x 20 1/2"

Figure 5 and 6 strands red embroidery floss. It was hand-quilted in the ditch of seams between blocks and I squares using blue quilting thread.

Figure 5
Make a square knot as shown.

Step 3. Sandwich batting between the stitched top and the backing piece; pin or baste layers together to hold. Quilt as desired by hand or machine.

Step 4. When quilting is complete, trim batting and backing fabric even with raw edges of quilt top.

Step 5. Bind edges with 1"-wide green print prepared binding strip referring to Binding Your Quilt on page 36.

Step 6. Sew a 5/8" button in the center of each I square to finish. ❖

Illustrated Guide to Scrap Miniature Magic **51**

Scrappy Hole in the Barn Door

Choose fabrics in a variety of colors and scales to create movement in this simple block pattern.

PROJECT SPECIFICATIONS
Skill Level: Beginner
Quilt Size: 13 1/2" x 16 1/2"
Block Size: 3" x 3"
Number of Blocks: 9
Techniques: Quick-cut triangles, strip piecing, straight block setting, straight borders and border cornerstone

Hole in the Barn Door
3" x 3" Block

MATERIALS
- 5 assorted dark pink prints 3 7/8" x 3 7/8" A squares
- 5" x 14" rectangle light blue print
- 5" x 12" rectangle 2 different pink solids
- 5" x 12" rectangle each green, brown, navy and red prints
- 8" x 11" strip navy-and-white floral
- 7" x 13" strip gray stripe 
- 7" x 11" strip brown stripe
- 1/8 yard brown print for binding
- Backing 16 1/2" x 19 1/2"
- Batting 15 1/2" x 18 1/2"
- Neutral color all-purpose thread
- White quilting thread
- Basic sewing tools and supplies

CUTTING

Step 1. Cut each A square in half on one diagonal to make A triangles.

Step 2. Cut three 3 7/8" x 3 7/8" B squares light blue print; cut each square in half on one diagonal to make B triangles. Set aside one triangle for another project.

Step 3. Cut two 1 5/8" x 1 5/8" C squares, one 7/8" x 10" D strip and one 2" x 2" E square from each pink solid.

Step 4. Cut two 1 5/8" x 1 5/8" F squares and one 7/8" x 10" G strip each from green, brown, navy and red prints. Stack by color.

Step 5. Cut two 2" x 9 1/2" H strips and four 2 1/2" x 2 1/2" K squares navy-and-white floral.

Step 6. Cut two 2 1/2" x 12 1/2" I strips gray stripe and two 2 1/2" x 9 1/2" J strips brown stripe.

Step 7. Cut 1"-wide strips brown print and join to create a 68" binding strip referring to Binding Your Quilt on page 36.

PIECING BLOCKS

Note: Use a 1/4" seam allowance; press seams before trimming. Press all seams in the direction of small arrows shown on figure drawings.

Step 1. Sew A to B as shown in Figure 1; repeat for five A/B units.

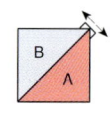

Figure 1
Sew A to B.

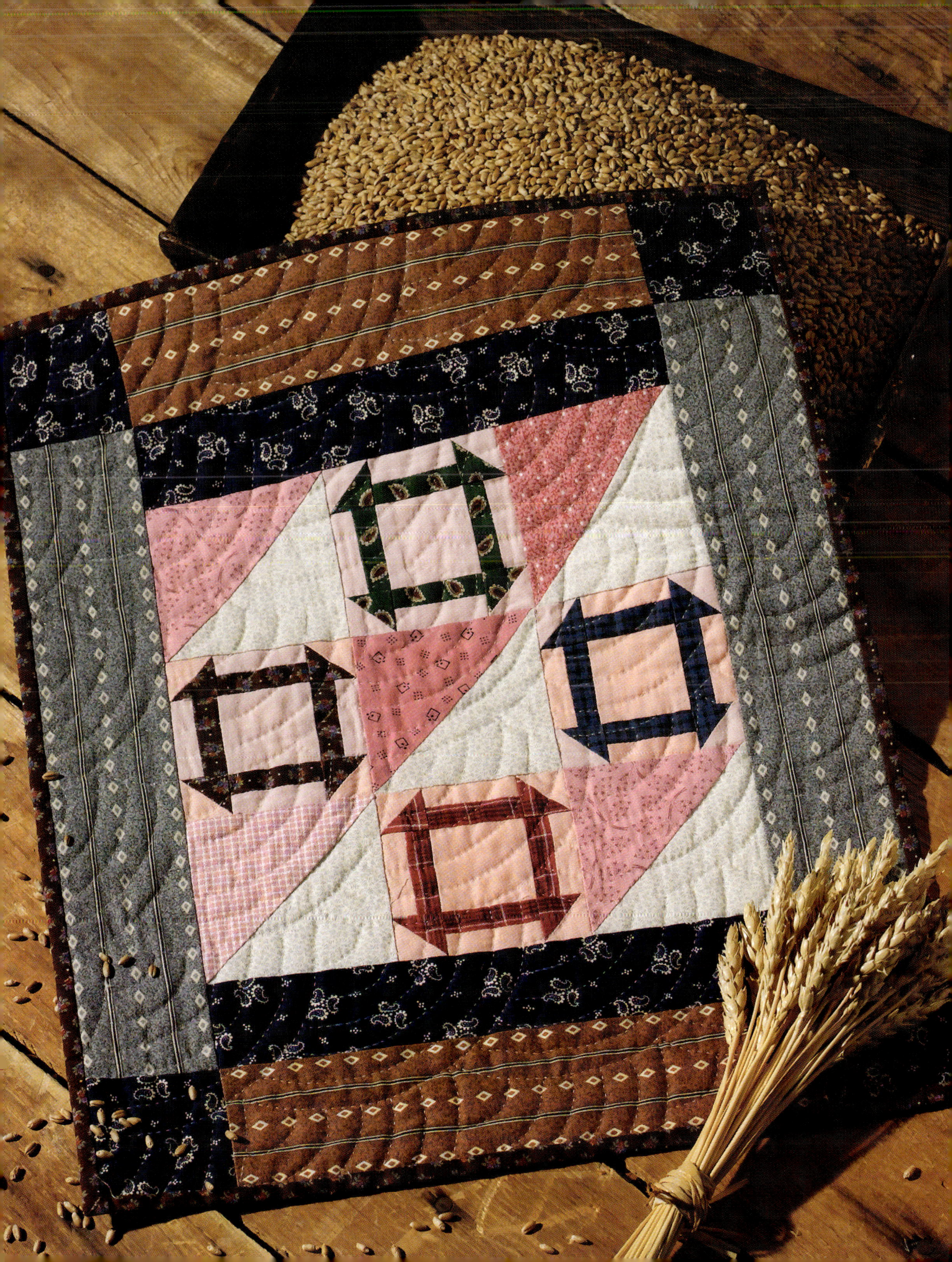

Step 2. Sew one D strip to one G strip with right sides together along length as shown in Figure 2; repeat for all D and G strips.

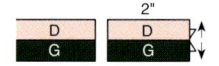

Figure 2
Sew D to G; subcut into 2" segments.

Step 3. Subcut the D/G strips into 2" segments, again referring to Figure 2.

Step 4. Cut each C and F square in half on one diagonal. Sew C to F as shown in Figure 3, making four identical C/F units for each block to total 16 units.

Figure 3
Sew C to F.

Step 5. Sew two matching C/F units to a matching D/G unit as shown in Figure 4; repeat for two matching units for each block to total eight.

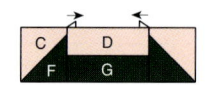

Figure 4
Sew 2 matching C/F units to a matching D/G unit.

Step 6. Sew a D/G unit to opposite sides of a matching E square as shown in Figure 5.

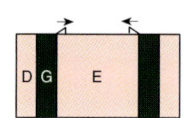

Figure 5
Sew a D/G unit to opposite sides of a matching E square.

Step 7. Sew a C/F/D/G unit to opposite sides of the D/G/E unit as shown in Figure 6 to complete one block. Repeat for four blocks.

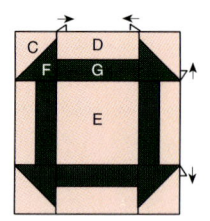

Figure 6
Join matching units to complete 1 block.

PIECING THE TOP

Step 1. Join two A/B units with one block to make an X row as shown in Figure 7; repeat for two X rows. Join two blocks with one A/B unit to make a Y row, again referring to Figure 7.

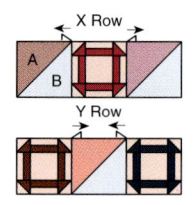

Figure 7
Join blocks and A/B units to make X and Y rows.

Step 2. Join the rows as shown in Figure 8 to complete the quilt top.

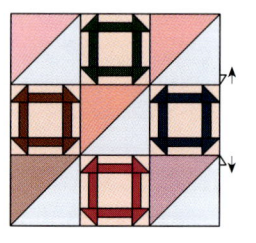

Figure 8
Join the rows.

Helpful Hints for Miniature Quiltmaking

- Use only high-quality, 100 percent cotton fabric for optimum finished results.
- If possible, coordinate fabric manufactured from same design line or collection because the thread count is usually identical, making for more manageable work.
- For the best visual results, select a variety of small-to-medium scale prints or designs in a simple color value range such as light, medium and dark.
- Accentuate small block or border pieces by using, for example, your lightest, brightest or darkest fabric for high contrast.
- New fabric does not need prewashing. The manufacturer's sizing provides for thread stability and crispness, making it easier and more accurate to cut and sew small pieces.
- Test dark fabric for colorfastness; if it runs, do not use.
- Cut and paste up or sew a test block to preview fabric selection and/or check sewing accuracy before cutting fabric and sewing the entire project.
- Before ironing wrinkled or limp fabric, liberally spray it with fabric sizing.
- Rotary-cut slowly and precisely with a sharp blade and small rulers.
- Use fine, long straight-head silk pins.
- A vintage Singer Featherweight sewing machine is ideal for small work because the feed dogs are close together.

Step 3. Sew H to J; repeat. Sew an H/J strip to the top and bottom of the quilt center referring to Figure 9.

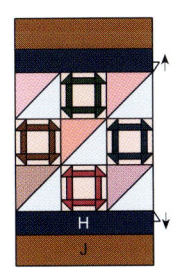

Figure 9
Sew an H/J strip to the top and bottom of the quilt center.

Step 4. Sew K to each end of each I strip as shown in Figure 10; sew a K/I strip to opposite long sides of the pieced center to complete the quilt top; press seams toward K/I.

Figure 10
Sew K to each end of each I strip.

FINISHING

Step 1. Press quilt top on both sides; check for proper seam pressing and trim all loose threads.

Step 2. Mark top for quilting if using patterned design. *Note: The quilt shown was hand-quilted in the pattern given over the entire top using white quilting thread.*

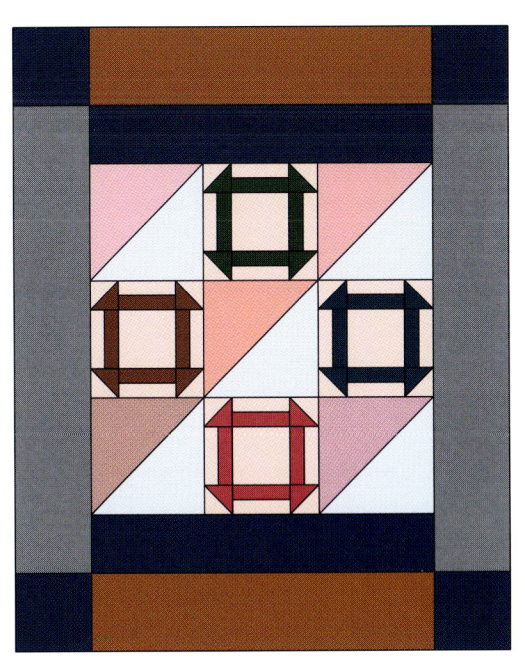

Scrappy Hole in the Barn Door
Placement Diagram
13 1/2" x 16 1/2"

Step 3. Sandwich batting between the stitched top and the backing piece, pin or baste layers together to hold. Quilt as desired by hand or machine.

Step 4. When quilting is complete, trim batting and backing fabric even with raw edges of quilt top.

Step 5. Bind edges with 1"-wide brown print prepared binding strips referring to Binding Your Quilt on page 36. ❖

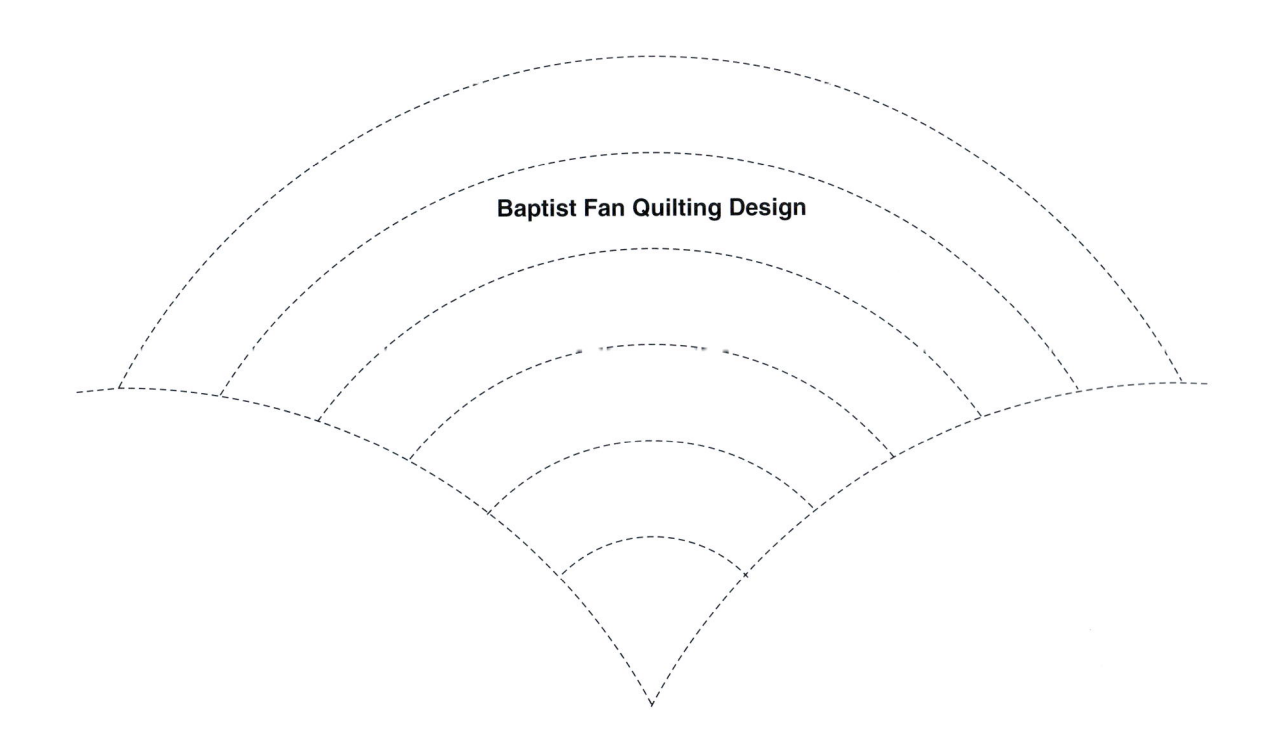

Baptist Fan Quilting Design

Illustrated Guide to Scrap Miniature Magic 55

Homecoming

Take a weekend off and stitch up a quilt of house blocks in any color combination.

PROJECT SPECIFICATIONS
Skill Level: Advanced beginner
Quilt Size: 16½" x 16½"
Block Size: 4¾" x 4¾"
Number of Blocks: 4
Techniques: Quick-cut triangles, straight block setting, sashing cornerstones, sashing and straight borders

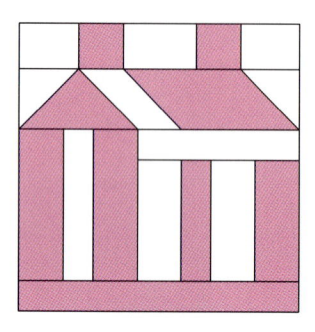

House
4 3/4" x 4 3/4" Block

MATERIALS
- 9" x 18" rectangle each four assorted prints for house prints
- 5" x 9" rectangle blue solid
- ½ fat quarter blue floral
- Fat quarter white solid
- ⅛ yard blue print for binding
- Backing 19½" x 19½"
- Batting 18½" x 18½"
- Neutral color all-purpose thread
- White quilting thread
- Basic sewing tools and supplies and Quilter's Rule™ Mini Triangle 45-degree ruler

CUTTING
Step 1. Cut the following from white solid: eight 1¼" x 1½" A rectangles; four 1¼" x 1¾" B rectangles; four 1⅞" x 1⅞" squares for C; four 1" x 3⅛" D strips; four 1" x 3" E strips; four 1" x 3¼" F strips; eight 1¼" x 2½" G strips; and twelve 1½" x 5¼" H strips.

Step 2. Cut the following from each of the house prints: two 1¼" x 1¼" I squares; one 2¼" x 2¼" J square; one 1½" x 4¼" K strip; two 1¼" x 3" L strips; one 1" x 2½" M strip; one 1¼" x 2½" N strip; and one 1" x 5¼" O strip.

Step 3. Cut nine 1½" x 1½" P squares.

Step 4. Cut two 2¼" x 13" Q strips and two 2¼" x 16½" R strips blue floral.

Step 5. Cut 1"-wide strips blue print and join to create a 74" binding strip referring to Binding Your Quilt on page 36.

PIECING BLOCKS
Note: Use a ¼" seam allowance; press seams before trimming. Press all seams in the direction of small arrows shown on figure drawings. Use the same house print pieces to complete one house block.

Step 1. To piece one block, join two A rectangles, two matching I squares and one B rectangle to make a 5¼" chimney unit as shown in Figure 1.

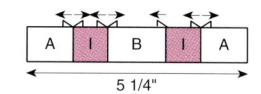

Figure 1
Join 2 A rectangles, 2 matching I squares and 1 B rectangle to make a 5 1/4" chimney unit.

Step 2. With right sides up and using the mini triangle tool, cut 45-degree triangles off each end of the D pieces to make a parallelogram as shown in Figure 2. Repeat with K strips, again referring to Figure 2.

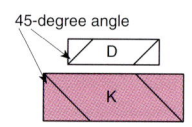

Figure 2
With right sides up, cut 45-degree triangles off each end of the D and K pieces to make parallelograms.

Step 3. Cut each C square in half on one diagonal to make C triangles; repeat with J to make J triangles.

Step 4. Join matching J and K pieces with D and two C triangles as shown in Figure 3 to make a roof unit.

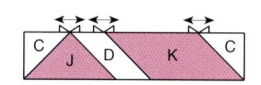

Figure 3
Join matching J and K pieces with D and 2 C triangles to make a roof unit.

Step 5. Join two matching L strips with E to make a door unit as shown in Figure 4.

Master Quilter's Workshop

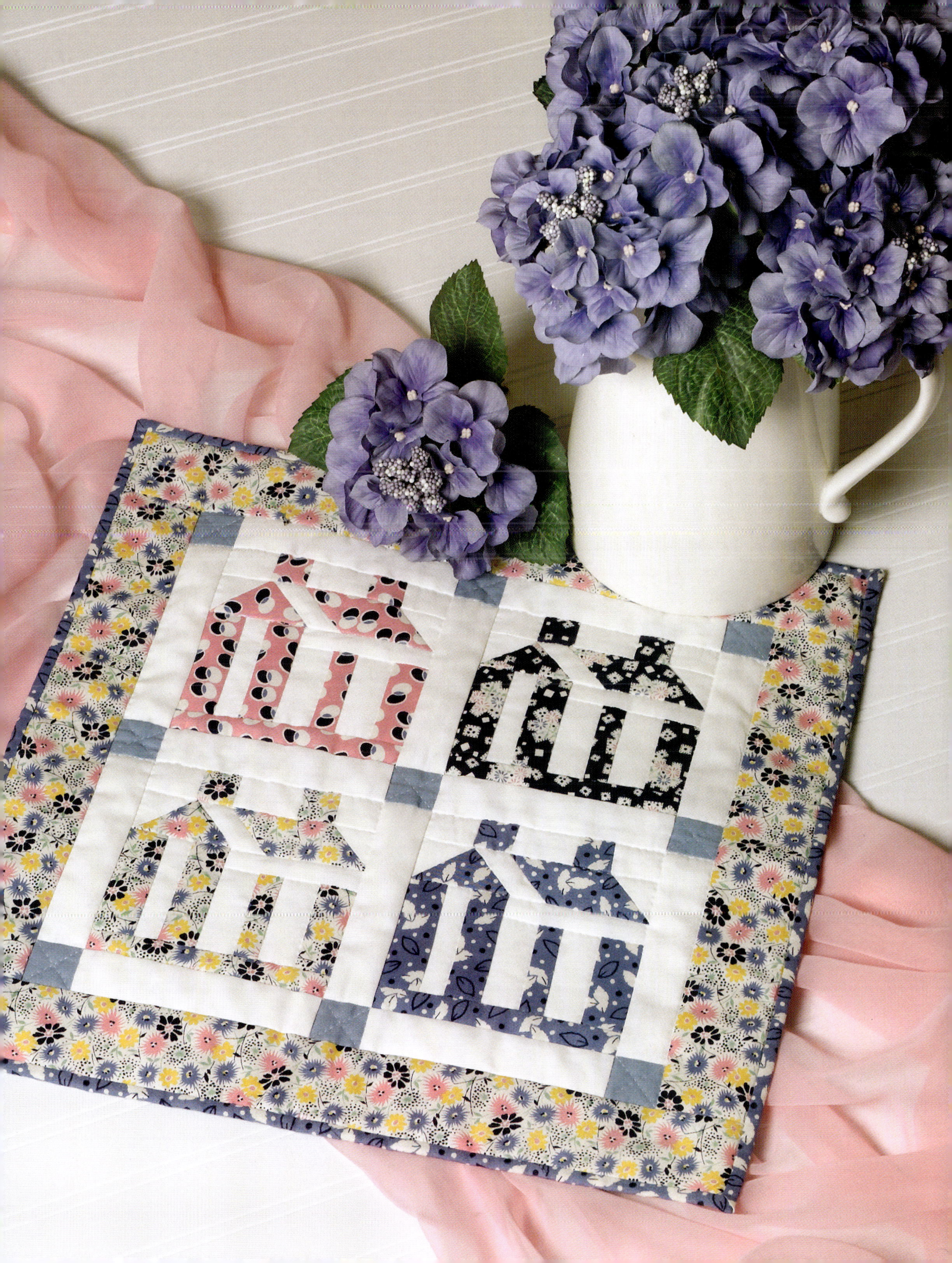

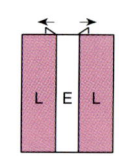

Figure 4
Join 2 matching L strips with E to make a door unit.

Step 6. Join two G strips with matching M and N strips and add F to make a window unit as shown in Figure 5.

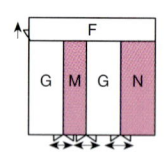

Figure 5
Join 2 G strips with matching M and N strips and add F to make a window unit.

Step 7. Join a matching door and window unit as shown in Figure 6.

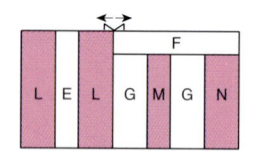

Figure 6
Join a matching door and window unit.

Step 8. Join the chimney, roof and house units as shown in Figure 7.

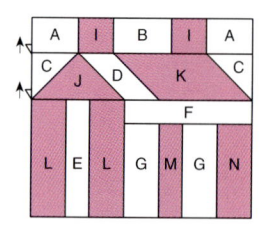

Figure 7
Join the chimney, roof and house units.

Step 9. Sew O to the bottom of the pieced unit to complete one House block as shown in Figure 8; repeat for four House blocks.

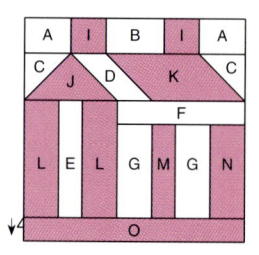

Figure 8
Sew O to the bottom of the pieced unit to complete 1 House block.

PIECING THE TOP

Step 1. Join two House blocks with three H strips to make a block row as shown in Figure 9; repeat for two block rows. Press seams toward H.

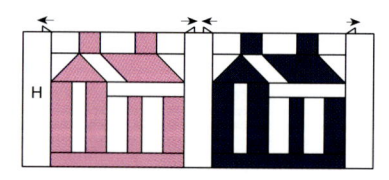

Figure 9
Join 2 House blocks with 3 H strips to make a block row.

Step 2. Join two H strips and three P squares to make a sashing row as shown in Figure 10; repeat for three sashing rows. Press seams toward H.

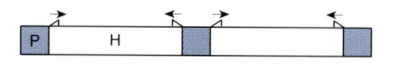

Figure 10
Join 2 H strips and 3 P squares to make a sashing row.

Step 3. Join the block rows with the sashing rows to complete the pieced center; press seams toward sashing rows.

Step 4. Sew Q to opposite sides and R to the top and

58 Master Quilter's Workshop

bottom of the pieced center; press seams toward Q and R to complete the pieced top.

FINISHING

Step 1. Press quilt top on both sides; check for proper seam pressing and trim all loose threads.

Step 2. Mark top for quilting if using patterned design. *Note: The quilt shown was hand-quilted in the ditch of seams and with an X through the center of each P square using cream hand-quilting thread.*

Step 3. Sandwich batting between the stitched top and the backing piece; pin or baste layers together to hold. Quilt as desired by hand or machine.

Step 4. When quilting is complete, trim batting and backing fabric even with raw edges of quilt top.

Step 5. Bind edges with 1"-wide blue print prepared binding strips referring to Binding Your Quilt on page 36. ❖

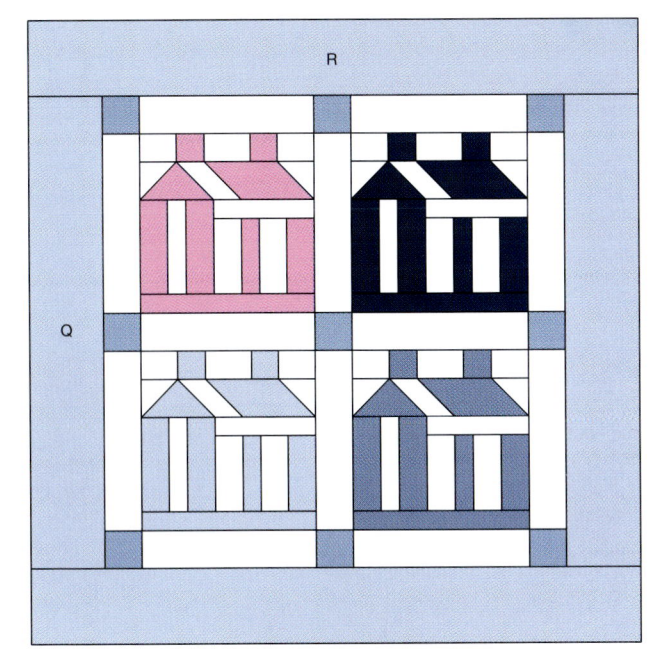

Homecoming
Placement Diagram
16 1/2" x 16 1/2"

Whirling Crowns

A whirling effect is achieved by rotating the position of the four blocks in the center of this quilt.

PROJECT SPECIFICATIONS
Skill Level: Advanced beginner
Quilt Size: 17" x 17"
Block Size: 4 1/2" x 4 1/2"
Number of Blocks: 4
Techniques: Bias-square triangles, three straight borders each with cornerstones

Whirling Crowns
4 1/2" x 4 1/2" Block

MATERIALS
- 1 fat quarter each gold, green, blue and red prints for darks
- 1 rectangle each 11" x 16" tan stripe and beige, cream and tan prints for lights for C
- 1/8 yard cream print for binding
- Backing 20" x 20"
- Batting 19" x 19"
- Neutral color all-purpose thread
- White quilting thread 
- Basic sewing tools and supplies, 3" x 18" ruler and 4" Baby Bias Square ruler

CUTTING

Note: Use the 3" x 18" ruler to cut 45-degree bias strips; reverse cutting direction if left-handed.

Step 1. Cut one 11" x 16" A rectangle from each dark print. Cut one 1 3/4" x 15" bias strip from each A rectangle as shown in Figure 1. Repeat with each light C fabric.

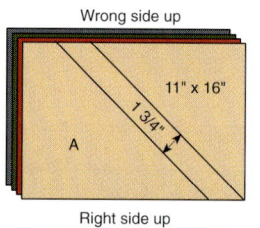

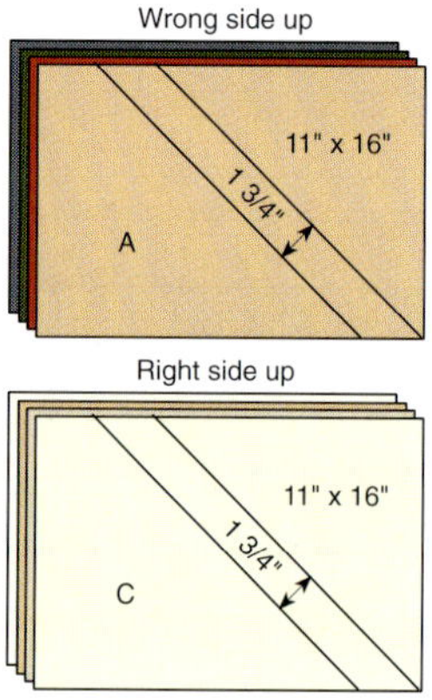

Figure 1
Cut one 1 3/4" x 15" bias strip from each A and C fabric.

Step 2. Cut one 3 7/8" x 3 7/8" B square from each dark print; cut each square in half on one diagonal to make B triangles. Set aside one B triangle from each fabric for another project.

Step 3. Cut four 1 3/4" x 9 1/2" F strips gold print.

Step 4. Cut four 1 3/4" x 12" G strips green print.

Step 5. Cut four 1 3/4" x 14 1/2" H strips blue print.

Step 6. Cut four 1 3/4" x 1 3/4" J squares red print.

Step 7. Cut one 3 7/8" x 3 7/8" D square and one 2" x 2" E square from each of the leftover light prints. Cut each D square in half on one diagonal to make D triangles; set aside one D triangle from each fabric for another project.

Step 8. Cut four 1 3/4" x 1 3/4" I squares from leftover beige print.

Step 8. Cut four 1 3/4" x 1 3/4" K squares from the leftover tan stripe.

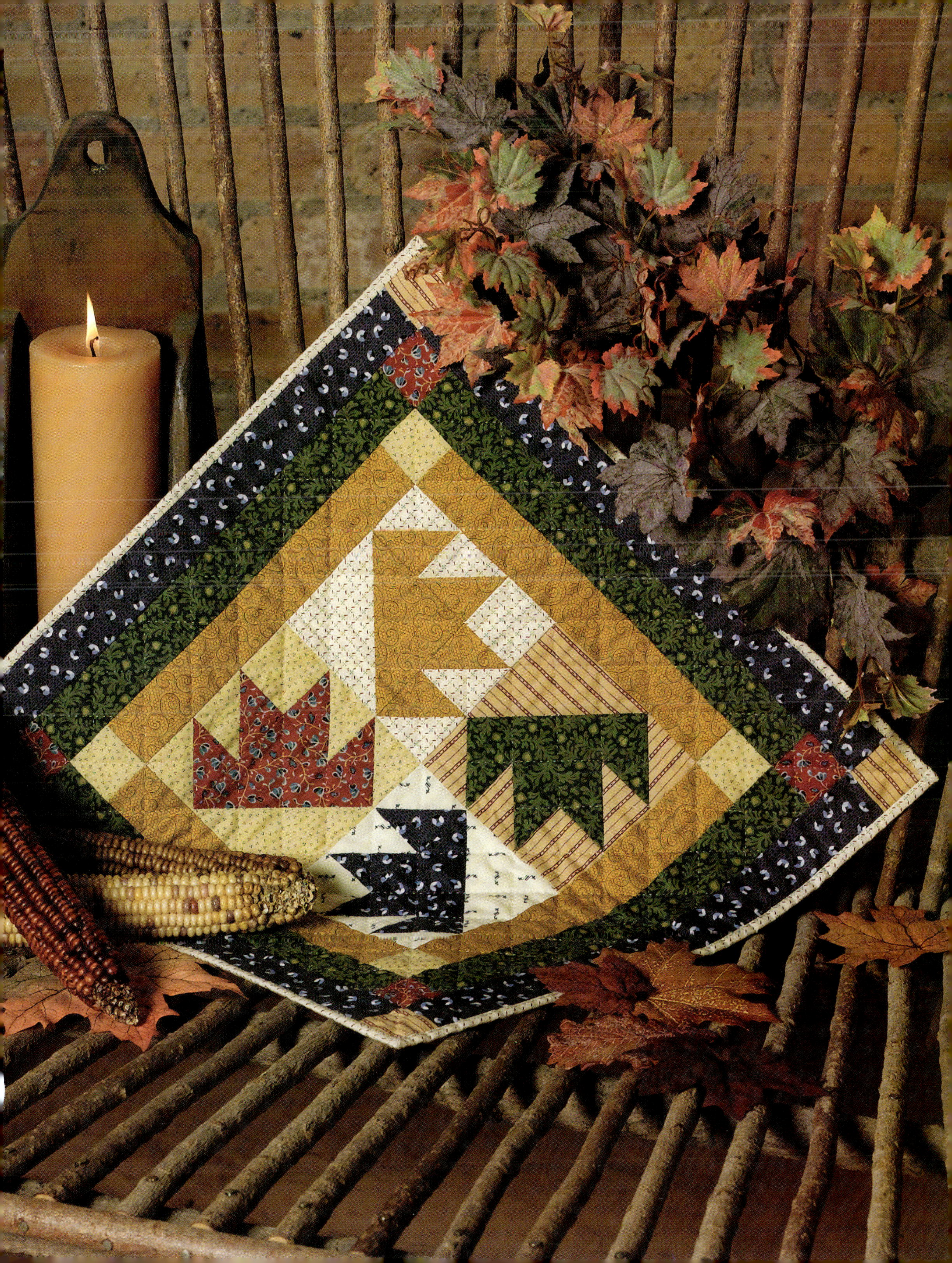

Step 9. Cut 1"-wide strips cream print and join to create a 76" binding strip referring to Binding Your Quilt on page 36.

PIECING BLOCKS

Note: Use 4" Baby Bias Square ruler to cut bias squares or prepare template A/B using pattern given. Use a 1/4" seam allowance; press seams before trimming. Press all seams in the direction of small arrows shown on figure drawings.

Step 1. Sew one A bias strip to one C bias strip with right sides together along length to make an A/C bias strip set as shown in Figure 2; repeat for one bias strip set in each color. Press seams open. *Note: It does not matter which combination you use as long as you have a light and a dark strip in each strip set.*

Figure 2
Sew 1 A bias strip to 1 C bias strip with right sides together along length to make an A/C bias strip set.

Step 2. Cut four 2" x 2" A/C bias squares from each strip set using bias ruler or template A/C, matching line on template to seam between strips as shown in Figure 3. Keep bias squares together in matching color sets.

Figure 3
Cut four 2" x 2" A/C bias squares from each strip set using bias ruler or template A/C, matching line on template to seam between strips.

Step 3. Join two matching A/C bias squares as shown in Figure 4; repeat for two units of each color combination.

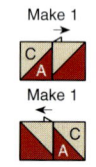

Figure 4
Join 2 matching A/C bias squares.

Step 4. Sew a B to D matching colors used in the A/C combinations as shown in Figure 5. Repeat for four B/D units.

Figure 5
Sew a B to D matching colors used in the A/C combinations.

Step 5. Join matching A/C and B/D units as shown in Figure 6.

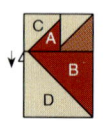

Figure 6
Join matching A/C and B/D units.

Step 6. Sew a matching E square to the A end of an A/C unit as shown in Figure 7; repeat for four A/C/E units.

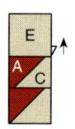

Figure 7
Sew a matching E square to the A end of an A/C unit.

Step 7. Sew a matching A/C/E unit to the A/C/B/D unit to complete one block as shown in Figure 8; repeat for four blocks.

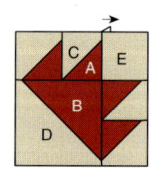

Figure 8
Join units to complete 1 block.

PIECING THE TOP

Step 1. Join two blocks as shown in Figure 9 to make a row; repeat for two rows.

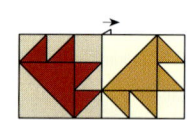

Figure 9
Join 2 blocks to make a block row.

Step 2. Join the block rows as shown in Figure 10.

62 *Master Quilter's Workshop*

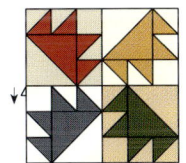

Figure 10
Join block rows.

Step 3. Referring to Figure 11, sew F to opposite sides of the pieced center; sew I to each end of the remaining F strips. Sew the I/F strips to the remaining sides of the pieced center.

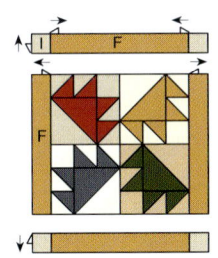

Figure 11
Sew F and I/F to the quilt center.

Step 4. Referring to Figure 12, sew G to opposite sides of the pieced center; sew J to each end of the remaining G strips. Sew the J/G strips to the remaining sides of the pieced center.

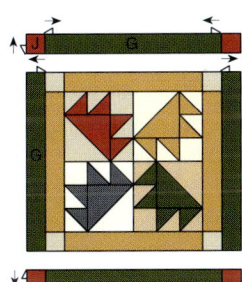

Figure 12
Sew G and J/G to the quilt center.

Step 5. Referring to Figure 13, sew H to opposite sides of the pieced center; sew K to each end of the remaining H strips. Sew the K/H strips to the remaining sides of the pieced center to complete the quilt top.

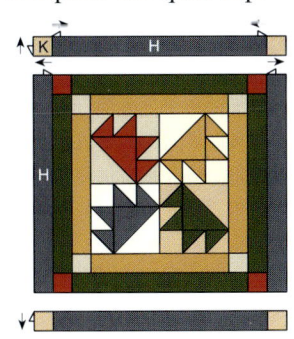

Figure 13
Sew H and K/H to the quilt center.

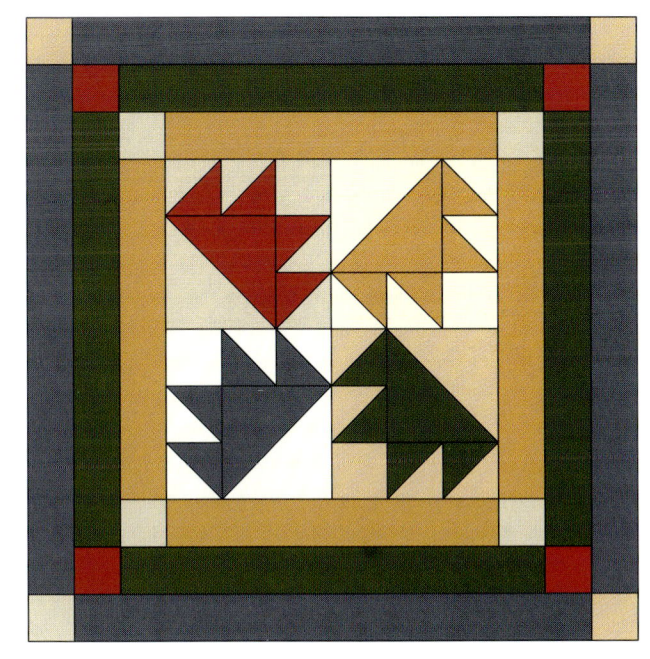

Whirling Crowns
Placement Diagram
17" x 17"

FINISHING

Step 1. Press quilt top on both sides; check for proper seam pressing and trim all loose threads.

Step 2. Mark top for quilting if using patterned design. *Note: The quilt shown was hand-quilted in a 1" diamond crosshatch grid through the entire quilt center including the F and G border strips, using white quilting thread.*

Step 3. Sandwich batting between the stitched top and the backing piece; pin or baste layers together to hold. Quilt as desired by hand or machine.

Step 4. When quilting is complete, trim batting and backing fabric even with raw edges of quilt top.

Step 5. Bind edges with 1"-wide cream print prepared binding strips referring to Binding Your Quilt on page 36. ❖

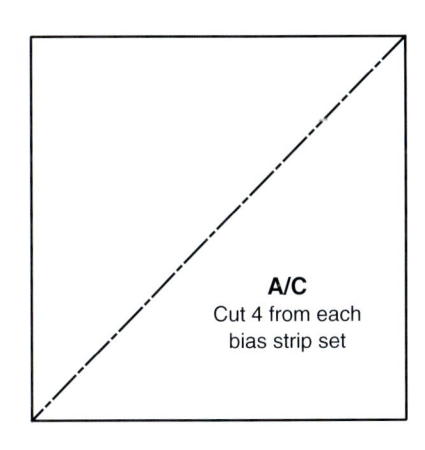

A/C
Cut 4 from each bias strip set

Illustrated Guide to Scrap Miniature Magic **63**

Dainty Basket

Tiny basket blocks set on point float on a light-colored background in this pretty basket quilt.

PROJECT SPECIFICATIONS
Skill Level: Intermediate
Quilt Size: 11" x 11"
Block Size: 2½" x 2½"
Number of Blocks: 5
Techniques: Bias squares, quick-cut triangles, diagonal block setting and one mitered border

Dainty Basket
2 1/2" x 2 1/2" Block

PROJECT NOTES
The basket bases in the sample shown are made with the border fabrics. This quilt is a good example of poor contrast between pieces making it difficult to see the design. A better choice for the basket bases would be the same blue stripe used in the basket top triangles or darker fabrics for both. We have provided an alternate Placement Diagram to help visualize how different the project would look with a change in fabrics.

MATERIALS
- 1 fat quarter tan mottled for background
- 1 fat quarter blue stripe
- 1 fat quarter floral print
- 13" x 13" lightweight batting
- 14" x 14" backing
- Neutral color all-purpose thread
- Cream quilting thread
- Basic sewing tools and supplies, 3" x 18" ruler and 4" Baby Bias Square ruler

CUTTING
Note: Use the 3" x 18" ruler to cut 45-degree bias strips; reverse cutting direction if left-handed.

Step 1. Cut one 11" x 18" rectangle tan mottled; place wrong side up on a flat surface. Cut four 1" x 15" A bias strips as shown in Figure 1.

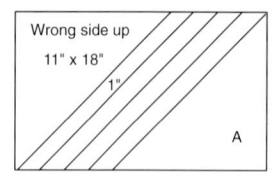

Figure 1
Cut four 1" x 15" A bias strips tan mottled.

Step 2. From the remaining tan mottled, cut five 1" x 1" B squares, three 2⅜" x 2⅜" C squares, ten 1" x 2" D pieces, three 1⅞" x 1⅞" E squares, one 4¾" x 4¾" I square and two 2⅝" x 2⅝" J squares.

Step 3. Cut two 11" x 16" rectangles blue stripe; place pieces right side up on a flat surface; referring to Figure 2, cut two 1" x 15" F bias strips from each piece, reversing direction of strips on each piece.

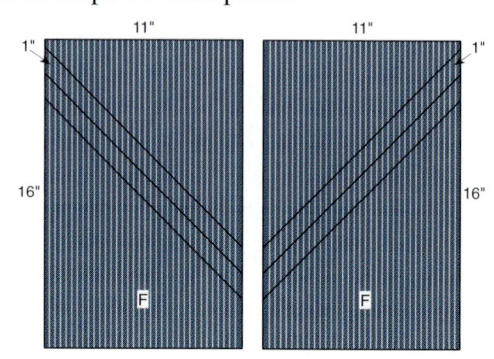

Figure 2
Cut two 1" x 15" F bias strips from each blue stripe rectangle.

Step 4. From the floral print cut three 2⅜" x 2⅜" G squares, five 1⅜" x 1⅜" H squares and four 2¼" x 13" K strips.

Step 5. Cut 1"-wide strips floral print and join to create a 52" binding strip referring to Binding Your Quilt on page 36.

PIECING BLOCKS
Note: Use 4" Baby Bias Square ruler to cut bias squares or prepare A/F template using pattern given. Use a ¼" seam allowance; press seams before trimming. Press all seams in the direction of small arrows shown on figure drawings.

Step 1. Sew one A bias strip to one F bias strip to make an A/F strip set; repeat for four strip sets.

Step 2. Prepare template for A/F bias square using pattern given. Cut 30 A/F 1" x 1" bias squares from strip set with 15 squares with stripes running in one direction and 15 squares with stripes running in the opposite direction as shown in Figure 3.

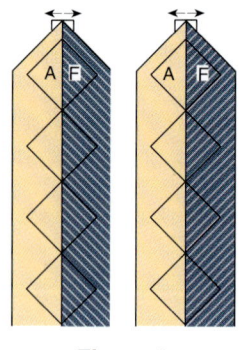

Figure 3
Cut A/F bias squares as shown.

Step 3. Cut C and G squares in half on one diagonal to make six each C and G triangles. Discard one triangle of each fabric.

Step 4. Sew C to G to make a C/G unit as shown in

64 *Master Quilter's Workshop*

Figure 4; repeat for five units. Press seams open and trim corner tails referring to Figure 5.

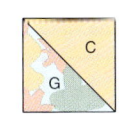

Figure 4
Sew C to G to make a C/G unit.

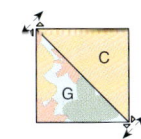

Figure 5
Press seams open and trim corner tails.

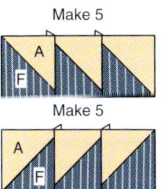

Figure 6
Join 3 matching A/F bias squares to make a set.

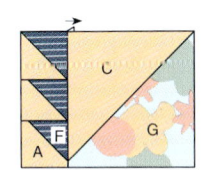

Figure 7
Sew 1 A/F set to 1 C/G square to make an A/F/C/G unit.

Step 5. Join three matching A/F bias squares to make a set as shown in Figure 6; repeat for 10 sets, again referring to Figure 6.

Step 6. Sew one A/F set to one C/G square to make an A/F/C/G unit as shown in Figure 7; repeat for five units.

Step 7. Join one A/F set and one B square to make an A/F/B unit as shown in Figure 8; repeat for five units.

Step 8. Sew one A/F/B unit to one A/F/C/G unit, match-

Illustrated Guide to Scrap Miniature Magic **65**

ing seams as shown in Figure 9; repeat for five units.

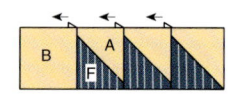

Figure 8
Join 1 A/F set and 1 B square to make an A/F/B unit.

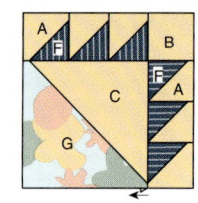

Figure 9
Sew 1 A/F/B unit to 1A/F/C/G unit, matching seams.

Step 9. Cut H squares in half on one diagonal to make 10 H triangles.

Step 10. Sew one D strip to one H triangle to make a set as shown in Figure 10; repeat for five sets and five sets reversed.

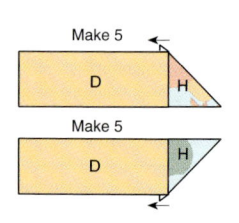

Figure 10
Sew 1 D strip to 1 H triangle; repeat for reverse units.

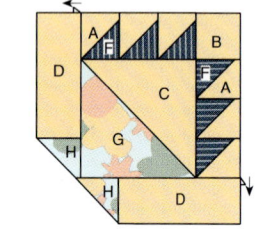

Figure 11
Sew a D/H and D/H reversed unit to a previously pieced unit.

Step 11. Sew a D/H and D/H reversed unit to the previously pieced units as shown in Figure 11.

Step 12. Cut E squares in half on one diagonal to make six E triangles; discard one triangle.

Step 13. Sew an E triangle to each previously pieced unit to complete five Dainty Basket blocks referring to Figure 12.

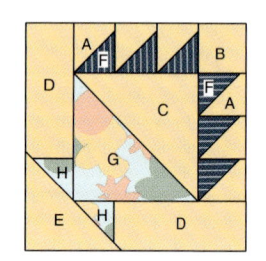

Figure 12
Sew an E triangle to a pieced unit to complete 1 Dainty Basket block.

PIECING THE TOP

Step 1. Cut the I square in half on both diagonals to make four I triangles.

Step 2. Arrange blocks and I triangles in three diagonal rows as shown in Figure 13; join in rows.

Step 3. Cut J squares in half on one diagonal to make four J triangles. Sew a J triangle to each corner of the pieced section to complete the pieced center, again referring to Figure 13.

Step 4. Sew a K strip to each side of the pieced center referring to Borders on page 29; trim excess. Press seams toward K.

FINISHING

Step 1. Press quilt top on both sides; check for proper seam pressing and trim all loose threads.

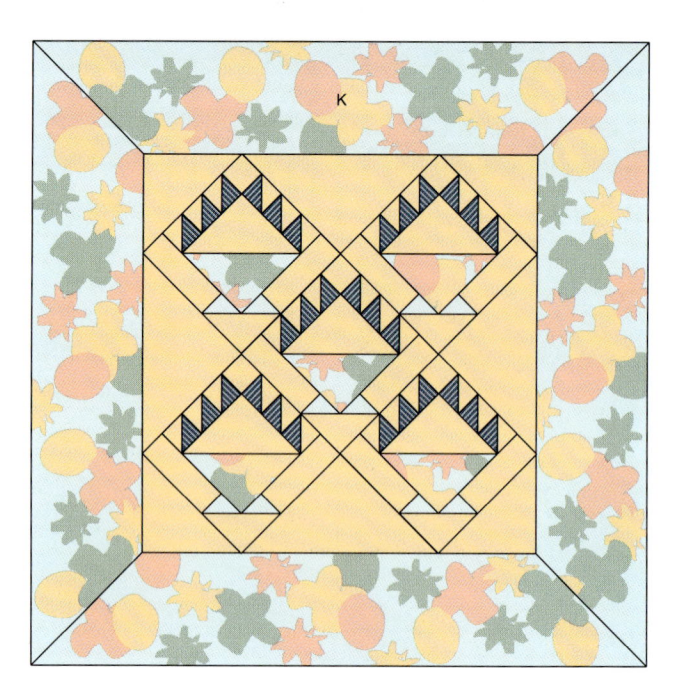

Dainty Basket
Placement Diagram
11" x 11"

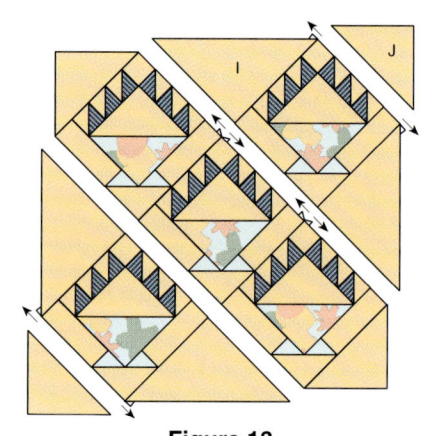

Figure 13
Arrange and join blocks and I triangles in 3 diagonal rows; add J.

Step 2. Sandwich batting between the stitched top and the backing piece; pin or baste layers together to hold. Quilt as desired by hand or machine. *Note: The quilt shown was hand-quilted in the ditch of seams, 1/4" from seams in C/G units and in the heart quilting design given with Kaleidoscope on page 115 on the border strips using cream quilting thread.*

Step 3. Sandwich batting between the stitched top and the backing piece; pin or baste layers together to hold. Quilt as desired by hand or machine.

Step 4. When quilting is complete, trim batting and backing fabric even with raw edges of quilt top.

Step 5. Bind edges with 1"-wide floral print prepared binding strips referring to Binding Your Quilt on page 36. ❖

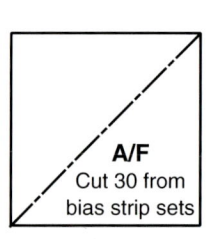

A/F
Cut 30 from bias strip sets

66 *Master Quilter's Workshop*

Spools Variation

A variety of scraps are used in this variation of an old favorite pattern.

PROJECT SPECIFICATIONS
Skill Level: Intermediate
Quilt Size: 10" x 12" (without prairie points)
Block Size: 2" x 2"
Number of Blocks: 12
Techniques: Strip piecing, straight block setting, straight border and prairie points

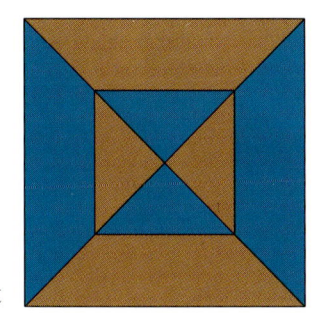

Spools Variation
2" x 2" Block

MATERIALS
- Fat quarter blue print for A
- 6" x 10" rectangle each yellow, brown, black and green prints for B
- 12" x 12" square brown floral for borders
- Fat quarter light green print for H prairie points
- Backing 12" x 14"
- Batting 12" x 14"
- Neutral color all-purpose thread
- White quilting thread
- Basic sewing tools and supplies, Quilter's Rule Mini Triangle 45-degree ruler

CUTTING
Step 1. Cut twelve 1" x 10" A strips blue print.

Step 2. Cut three 1" x 10" B strips each yellow, brown, black and green prints.

Step 3. Cut two 2½" x 8½" F strips and two 2½" x 10½" G strips brown floral.

Step 4. Cut forty-four 1½" x 1½" H squares light green print.

PIECING BLOCKS
Note: Use ¼" seam allowance; press seams before trimming. Press all seams in the direction of small arrows shown on figure drawings.

Step 1. Sew one A strip to each B strip to make an A/B strip set as shown in Figure 1; repeat for three strip sets of each combination.

Figure 1
Sew 1 A strip to each B strip to make an A/B strip set.

Step 2. Prepare template for A/B using pattern given. *Note: Pattern given includes a ¼" seam allowance.* Cut four A/B units, alternating placement of A as shown in Figure 2. *Note: If using the Quilter's Rule Mini Triangle 45-degree ruler, cut length along long edge 3¼" referring to Figure 2.*

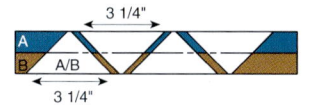

Figure 2
Cut A/B units from each strip set.

Step 3. Join two matching-color A/B units, alternating placement as shown in Figure 3; repeat for all A/B units.

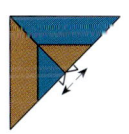

Figure 3
Join matching-color A/B units, alternating placement.

Figure 4
Join 2 matching-color units to complete 1 block.

Step 4. Join two matching-color units to complete one block as shown in Figure 4; repeat for 12 blocks.

PIECING THE TOP
Step 1. Join three blocks to complete an X row referring to Figure 5; repeat for two X rows. Repeat with remaining blocks to complete two Y rows.

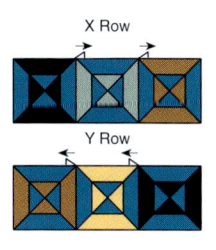

Figure 5
Join blocks to make X and Y rows.

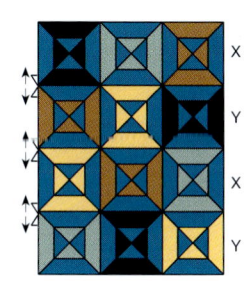

Figure 6
Join rows to complete the pieced center.

Step 2. Join the rows, alternating X and Y rows as shown in Figure 6 to complete the quilt center.

Step 3. Sew F to opposite long sides and G to the top and bottom of the pieced center; press seams toward F and G.

Illustrated Guide to Scrap Miniature Magic

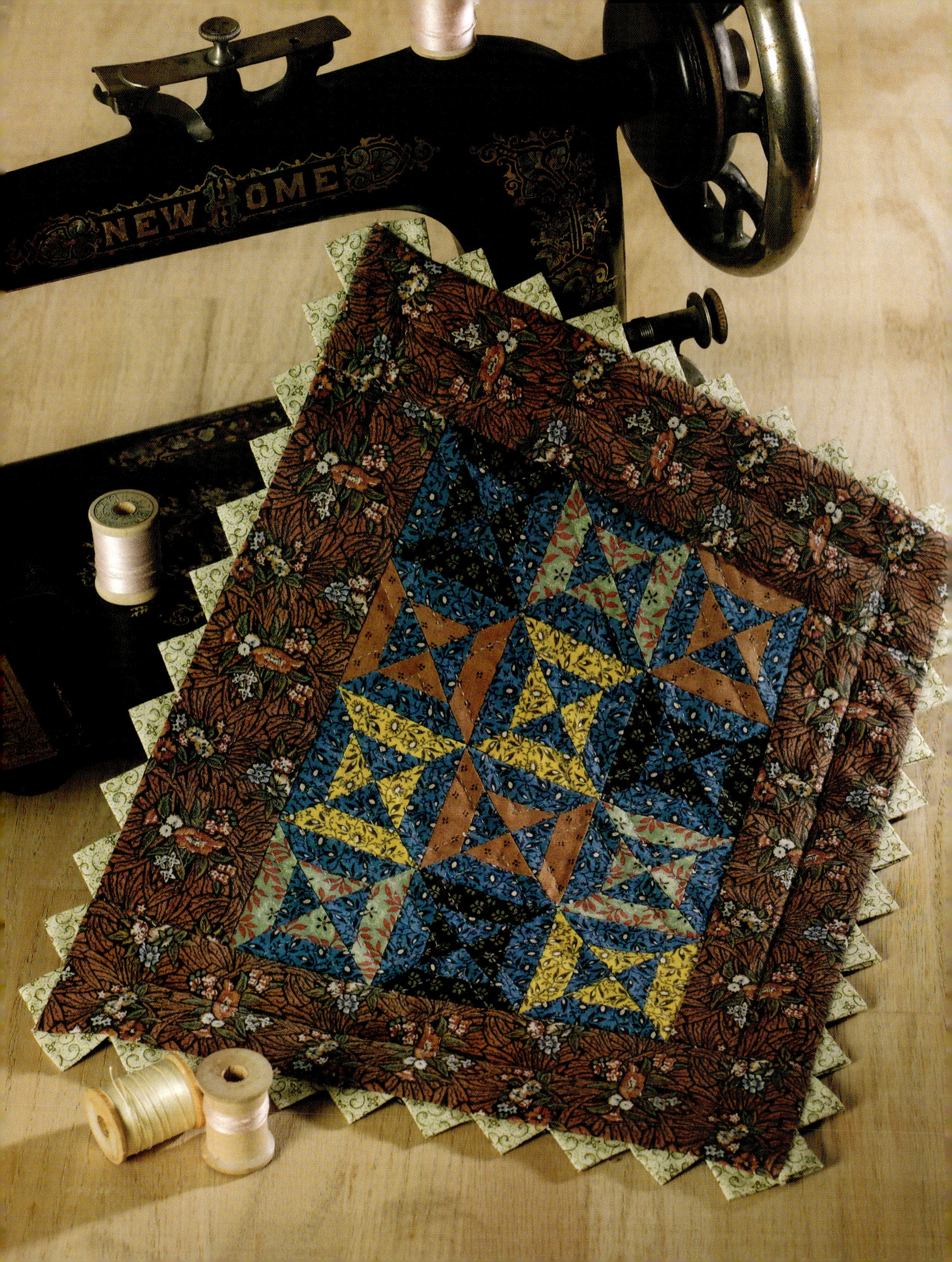
NEW HOME

FINISHING

Step 1. Press quilt top on both sides; check for proper seam pressing and trim all loose threads.

Step 2. Mark top for quilting if using patterned design. *Note: The quilt shown was hand-quilted 1/4" from A/B seams and straight through the border center using white quilting thread.*

Step 3. Referring to Figure 7 to make prairie points, fold each H square in half on one diagonal with wrong sides together; fold again and press. Repeat to make 44 prairie points.

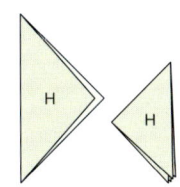

Figure 7
Fold each H square in half on 1 diagonal with wrong sides together; fold again.

Step 4. Stack all H prairie points with folds in the same direction. Arrange 12 H prairie points along each long side edge as shown in Figure 8, beginning 1/4" from quilt corner and overlapping edges at the seam allowance 1/4" as shown in Figure 9; baste in place to hold. Stitch in place with a 1/4" seam allowance.

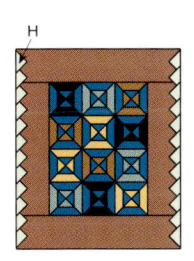

Figure 8
Arrange 12 H prairie points along each long side edge.

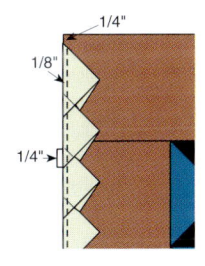

Figure 9
Overlap edges at the seam allowance; baste in place 1/8" from edge.

Step 5. Flip the prairie points to the outside and seam allowance to back of top; press flat. Baste 1/8" through seam on the right side of the top to hold flat as shown in Figure 10.

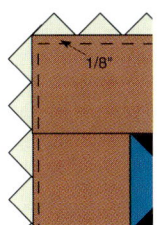

Figure 10
Baste 1/8" through seam on the right side to hold flat.

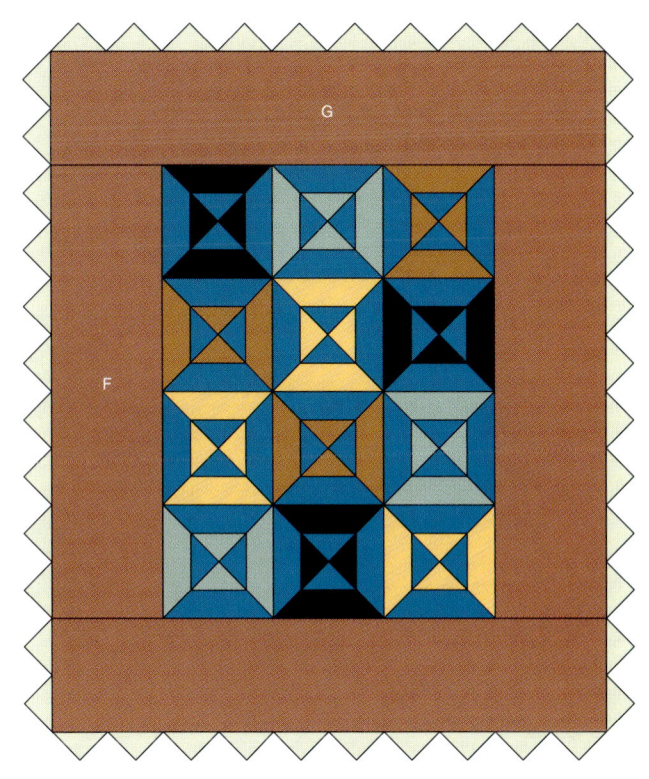

Spools Variation
Placement Diagram
10" x 12"
(without prairie points)

Step 6. Repeat on the top and bottom edges with 10 H prairie points.

Step 7. Lay backing and batting on the completed top; trim batting to the exact same size as the completed top and backing 1/4" larger than the quilt top all around.

Step 8. Press under backing edges 1/4" all around; place right side down on a flat surface. Place batting inside folded-under seam allowance edges of backing and the completed top on the batting; baste around edges to hold.

Step 9. Hand-stitch backing in place all around, covering seams of prairie points as you stitch. Remove all basting.

Step 10. Quilt on marked lines or as desired to complete the quilt. ❖

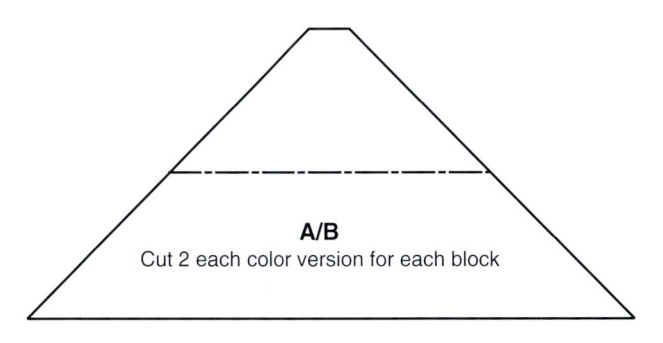

A/B
Cut 2 each color version for each block

Illustrated Guide to Scrap Miniature Magic **69**

Swedish Chain

Strip-pieced segments make even these tiny 1 1/2"-square blocks easy to stitch.

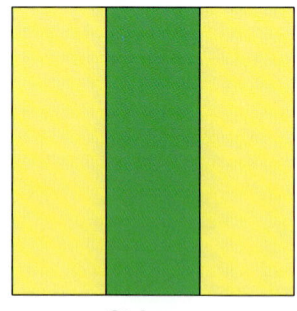

Strippy
1 1/2" x 1 1/2" Block

Nine-Patch
1 1/2" x 1 1/2" Block

PROJECT SPECIFICATIONS
Skill Level: Intermediate
Quilt Size: 13 3/4" x 15 7/8"
Block Size: 1 1/2" x 1 1/2"
Number of Blocks: 32
Techniques: Strip piecing, quick-cut triangles, diagonal and floating block settings and one straight border

MATERIALS
- 5 strips blue solid 1" x 14" for A
- 4 strips yellow solid 1" x 14" for B
- 20 assorted light print scraps 3" x 3"
- 20 assorted 2" x 3" dark print scraps
- 1/2 fat quarter violet solid
- 12" x 16" rectangle yellow-and-green print
- 1/8 yard yellow solid for binding
- Backing 17" x 19"
- Batting 16" x 18"
- Neutral color all-purpose thread
- White quilting thread
- Basic sewing tools and supplies

CUTTING
Step 1. Cut two 1" x 2" C pieces from each of the 3" x 3" squares assorted light prints for a total of 40 C rectangles.

Step 2. Cut one 1" x 2" D piece from each of the assorted dark prints for 20 D rectangles.

Step 3. Cut four 4" x 4" E squares and two 2 3/4" x 2 3/4" F squares violet solid.

Step 4. Cut two 2 1/2" x 11 7/8" G and two 2 1/2" x 13 3/4" H strips yellow-and-green print.

Step 5. Cut 1"-wide strips yellow solid and join to create a 68" binding strip referring to Binding Your Quilt on page 36.

PIECING BLOCKS
Note: Use a 1/4" seam allowance; press seams before trimming. Press all seams in the direction of small arrows shown on figure drawings.

Step 1. Referring to Figure 1, sew a B strip between two A strips with right sides together along length to make an A/B/A strip set; repeat for two strip sets. Subcut into 1" segments. You will need 24 A/B/A segments.

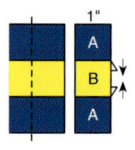

Figure 1
Sew a B strip between 2 A strips with right sides together along length to make an A/B/A strip set; subcut into 1" segments.

Step 2. Referring to Figure 2, sew an A strip between two B strips to make a B/A/B strip set; subcut into 1" segments. You will need 12 B/A/B segments.

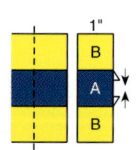

Figure 2
Sew an A strip between 2 B strips to make a B/A/B strip set; subcut into 1" segments.

Step 3. Sew a B/A/B segment between two A/B/A segments to complete one Nine-Patch block as shown in Figure 3; repeat for 12 blocks.

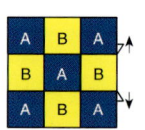

Figure 3
Sew a B/A/B segment between 2 A/B/A segments to complete 1 Nine-Patch block.

70 Master Quilter's Workshop

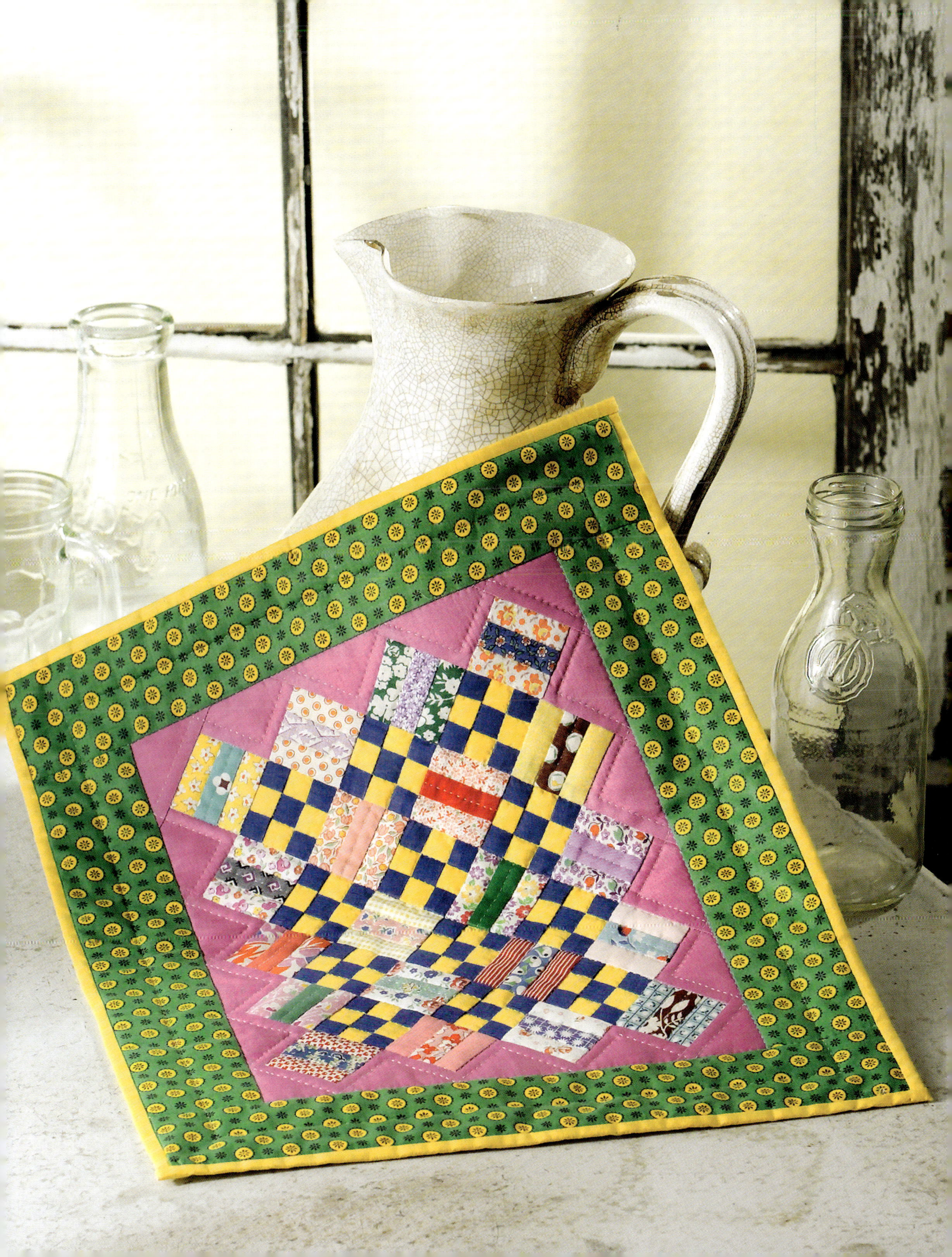

Step 4. Sew D between two C pieces to complete one Strippy block as shown in Figure 4; repeat for 20 blocks.

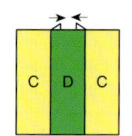

Figure 4
Sew D between 2 C pieces to complete 1 Strippy block.

PIECING THE TOP

Step 1. Cut each E square in half on both diagonals to make oversized E triangles; you will need 14 E triangles; set aside two E triangles for another project.

Step 2. Arrange the Nine-Patch and Strippy blocks with E in diagonal rows referring to Figure 5; join blocks in rows, again referring to Figure 5.

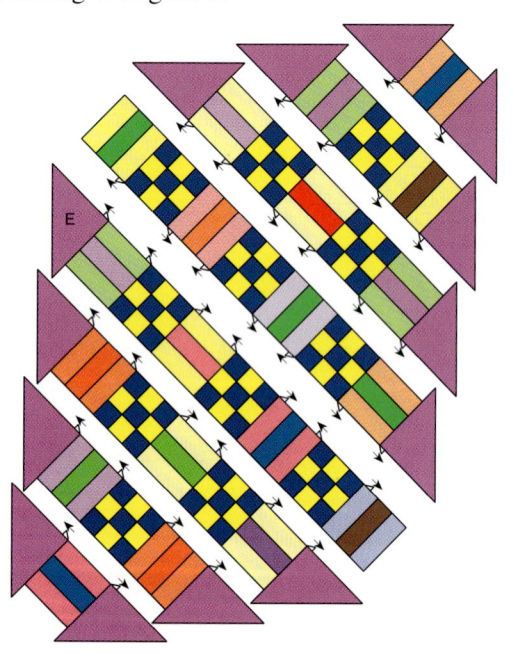

Figure 5
Arrange the Nine-Patch and Strippy blocks with E in diagonal rows; join blocks in rows.

Step 3. Join the rows as shown in Figure 6; press seams in one direction.

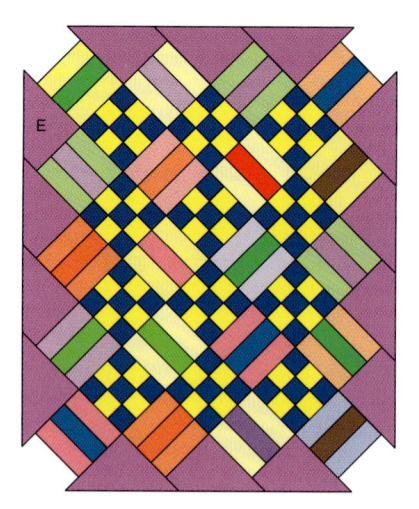

Figure 6
Join the rows.

Step 4. Cut each F square in half on one diagonal to make F corner triangles. Sew F to each corner of the pieced top as shown in Figure 7.

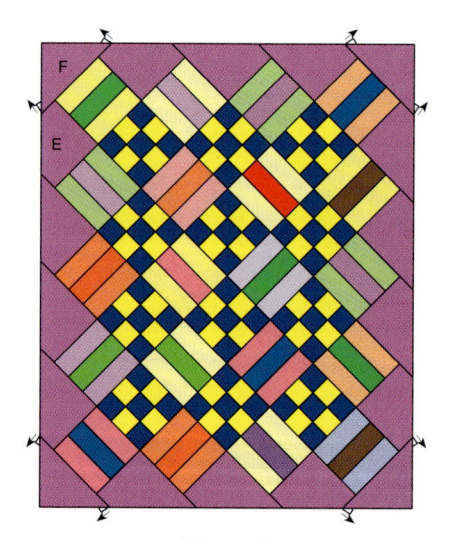

Figure 7
Sew F to each corner of the pieced top.

Helpful Hints for Miniature Quiltmaking

- Use the same sewing machine to stitch the entire project to guarantee identical seams throughout.
- For a superior seam guide, place rotary-cut strip of adhesive moleskin precisely ¼" to the right of the machine needle, using a clear ruler as a placement guide.
- Use the same fine thread for both bobbin and top of machine, such as Mettler Metrosene Plus.
- Sew slowly with an accurate and consistent ¼"-wide seam allowance.

- Sew the entire seam length—no need to backstitch to start or finish a seam.
- Sew about 16–18 stitches per inch for strip piecing. Sew about 12–14 stitches per inch for remainder of sewing. Avoid too-small stitches, which are difficult to rip out.
- Trim excess bulk from intersecting seams to ⅛" before seaming. Once any seam is trimmed, it is difficult to rip and resew.
- The ironing surface should have a minimum of padding for ideal pressing.

Swedish Chain
Placement Diagram
13 3/4" x 15 7/8"

Step 5. Trim edges to leave ⅝" beyond block points all around as shown in Figure 8.

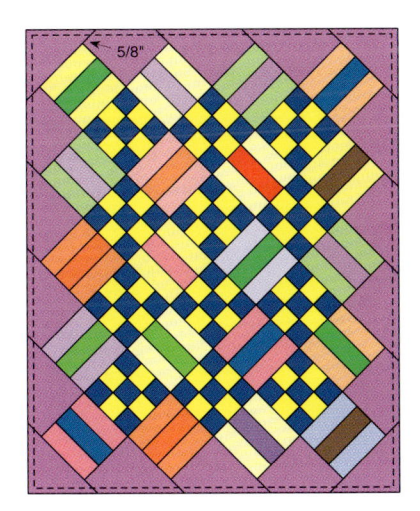

Figure 8
Trim edges to leave 5/8" beyond block points.

Step 6. Sew G to opposite long sides and H to the top and bottom of the pieced top; press seams toward strips.

FINISHING
Step 1. Press quilt top on both sides; check for proper seam pressing and trim all loose threads.

Step 2. Mark top for quilting if using patterned design. *Note: The quilt shown was hand-quilted in the ditch of seams between blocks, down the center of each Strippy block and border strip and ¼" from seams on each E and F triangle using white quilting thread.*

Step 3. Sandwich batting between the stitched top and the backing piece; pin or baste layers together to hold. Quilt as desired by hand or machine.

Step 4. When quilting is complete, trim batting and backing fabric even with raw edges of quilt top.

Step 5. Bind edges with 1"-wide yellow solid prepared binding strips referring to Binding Your Quilt on page 36. ❖

Illustrated Guide to Scrap Miniature Magic **73**

Fiery Baskets

Bright, miniature fabric basket blocks float on a white background in this tiny square quilt.

PROJECT SPECIFICATIONS

Skill Level: Intermediate
Quilt Size: 14 1/8" x 14 1/8"
Block Size: 3 3/4" x 3 3/4"
Number of Blocks: 4
Techniques: Bias squares, quick-cut triangles, diagonal block setting, one straight border with pieced cornerstones and pieced binding

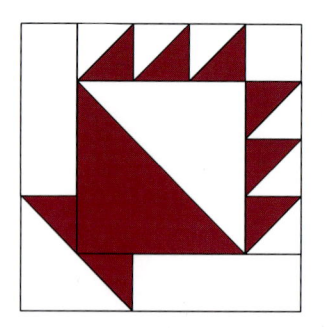

MATERIALS

- 1 fat quarter bright print
- 1/4 yard pink print
- 1/2 yard white solid
- Backing 17" x 17"
- Batting 16 1/2" x 16 1/2"
- Neutral color all-purpose thread
- White quilting thread
- Basic sewing tools and supplies

CUTTING

Step 1. Cut one 11" x 18" A piece bright print.

Step 2. Cut two 3 1/8" x 3 1/8" B squares, four 1 5/8" x 1 5/8" C squares and two 2 3/4" x 2 3/4" L squares from the remaining bright print.

Step 3. Cut one 11" x 18" D piece white solid.

Step 4. Cut four 1 1/4" x 1 1/4" E squares, two 3 1/8" x 3 1/8" F squares, one 2 3/4" x 12" G piece, two 2 3/8" x 2 3/8" H squares, two 6 1/4" x 6 1/4" I squares, two 2 3/4" x 2 3/4" J squares and four 1" x 11" K strips from the remaining white solid.

Step 5. Cut four 2" x 11" M strips and eight 1" x 3" N strips bright print.

PIECING BLOCKS

Note: Use 4" Baby Bias Square ruler to cut bias squares or prepare template A/D using pattern given. Use a 1/4" seam allowance. Press seams before trimming. Press all seams in the direction of small arrows shown on figure drawings.

Step 1. Layer the A and D pieces with right sides together; cut four 1 1/4" x 15" bias strips (four from each fabric) as shown in Figure 1.

Step 2. Sew one A bias strip to one D bias strip with right sides together along length to make an A/D bias strip set as shown in Figure 2; repeat for four sets.

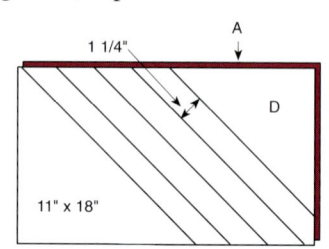

Figure 1
Layer the A and D pieces with right sides together; cut four 1 1/4" x 15" pieces.

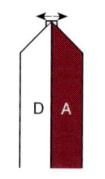

Figure 2
Sew 1 A bias strip to 1 D bias strip with right sides together along length to make an A/D bias strip set.

Step 3. Cut twenty-four 1 1/4" x 1 1/4" A/D bias squares from strip sets using bias ruler or template A/D, matching line on template to seam between strips as shown in Figure 3.

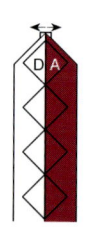

Figure 3
Cut A/D units from the bias strip set.

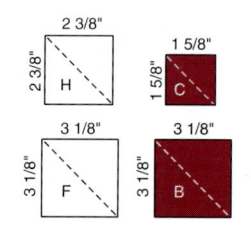

Figure 4
Cut B, C, F and H squares in half on 1 diagonal.

Step 4. Cut each B square in half on one diagonal to make four B triangles. Repeat with C squares for C triangles, F squares for F triangles and H squares for H triangles as shown in Figure 4.

Step 5. Sew B to F to make a B/F unit as shown in Figure 5; repeat for four units;

Step 6. Join three A/D bias squares to make a set as shown in Figure 6; repeat for four sets.

74 *Master Quilter's Workshop*

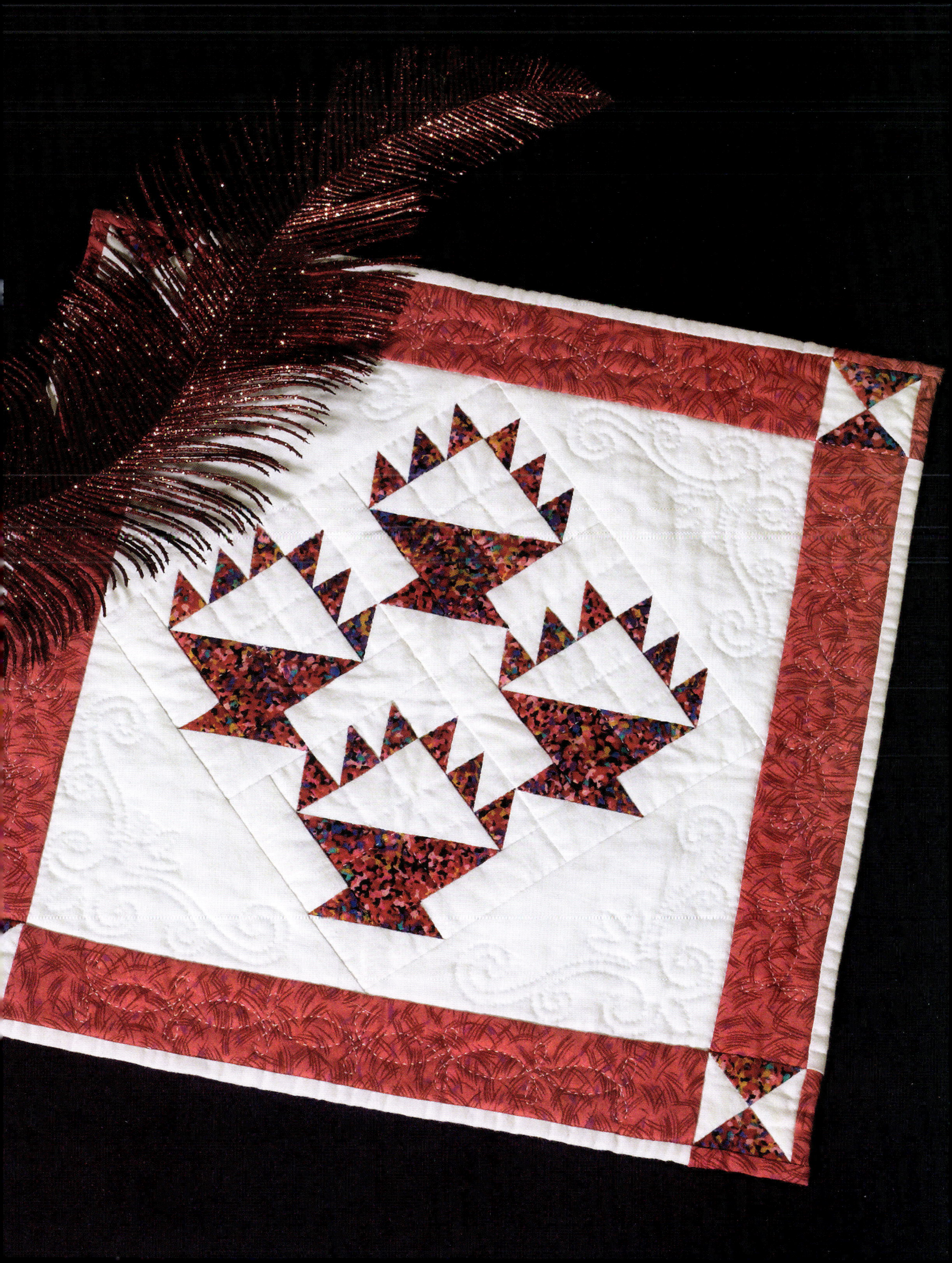

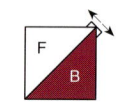

Figure 5
Sew B to F to make a B/F unit.

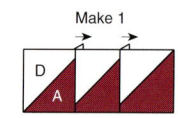

Figure 6
Make 1
Join 3 A/D bias squares to make a set.

Step 7. Sew an A/D set to the left side of one B/F unit as shown in Figure 7; repeat for four units.

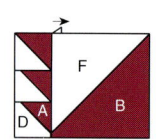

Figure 7
Sew an A/D set to the left side of 1 B/F unit.

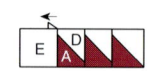

Figure 8
Join 1 E square and 3 A/D bias squares to make an E/A/D unit.

Step 8. Join one E square and three A/D bias squares to make an E/A/D unit as shown in Figure 8; repeat for four units.

Step 9. Sew an E/A/D unit to the top of the A/D/B/F unit as shown in Figure 9.

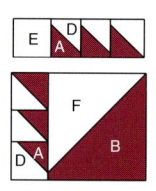

Figure 9
Sew an E/A/D unit to the top of the A/D/B/F unit.

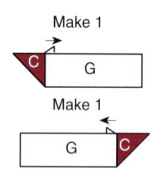

Figure 10
Make 1
Make 1
Sew C to G.

Step 10. Cut the G strip into eight 1¼" segments.

Step 11. Sew C to G as shown in Figure 10; repeat for two units. Sew a C/G unit to the B sides of the completed unit as shown in Figure 11.

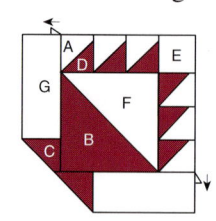

Figure 11
Sew a C/G unit to the B sides of the completed unit.

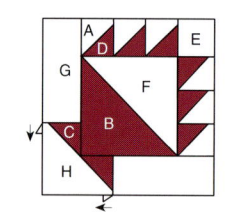

Figure 12
Sew H to the completed unit to complete 1 block.

Step 12. Sew H to the completed unit to complete one block as shown in Figure 12; repeat for four blocks.

PIECING THE TOP

Step 1. Join two blocks to make a row as shown in Figure 13; repeat for two rows.

Step 2. Join the rows to complete the block center section as shown in Figure 14.

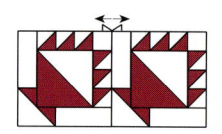

Figure 13
Join 2 blocks to make a row.

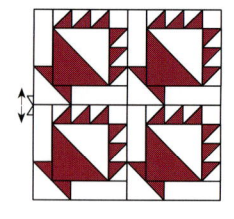

Figure 14
Join the rows to complete the block center.

Step 3. Cut each I square in half on one diagonal to make four I triangles. Sew I to each side of the pieced block center section to complete the quilt center as shown in Figure 15.

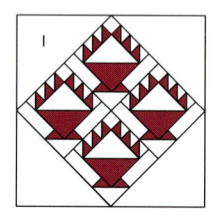

Figure 15
Sew I to each side of the pieced block center section to complete the quilt center.

Step 4. Sew M to opposite sides of the pieced center; press seams toward strips.

Step 5. Cut each J and L square in half on both diagonals to make four each J and L triangles.

Step 6. Sew J to L as shown in Figure 16; repeat for eight units. Join two J/L units, again referring to Figure 16. Repeat for four units.

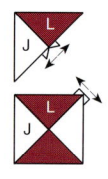

Figure 16
Sew J to L; join 2 units.

Step 7. Sew a J/L unit to each end of the remaining M strips as shown in Figure 17.

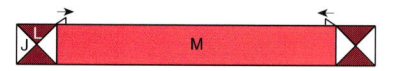

Figure 17
Sew a J/L unit to each end of the remaining M strips.

Step 8. Sew the J/L/M strips to the remaining sides of the pieced center; press seams toward strips.

FINISHING

Step 1. Press quilt top on both sides; check for proper seam pressing and trim all loose threads.

76 *Master Quilter's Workshop*

Step 2. Mark top for quilting using designs given for I and M strips. *Note: The quilt shown was hand-quilted in the ditch of seams and as shown in Figure 18 using white quilting thread.*

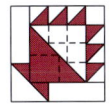

Figure 18
Quilt blocks as shown.

Step 3. Sandwich batting between the stitched top and the backing piece; pin or baste layers together to hold. Quilt as desired by hand or machine.

Step 4. When quilting is complete, trim batting and backing fabric even with raw edges of quilt top.

Step 5. Sew an N strip to each end of each K strip as shown in Figure 19. Press under ¼" on one long edge of each strip. Sew the shorter strips to opposite sides and longer strips to the top and bottom, matching seams between K and N to seams between M and J/L at each corner and referring to Binding Your Quilt on page 36. ❖

Figure 19
Sew an N strip to each end of each K strip.

Fiery Baskets
Placement Diagram
14 1/8" x 14 1/8"

A/D
Cut 24 from bias strip sets

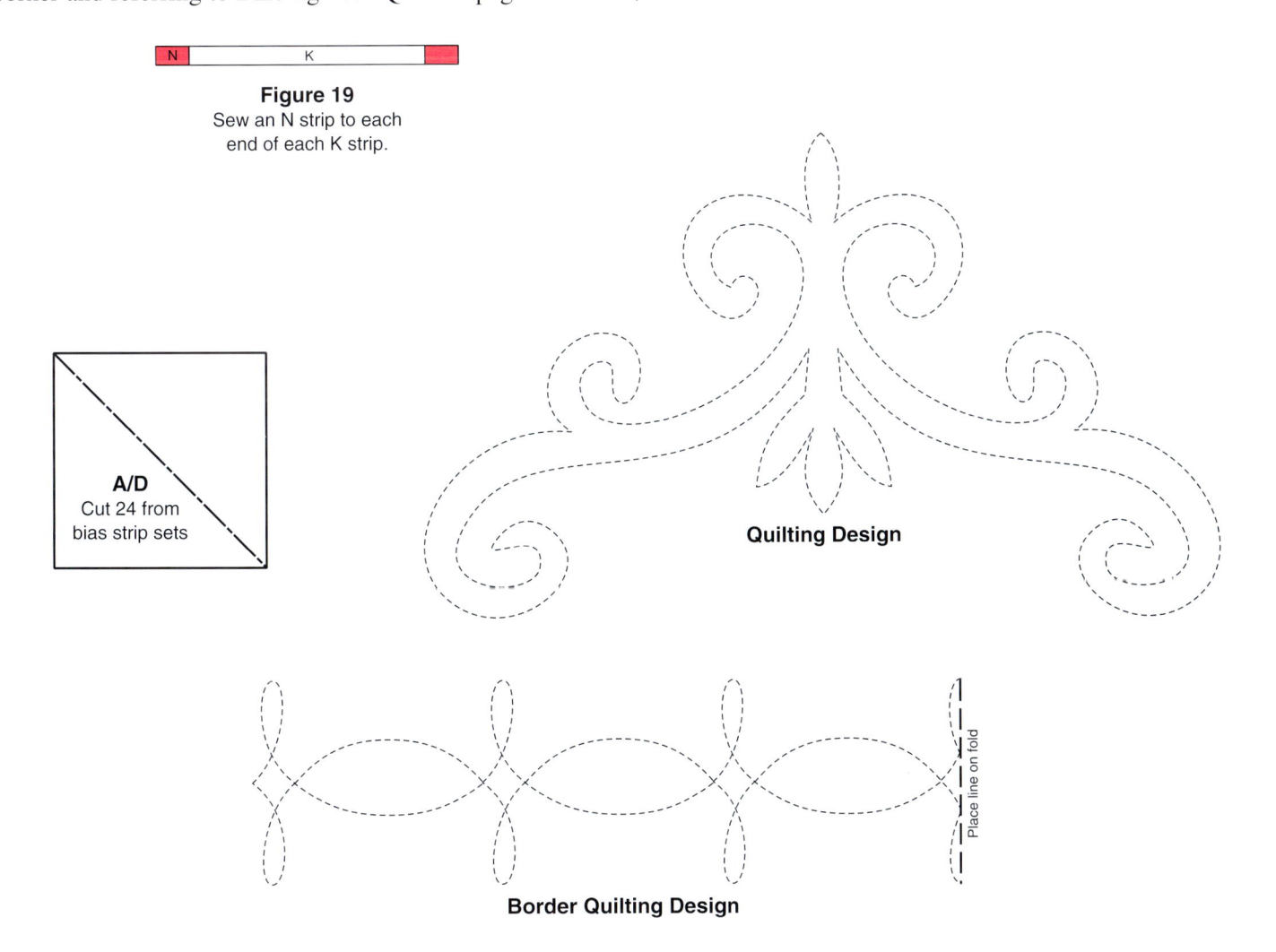

Quilting Design

Border Quilting Design

Place line on fold

Illustrated Guide to Scrap Miniature Magic

Radiant Bear Paw

Glowing colors combined with dark colors set the mood for this unusual setting of Bear Paw blocks.

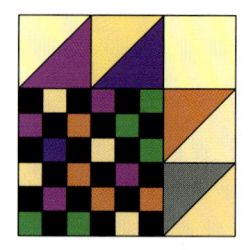

Bear Paw
2 1/4" x 2 1/4" Block

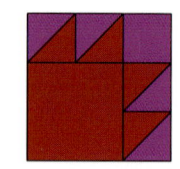

Corner Bear Paw
1 1/2" x 1 1/2" Block

PROJECT SPECIFICATIONS
Skill Level: Advanced
Quilt Size: 11¼" x 14¼"
Block Size: 1½" x 1½" and 2¼" x 2¼"
Number of Blocks: 8
Techniques: Bias squares, straight sashings, straight border with border cornerstone blocks

MATERIALS
- 7" x 10" rectangle 4 assorted dark prints for A
- 7" x 10" rectangle 4 assorted light prints for B
- 5" x 7" rectangle rust solid
- 6" x 6" square black check
- Fat quarter purple solid
- ½ fat quarter dark green solid
- 4" x 9" rectangle rust-and-black floral
- 9" x 18" rectangle gold print for J
- 9" x 18" rectangle purple-and-black plaid for K
- ½ fat quarter rust print
- ⅛ yard black print for binding
- Backing 14" x 17"
- Batting 13" x 16"
- Neutral color all-purpose thread
- Cream quilting thread
- Basic sewing tools and supplies, 3" x 18" ruler and 4" Baby Bias Square ruler

CUTTING
Note: Use the 3" x 18" ruler to cut 45-degree bias strips; reverse cutting direction if left-handed.

Step 1. Layer one A and one B rectangle with right sides together; cut one 1¼" x 10" bias strip from the layered fabrics as shown in Figure 1; repeat for each A and B fabric.

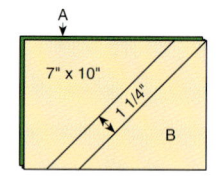

Figure 1
Layer 1 A and 1 B rectangle with right sides together; cut one 1 1/4" x 10" bias strip from the layered fabrics.

Step 2. Cut one 1¼" x 1¼" D square from the remainder of each of the B fabrics.

Step 3. Cut four 1¼" x 2¾" E strips, four 1¼" x 3½" F strips, one 7" x 15" O rectangle, four 1" x 1" Q squares, four 1" x 2" R pieces and four 1" x 2½" S pieces from purple solid.

Step 4. Cut four 1¼" x 3½" G strips rust solid.

Step 5. Cut one 1¼" x 1¼" H square, two 2½" x 10¼" L strips and two 2½" x 7¼" M strips dark green solid.

Step 6. Cut two 1¼" x 7¼" I strips rust-and-black floral.

Step 7. Cut one 7" x 15" N rectangle and four 1½" x 1½" P squares rust print.

Step 8. Cut four 2" x 2" C squares black check.

Step 9. Cut 1"-wide strips black print and join to create a 59" binding strip referring to Binding Your Quilt on page 36.

PIECING BEAR PAW BLOCKS
Note: Use the 4" Baby Bias Square ruler to cut bias squares or prepare template A/B-J/K using pattern given. Use a ¼" seam allowance; press seams before trimming. Press all seams in the direction of small arrows shown on figure drawings.

Step 1. Sew an A strip to a B strip as shown in Figure 2 to make an A/B bias strip set; repeat for all A and B strips.

Step 2. Cut four 1¼" x 1¼" A/B bias squares from each strip set using bias ruler or template A/B-J/K, matching line on template with seam of strip as shown in Figure 3 to total 16 A/B bias squares.

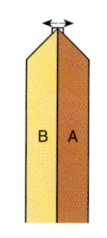

Figure 2
Sew an A strip to a B strip to make an A/B bias strip set.

78   Master Quilter's Workshop

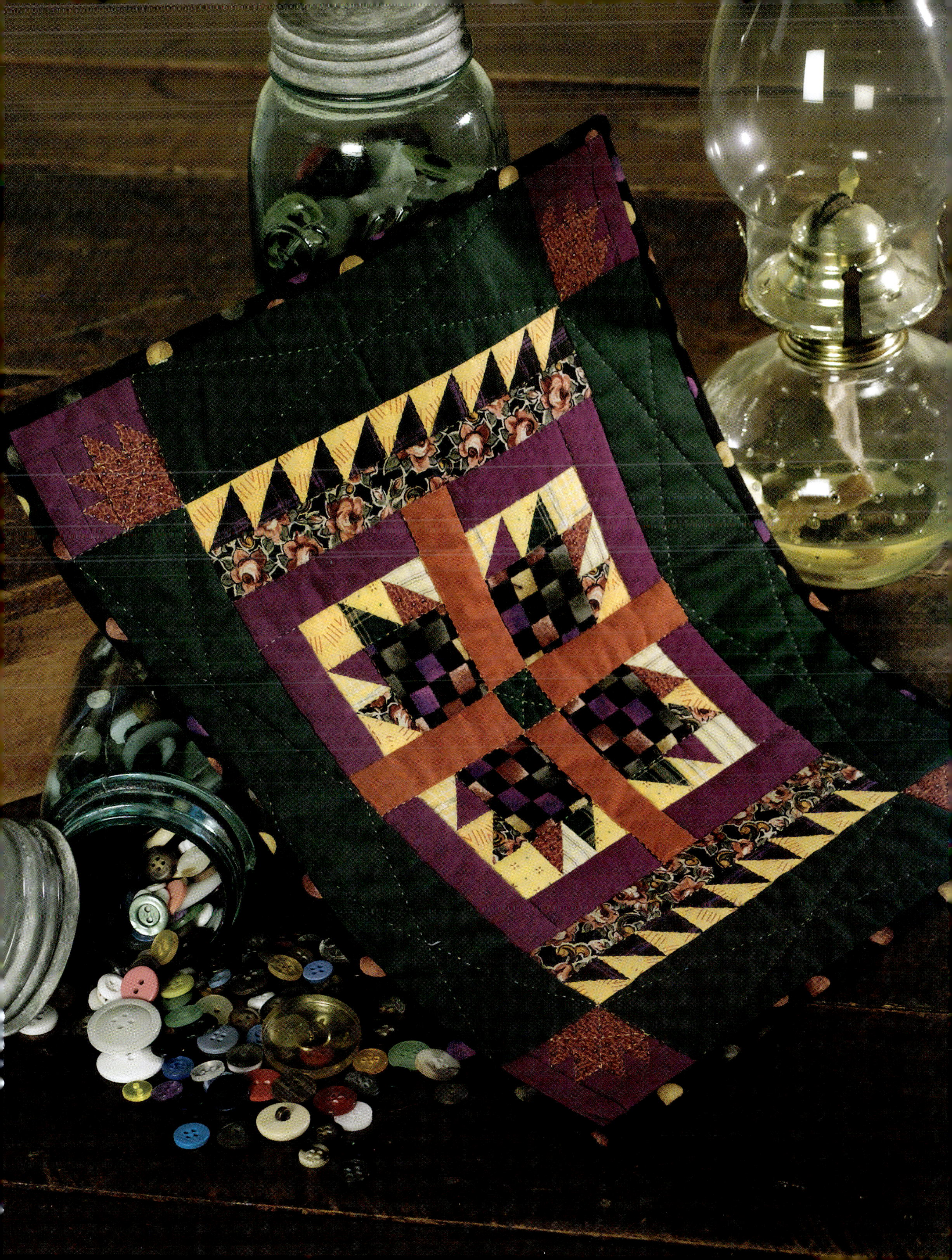

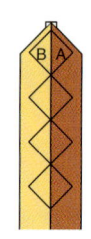

Figure 3
Cut 1 1/4" x 1 1/4" bias squares from strip sets, aligning line on template with seam of strip.

Step 3. Join two assorted A/B bias squares as shown in Figure 4; repeat for eight units.

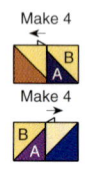

Figure 4
Join 2 assorted A/B bias squares.

Step 4. Sew one A/B unit to a C square as shown in Figure 5; repeat for four units.

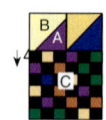

Figure 5
Sew 1 A/B unit to a C square.

Step 5. Sew D to the A side of an A/B unit as shown in Figure 6. Sew to the A/B/C unit to complete one block as shown in Figure 7; repeat for four Bear Paw blocks.

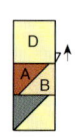

Figure 6
Sew D to the A side of an A/B unit.

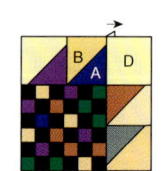

Figure 7
Join the units to complete 1 Bear Paw block.

PIECING CORNER BLOCKS

Note: Use the 3" x 18" ruler to cut 45-degree bias strips; reverse cutting direction if left-handed. Use the 4" Baby Bias Square ruler to cut bias squares or prepare template N/O using pattern given. Use a 1/4" seam allowance; press seams before trimming. Press all seams in the direction of small arrows shown on figure drawings.

Step 1. Layer the N and O rectangles with right sides together; cut three 1" x 10" bias strips from the layered fabrics as shown in Figure 8.

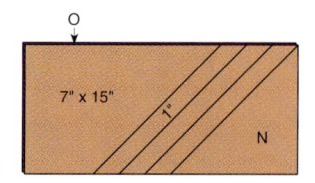

Figure 8
Layer the N and O rectangles with right sides together; cut three 1" x 10" bias strips from the layered fabrics.

Step 2. Sew an N strip to an O strip as shown in Figure 9 to make an N/O bias strip set; repeat for three bias strip sets.

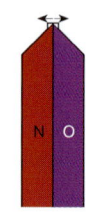

Figure 9
Sew an N strip to an O strip to make an N/O bias strip set.

Step 3. Cut sixteen 1" x 1" N/O bias squares from the strip sets using bias ruler or N/O template, matching line on N/O with seam as shown in Figure 10.

Figure 10
Cut 1" x 1" N/O bias squares from strip sets, aligning line on N/O with seam.

Step 4. Complete four Corner Bear Paw blocks as in Steps 3–5 in Piecing Bear Paw Blocks and referring to Figure 11 for alphabetical arrangement of pieces.

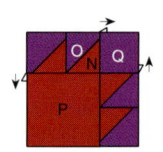

Figure 11
Join units as shown to complete 1 Corner Bear Paw block.

PIECING THE TOP

Step 1. Sew E to one side of a Bear Paw block and F to

80   Master Quilter's Workshop

the adjacent side referring to Figure 12 for positioning of pieces. Repeat for four E/F block units.

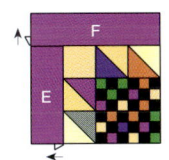

Figure 12
Sew E to 1 side of a Bear Paw block and F to the adjacent side.

Step 2. Join two E/F block units with G referring to Figure 13; repeat for two units.

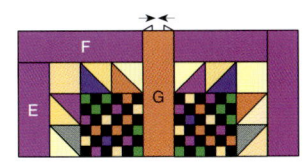

Figure 13
Join 2 E/F block units with G.

Step 3. Sew H between two G strips as shown in Figure 14.

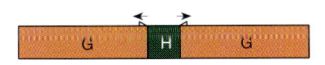

Figure 14
Sew H between 2 G strips.

Step 4. Join the two block units with the G/H unit as shown in Figure 15.

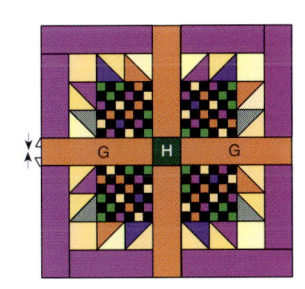

Figure 15
Join the 2 block units with the G/H unit.

Step 5. Sew I to the top and bottom referring to Figure 16.

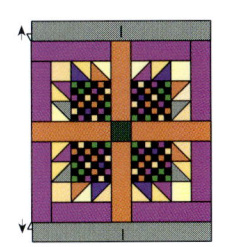

Figure 16
Sew I to the top and bottom.

Step 6. Layer the J and K rectangles with right sides together; cut three 1 1/4" x 12" bias strips from the layered fabrics as for A/B and N/O.

Step 7. Sew a J strip to a K strip as shown in Figure 17 to make a J/K bias strip set; repeat for three bias strip sets.

Figure 17
Sew a J strip to a K strip to make a J/K bias strip set.

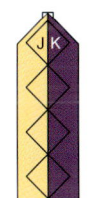

Figure 18
Using the A/B-J/K template, cut 1 1/4" x 1 1/4" J/K bias squares from the strip sets, aligning line on template with seam of strips.

Step 8. Using the bias ruler or A/B-J/K template, cut eighteen 1 1/4" x 1 1/4" J/K bias squares from the strip sets, matching line on template with seam of strips referring to Figure 18.

Step 9. Join nine J/K bias squares to make a strip as shown in Figure 19; repeat for two strips.

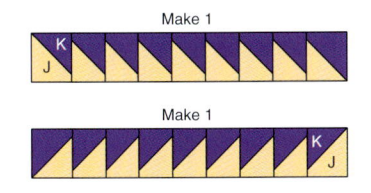

Make 1

Make 1

Figure 19
Join 9 J/K bias squares to make a strip.

Illustrated Guide to Scrap Miniature Magic **81**

Step 10. Sew a strip to the I sides of the pieced section as shown in Figure 20.

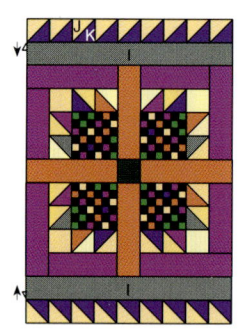

Figure 20
Sew a strip to the I sides of the pieced section.

Step 11. Sew L to opposite long sides of the pieced section; press seams toward L.

Step 12. Sew R to one side of a Corner Bear Paw block and S to the adjacent side referring to Figure 21 for positioning of pieces. Repeat for four R/S block units.

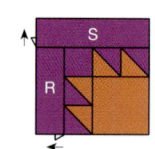

Figure 21
Sew R to 1 side of a Corner Bear Paw block and S to the adjacent side.

Step 13. Sew an R/S block unit to each end of each M strip as shown in Figure 22.

Figure 22
Sew an R/S block unit to each end of each M strip.

Step 14. Sew the M/block strips to the top and bottom of the pieced center; press seams toward M/block strips.

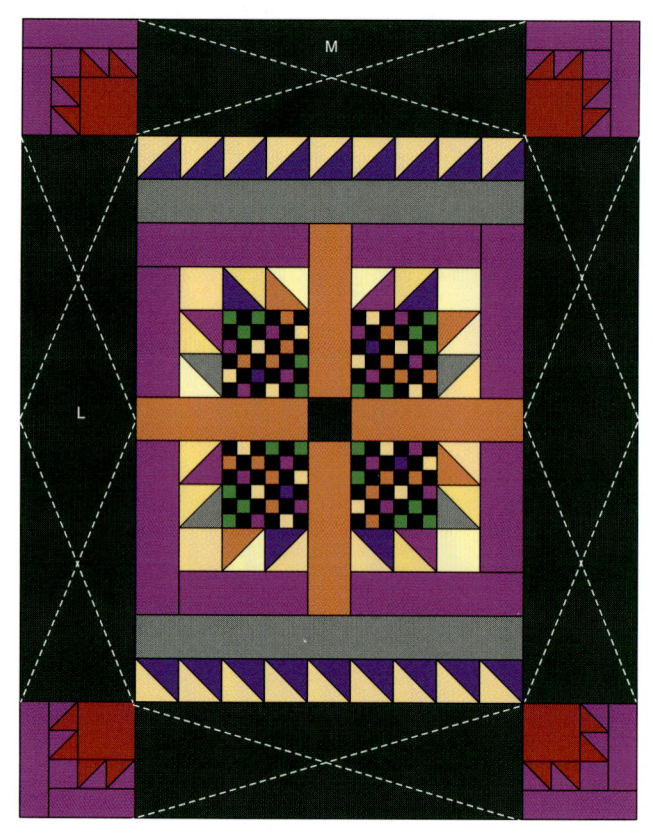

Radiant Bear Paw
Placement Diagram
11 1/4" x 14 1/4"

FINISHING

Step 1. Press quilt top on both sides; check for proper seam pressing and trim all loose threads.

Step 2. Mark top for quilting if using patterned design. *Note: The quilt shown was hand-quilted in the ditch of block seams, in a large X design from corner to corner in M and in large X designs from corner to center on L using cream quilting thread.*

Step 3. Sandwich batting between the stitched top and the backing piece; pin or baste layers together to hold. Quilt as desired by hand or machine.

Step 4. When quilting is complete, trim batting and backing fabric even with raw edges of quilt top.

Step 5. Bind edges with 1"-wide black print prepared binding strips referring to Binding Your Quilt on page 36. ❖

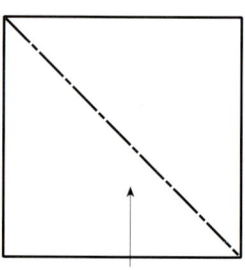

A/B–J/K
Cut 4 from each A/B bias strip set. Cut 6 from each J/K bias strip set

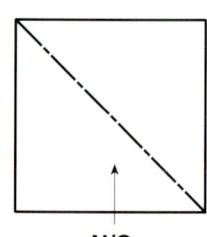

N/O
Cut 4 from each N/O bias strip set

Churn Dash Delight

Red and green combine with a light background to make a mini that is a perfect holiday accent piece.

PROJECT SPECIFICATIONS
Skill Level: Advanced
Quilt Size: 12" x 14½"
Block Size: 2½" x 2½"
Number of Blocks: 6
Techniques: Bias squares, strip piecing, one border with cornerstones

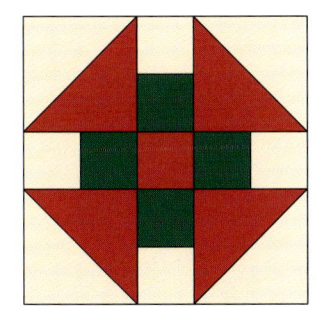

Churn Dash
2 1/2" x 2 1/2" Block

PROJECT NOTES
The Churn Dash block has always been a big hit with quilters. It can be set on point in a different quilt plan. Choose a good color contrast for the small-size blocks.

MATERIALS
- 1 fat quarter beige solid
- 1 fat quarter red print
- 6" x 10" rectangle green print
- ⅛ yard green-with-gold print
- ⅛ yard beige plaid
- 14" x 16½" lightweight batting
- 15" x 17½" backing
- Neutral color all-purpose thread
- Cream and red quilting thread
- Basic sewing tools and supplies, 3" x 18" ruler and 4" Baby Bias Square ruler

CUTTING
Note: Use the 3" x 18" ruler to cut 45-degree bias strips; reverse cutting direction if left-handed.

Step 1. Cut an 11" x 18" rectangle beige solid; subcut into four 1½" x 15" bias strips for A referring to Figure 1. From remaining fabric, cut four 1" x 8" strips for B.

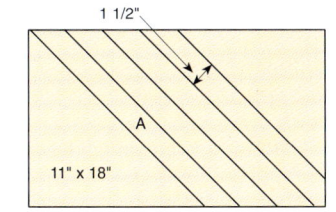

Figure 1
Cut 1 1/2" x 15" bias strips.

Step 2. Cut an 11" x 18" rectangle red print; lay the red print rectangle wrong side up on a flat surface; cut four 1½" x 15" bias strips for C as shown in Figure 2. Cut one 1" x 8" strip from remaining fabric for D and four 2½" x 2½" squares for I.

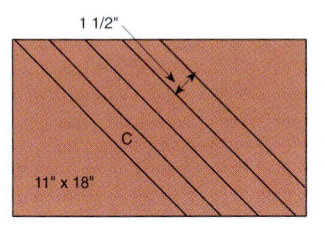

Figure 2
Lay red print wrong side up;
cut 1 1/2" x 15" bias strips.

Step 3. Cut four 1" x 8" strips green print for E.

Step 4. Cut six 3" x 3" squares beige plaid for F.

Step 5. Cut two strips each 2½" x 10½" G and 2½" x 8" F green-with-gold print.

Step 6. Cut 1"-wide strips red print and join to create a 62" binding strip referring to Binding Your Quilt on page 36.

PIECING BLOCKS
Note: Use 4" Baby Bias Square ruler to cut bias squares or prepare A/C template using pattern given. Use a ¼" seam allowance; press seams before trimming. Press all seams in the direction of small arrows shown on figure drawings.

Step 1. Join A and C bias strips with right sides together along length; repeat for four strip sets. Cut twenty-four 1½" x 1½" A/C bias squares using bias ruler or template A/C, matching line on template to seam between strips as shown in Figure 3.

Step 2. Join one B and E strip with right sides together along length; repeat for two strip sets. Trim seams to ⅛", press and cut into 1"-wide B/E segments as shown in Figure 4.

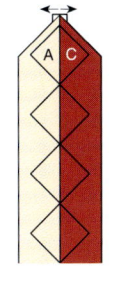

Figure 3
Match line on template to seam on strip and cut to make A/C units.

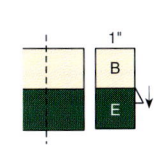

Figure 4
Cut into 1"-wide B/E segments.

Illustrated Guide to Scrap Miniature Magic **83**

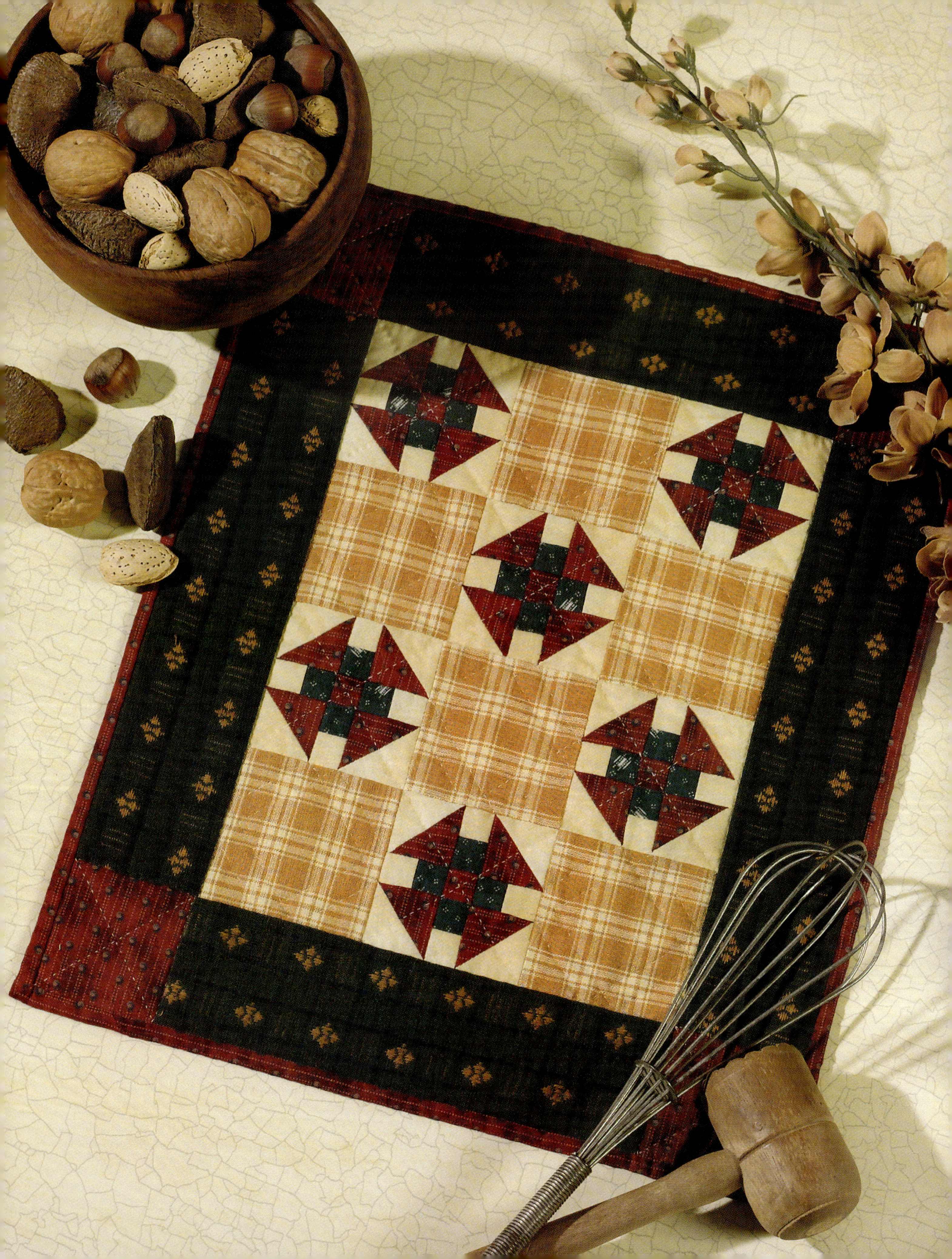

Step 3. Join two A/C units with one B/E segment as shown in Figure 5; repeat for 12 units.

Step 4. Join 1" x 8" strips with right sides together to make a B/E/D/E/B strip set; trim seams to $1/8$" and press. Cut six 1" segments from the strip.

Step 5. Sew a B/E/D/E/B segment between two A/C/B/E units, matching seams as shown in Figure 6 to complete one block; repeat for six blocks.

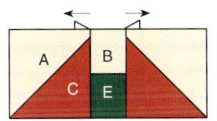

Figure 5
Join 2 A/C units with 1 B/E segment.

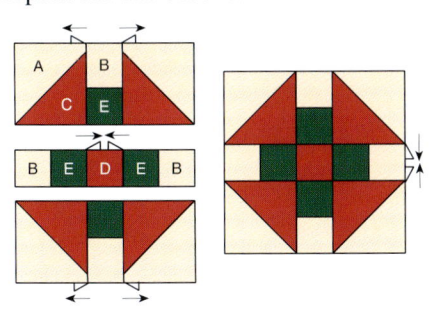

Figure 6
Join units as shown to complete 1 block.

PIECING THE TOP

Step 1. Join two blocks with F to make a row as shown in Figure 7; repeat for two rows and press.

Step 2. Join two F squares with one block to make a row, again referring to Figure 7; repeat for two rows and press.

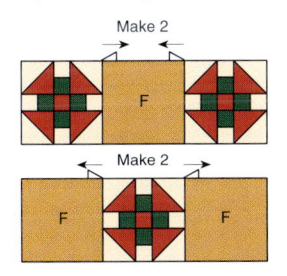

Figure 7
Join blocks with F to make rows as shown.

Step 3. Join the rows referring to the Placement Diagram for positioning; press seams in one direction.

Step 4. Sew a G strip to opposite long sides of the pieced center; press. Sew I to each end of each H strip; press.

Step 5. Sew an H/I strip to the top and bottom of the pieced center to complete the top.

FINISHING

Step 1. Press quilt top on both sides; check for proper seam pressing and trim all loose threads.

Step 2. Mark top for quilting. *Note: The quilt shown was hand-quilted in a diagonal grid through the centers and from seam points on blocks to border strips as shown in Figure 8, in an X on I squares and in the ditch of seams using cream* quilting thread. Red quilting thread was used to hand-quilt two centered lines $1/2$" apart on each G and H border strip.

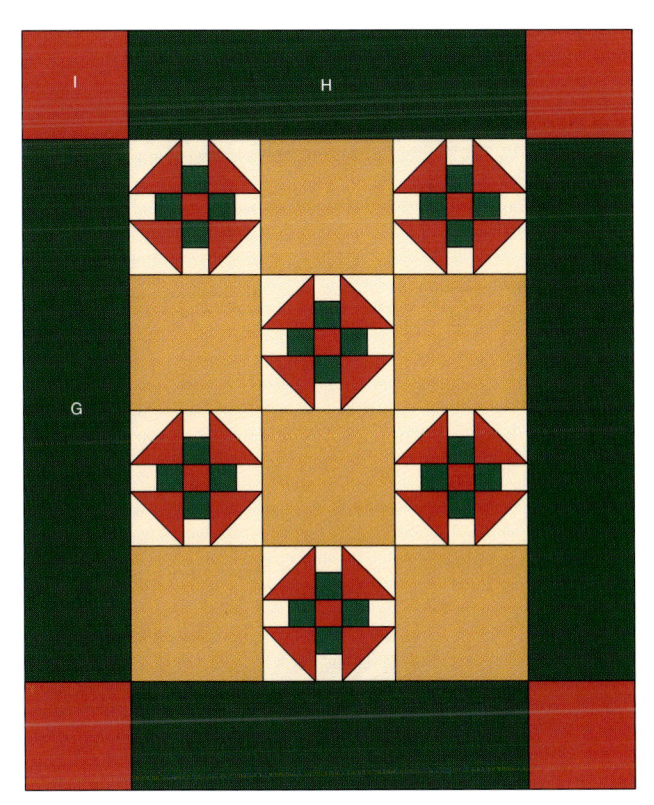

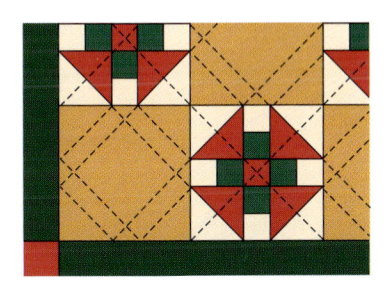

Churn Dash Delight
Placement Diagram
12" x 14 1/2"

Figure 8
Quilt the center section as shown.

Step 3. Sandwich batting between the stitched top and the backing piece; pin or baste layers together to hold. Quilt as desired by hand or machine.

Step 4. When quilting is complete, trim batting and backing fabric even with raw edges of quilt top.

Step 5. Bind edges with 1"-wide red print prepared binding strips referring to Binding Your Quilt on page 36. ❖

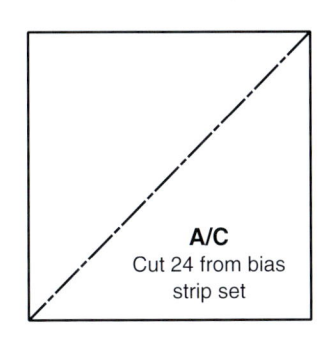

A/C
Cut 24 from bias strip set

Illustrated Guide to Scrap Miniature Magic **85**

Crown of Thorns

Four tiny blocks look like they are floating in the white solid background.

PROJECT SPECIFICATIONS

Skill Level: Advanced
Quilt Size: 14¼" x 14¼"
Block Size: 2¼" x 2¼"
Number of Blocks: 4
Techniques: Bias squares, quick-cut triangle, straight sashing and one straight border with cornerstones

MATERIALS

- ½ fat quarter dark green print
- Fat quarter gold print
- ⅛ yard green print for binding
- ½ yard white solid
- ½ yard red-and-gold print
- 16" x 16" lightweight batting
- 17" x 17" backing
- Neutral color all-purpose thread
- White quilting thread
- Basic sewing tools and supplies, 3" x 18" ruler and 4" Baby Bias Square ruler

Crown of Thorns
2 1/4" x 2 1/4" Block

CUTTING

Note: Use the 3" x 18" ruler to cut 45-degree bias strips; reverse cutting direction if left-handed.

Step 1. Cut one 11" x 18" A rectangle, four 1¼" x 2¾" E pieces and four 2½" x 2½" L squares gold print.

Step 2. Cut one 11" x 18" B rectangle, two 2⅜" x 2⅜" C squares, five 1¼" x 1¼" D squares, two 2" x 5¾" F strips, two 2" x 8¾" G strips and two 11" x 18" J rectangles white solid.

Step 3. Cut two 2⅜" x 2⅜" H squares and two 11" x 18" I rectangles red-and-gold print.

Step 4. Cut four 2½" x 10¼" K strips dark green print.

Step 5. Cut two 1" by fabric width strips red-and-gold print to create a 65" binding strip referring to Binding Your Quilt on page 36.

PIECING BLOCKS

Note: Use 4" Baby Bias Square ruler to cut bias squares or prepare A/B (I/J) template using pattern given. Use a ¼" seam allowance; press seams before trimming. Press all seams in the direction of small arrows shown on figure drawings.

Step 1. Layer an A and B rectangle with right sides together; cut three 1¼" x 15" bias strips of each fabric as shown in Figure 1.

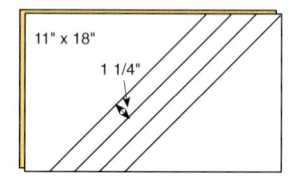

Figure 1
Layer an A and B rectangle with right sides together; cut three 1 1/4" x 15" bias strips of each fabric.

Step 2. Sew one A bias strip to one B bias strip with right sides together along length to make an A/B strip set; repeat for three strip sets. Press seams open.

Step 3. Cut sixteen 1¼" x 1¼" A/B bias squares from sets using bias ruler or template A/B (I/J), matching line on template to seam between strips as shown in Figure 2.

Step 4. Join two A/B units to make a set as shown in Figure 3; repeat for four sets.

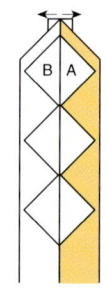

Figure 2
Cut 1 1/4" x 1 1/4" A/B bias squares from sets using bias ruler or template A/B (I/J), matching line on template to seam between strips.

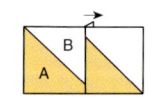

Figure 3
Join 2 A/B units to make a set.

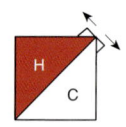

Figure 4
Sew C to H to make a C/H unit.

Step 5. Cut each C square in half on one diagonal to make four C triangles; repeat with H squares to make four H triangles.

Step 6. Sew C to H to make a C/H unit as shown in Figure 4; repeat for four units.

86 Master Quilter's Workshop

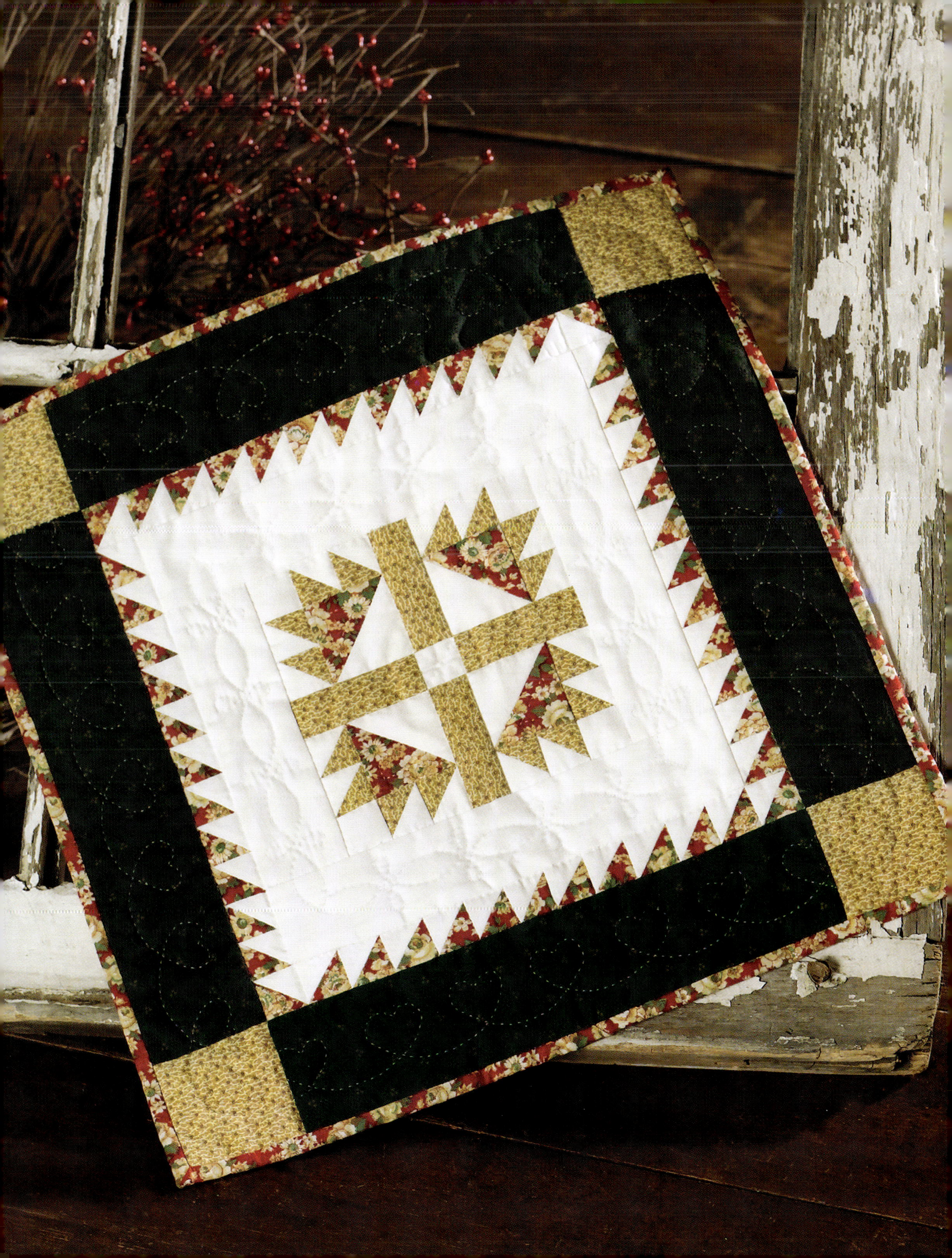

Step 7. Sew an A/B set to a C/H unit as shown in Figure 5; repeat for four units.

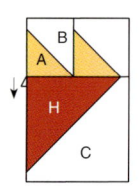

Figure 5
Sew an A/B set to a C/H unit.

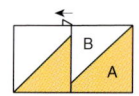

Figure 6
Join 2 A/B units to make a set.

Step 8. Join two A/B units to make a set as shown in Figure 6; repeat for four sets.

Step 9. Sew D to each set as shown in Figure 7.

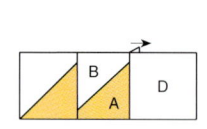

Figure 7
Sew D to each set.

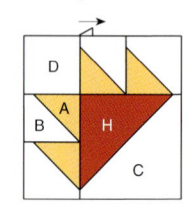

Figure 8
Join the pieced units to complete 1 Crown of Thorns block.

Step 10. Join the pieced units as shown in Figure 8 to complete one Crown of Thorns block; repeat for four blocks.

Step 11. Join two blocks with E to make a block row as shown in Figure 9; repeat for two block rows.

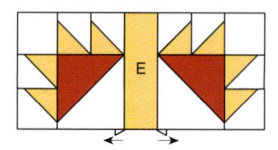

Figure 9
Join 2 blocks with E to make a block row.

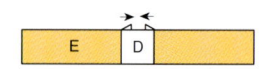

Figure 10
Join 2 E pieces with D to make a sashing row.

Step 12. Join two E pieces with D to make a sashing row as shown in Figure 10.

Step 13. Join the block rows with the sashing row as shown in Figure 11.

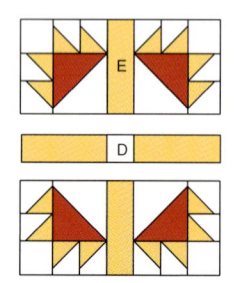

Figure 11
Join the block rows with the sashing row.

Step 14. Sew F to two opposite sides and G to the remaining sides of the pieced section to complete the pieced center as shown in Figure 12.

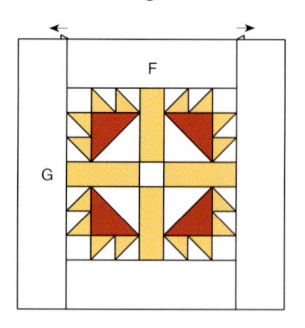

Figure 12
Sew F to 2 opposite sides and G to the remaining sides of the pieced section to complete the pieced center.

PIECING THE TOP

Step 1. Layer one each I and J rectangles with right sides together; cut three 1 1/4" x 15" bias strips of each fabric. Repeat with second I and J rectangles.

Step 2. Sew one I bias strip to one J bias strip with right sides together along length to make an I/J strip set; repeat for six strip sets. Press seams open.

Step 3. Cut forty-eight 1 1/4" x 1 1/4" I/J bias squares from sets using bias ruler or template A/B (I/J), matching line on template to seam between strips as for Step 3 in Piecing Blocks.

Step 4. Join 11 I/J units to make a strip as shown in Figure 13; repeat for two strips. Sew strips to opposite sides of the pieced center referring to Figure 14.

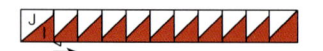

Figure 13
Join 11 I/J units to make strips as shown.

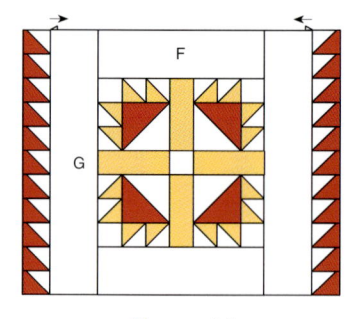

Figure 14
Sew strips to opposite sides of the pieced center.

Step 5. Join 13 I/J units to make a strip referring to Figure 15; repeat for two strips. Sew the strips to the top and bottom of the pieced center referring to Figure 16. *Note: The sample has one reversed I/J strip. The instructions given make all rows with I/J pieces positioned the same to create four matching corners.*

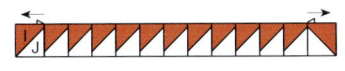

Figure 15
Join 13 I/J units to make strips.

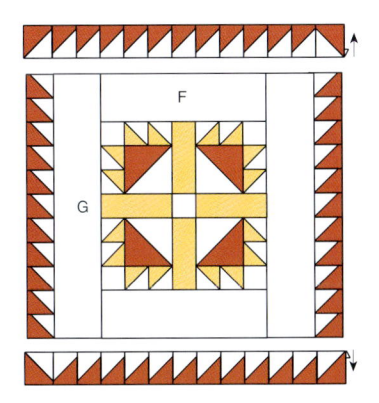

Figure 16
Sew the strips to the top and bottom of the pieced center.

Step 6. Sew K to opposite sides of the pieced section; press seams toward K. Sew L to each end of the remaining K pieces; sew to the top and bottom of the pieced section to complete the quilt top; press seams toward K and then toward K/L.

FINISHING

Step 1. Press quilt top on both sides; check for proper seam pressing and trim all loose threads.

Step 2. Mark top for quilting using border design given on F and G strips and heart design given for Kaleidoscope on page 117 on the K and L pieces. *Note: The quilt shown was hand-quilted 1/4" inside each H triangle, in the ditch of all seams and on the marked designs using white quilting thread.*

Step 3. Sandwich batting between the stitched top and the backing piece; pin or baste layers together to hold. Quilt as desired by hand or machine.

Step 4. When quilting is complete, trim batting and backing fabric even with raw edges of quilt top.

Step 5. Bind edges with 1"-wide red-and-gold print prepared binding strip referring to Binding Your Quilt on page 36 to finish. ❖

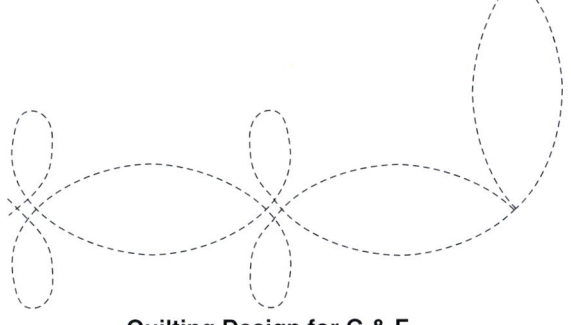

Quilting Design for G & F

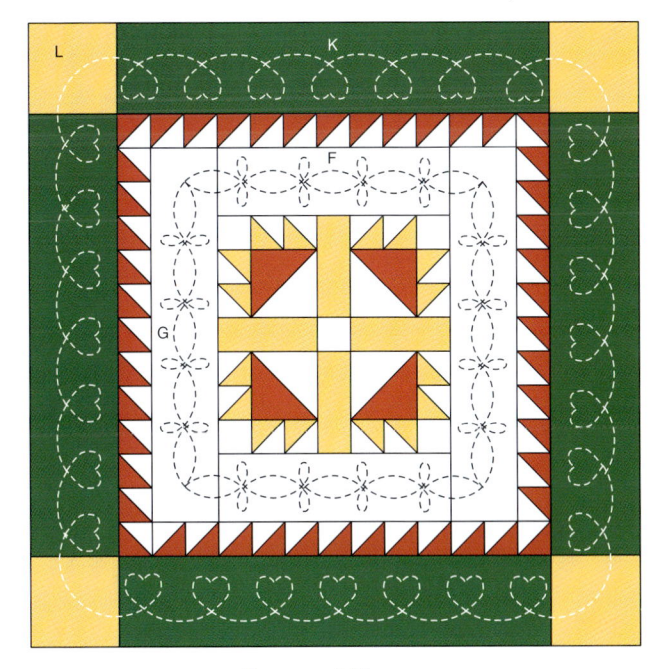

Crown of Thorns
Placement Diagram
14 1/4" x 14 1/4"

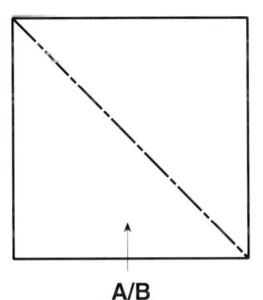

A/B (I/J)
Cut 16 A/B and 48 I/J from bias strip sets

Illustrated Guide to Scrap Miniature Magic **89**

Clothing

Vintage fabrics create the pieces of clothing featured in the tiny paper-pieced blocks in this miniature quilt.

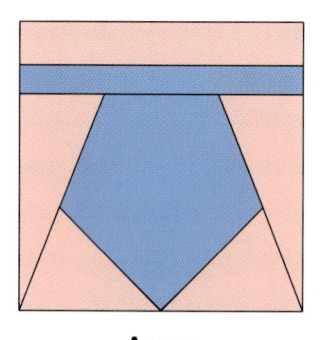

Apron
2 1/2" x 2 1/2" Block

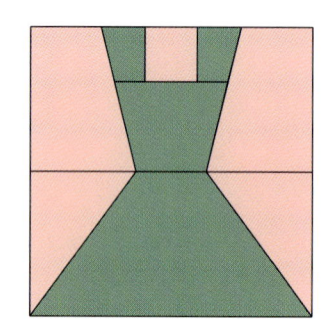

Dress
2 1/2" x 2 1/2" Block

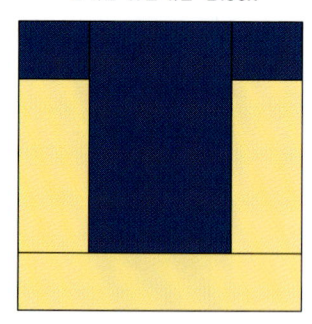

Shirt
2 1/2" x 2 1/2" Block

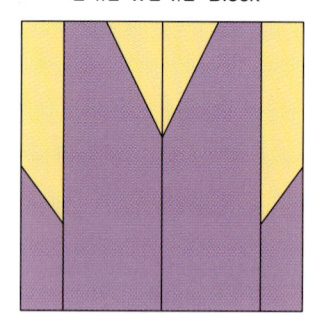

Vest
2 1/2" x 2 1/2" Block

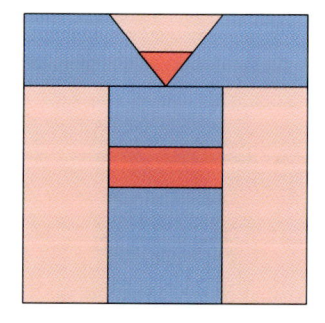

Kimono
2 1/2" x 2 1/2" Block

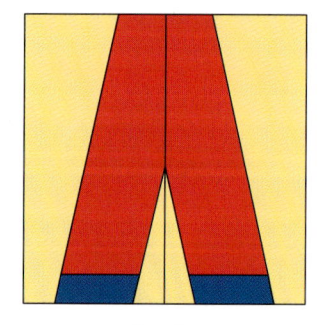

Pants
2 1/2" x 2 1/2" Block

PROJECT SPECIFICATIONS
Skill Level: All levels
Quilt Size: 9¾" x 13"
Block Size: 2½" x 2½"
Number of Blocks: 6
Techniques: Machine paper-foundation piecing for flip-and-sew method

MATERIALS
- Assorted vintage scraps for apron, vest, shirt, kimono, dress, pants and block backgrounds
- 8" x 11" rectangle green solid
- ½ fat quarter blue/rust/green vintage floral print for border
- 8" x 11" rectangle white vintage print for binding
- 12" x 15" lightweight batting
- 13" x 16" backing
- Neutral color all-purpose thread
- Cream quilting thread
- 3 (¼") buttons to match vest fabric
- Small red satin rose
- Basic sewing tools and supplies

CUTTING
Step 1. Cut three 1¼" x 3" A and two 1¼" x 6¼" B pieces green solid.

Step 2. Cut two 2¼" x 9½" C strips and two 2¼" x 9¾" D strips blue/rust/green vintage floral print.

Step 3. Cut 1"-wide strips white print to create a 54" binding strip referring to Binding Your Quilt on page 36.

PIECING BLOCKS
Note: Use a ¼" seam allowance; press seams before trimming. Press all seams in the direction of small arrows shown on figure drawings.

Step 1. Refer to Machine Paper-Foundation Piecing on page 38 for tracing and sewing instructions.

Step 2. Complete one block of each pattern; join pieced sections as necessary to complete blocks. *Note: Colors to match sample are indicated on blocks. You may change to use colors of your vintage fabrics.*

PIECING THE TOP
Step 1. Join two blocks with an A strip to complete one row referring to Figure 1 and the Placement Diagram for positioning of blocks; repeat for three rows.

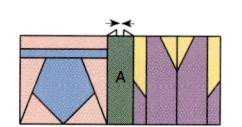

Figure 1
Join 2 blocks with A.

90 *Master Quilter's Workshop*

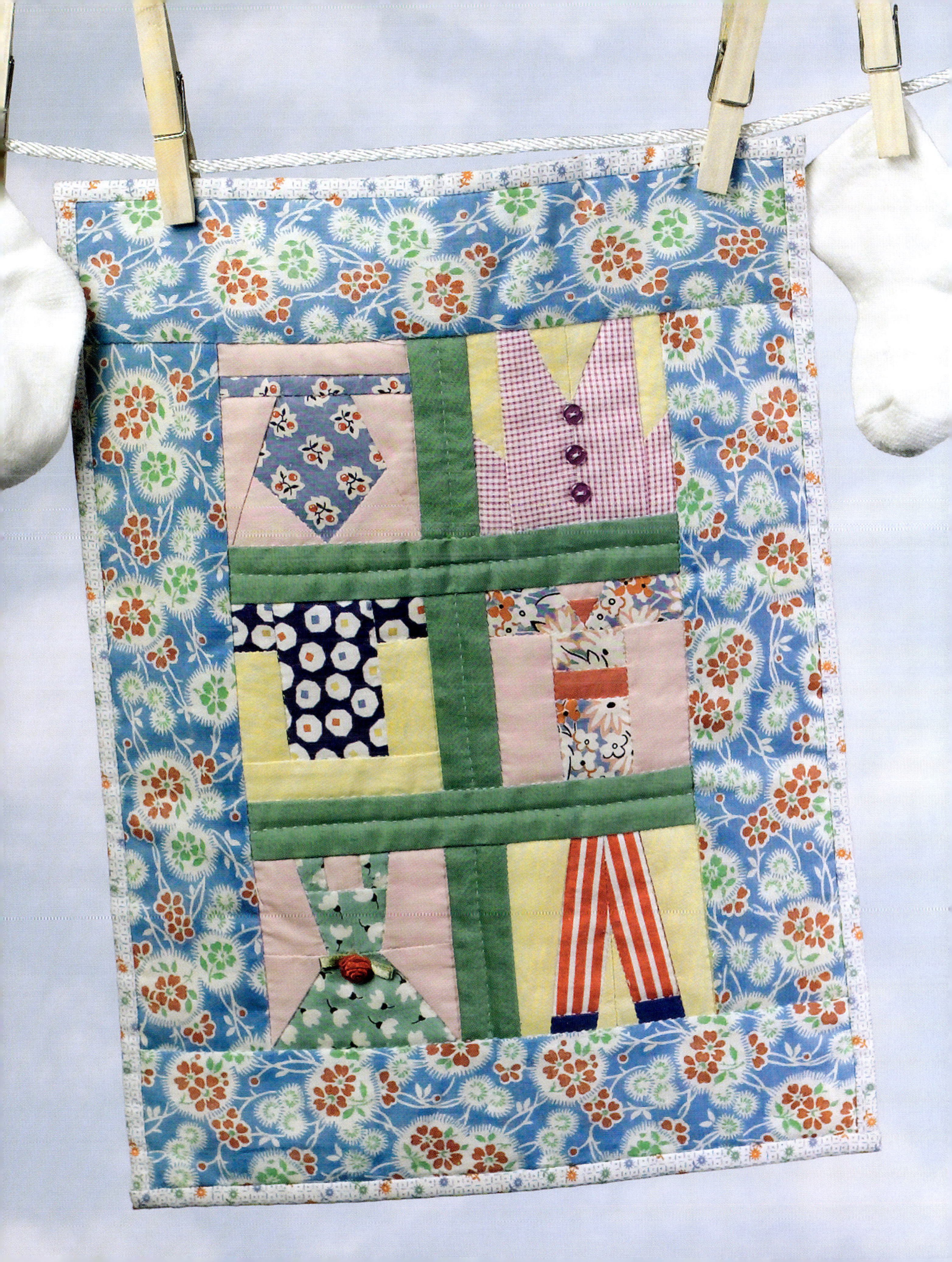

Step 2. Join the rows with B strips, again referring to the Placement Diagram; press seams toward strips.

Step 3. Sew C strips to opposite long sides and D strips to the top and bottom of the pieced center; press seams toward strips.

FINISHING

Step 1. Press quilt top on both sides; check for proper seam pressing and trim all loose threads.

Step 2. Mark top for quilting. *Note: The quilt shown was hand-quilted in the ditch of block seams and through the center of each sashing strip using cream quilting thread.*

Step 3. Sandwich batting between the stitched top and the backing piece; pin or baste layers together to hold. Quilt as desired by hand or machine.

Step 4. When quilting is complete, trim batting and backing fabric even with raw edges of quilt top.

Step 5. Bind edges with 1"-wide white print prepared binding strips referring to Binding Your Quilt on page 36.

Step 6. Sew the three 1/4" buttons to the center of the Vest block and the small red satin rose to the waistline of the Dress block to finish. ❖

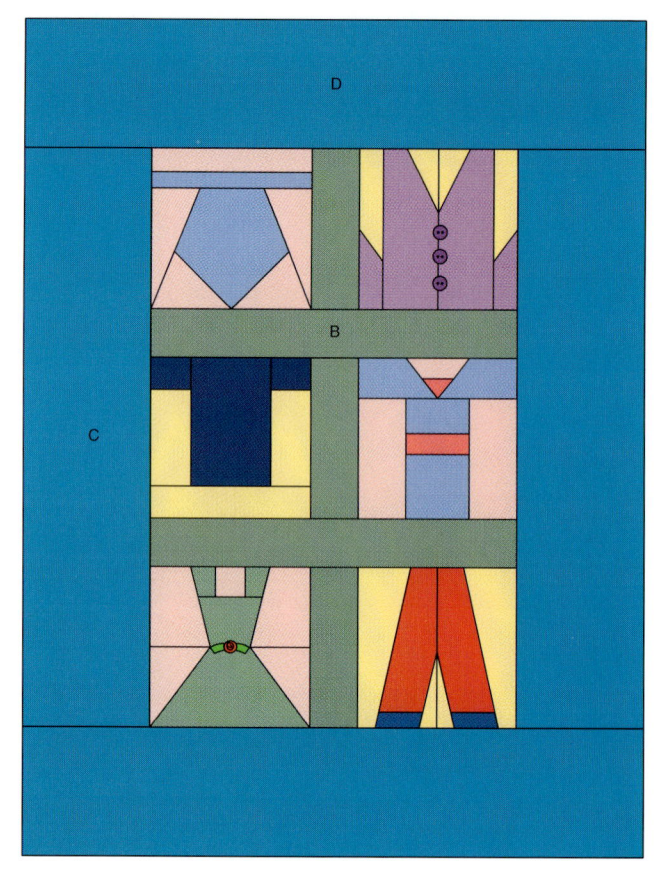

Clothing
Placement Diagram
9 3/4" x 13"

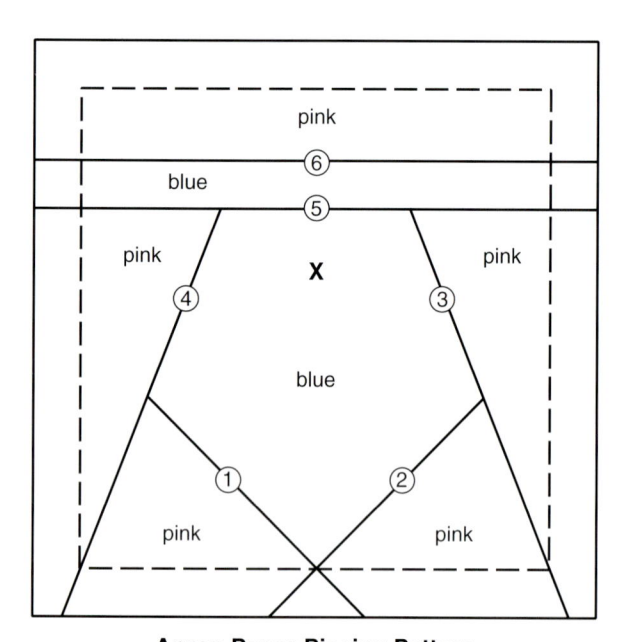

Apron Paper-Piecing Pattern

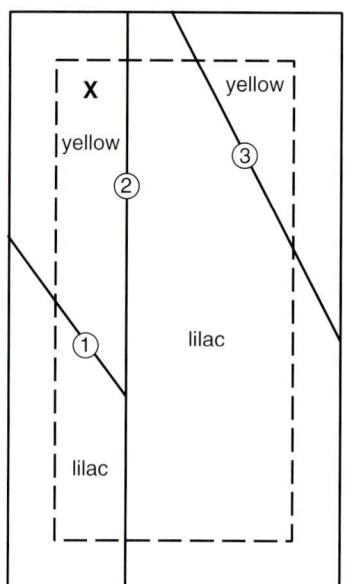

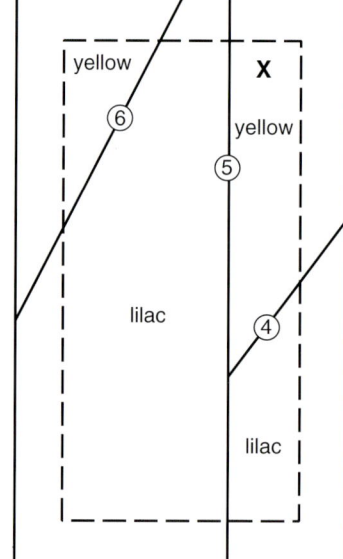

Vest Paper-Piecing Patterns

92 *Master Quilter's Workshop*

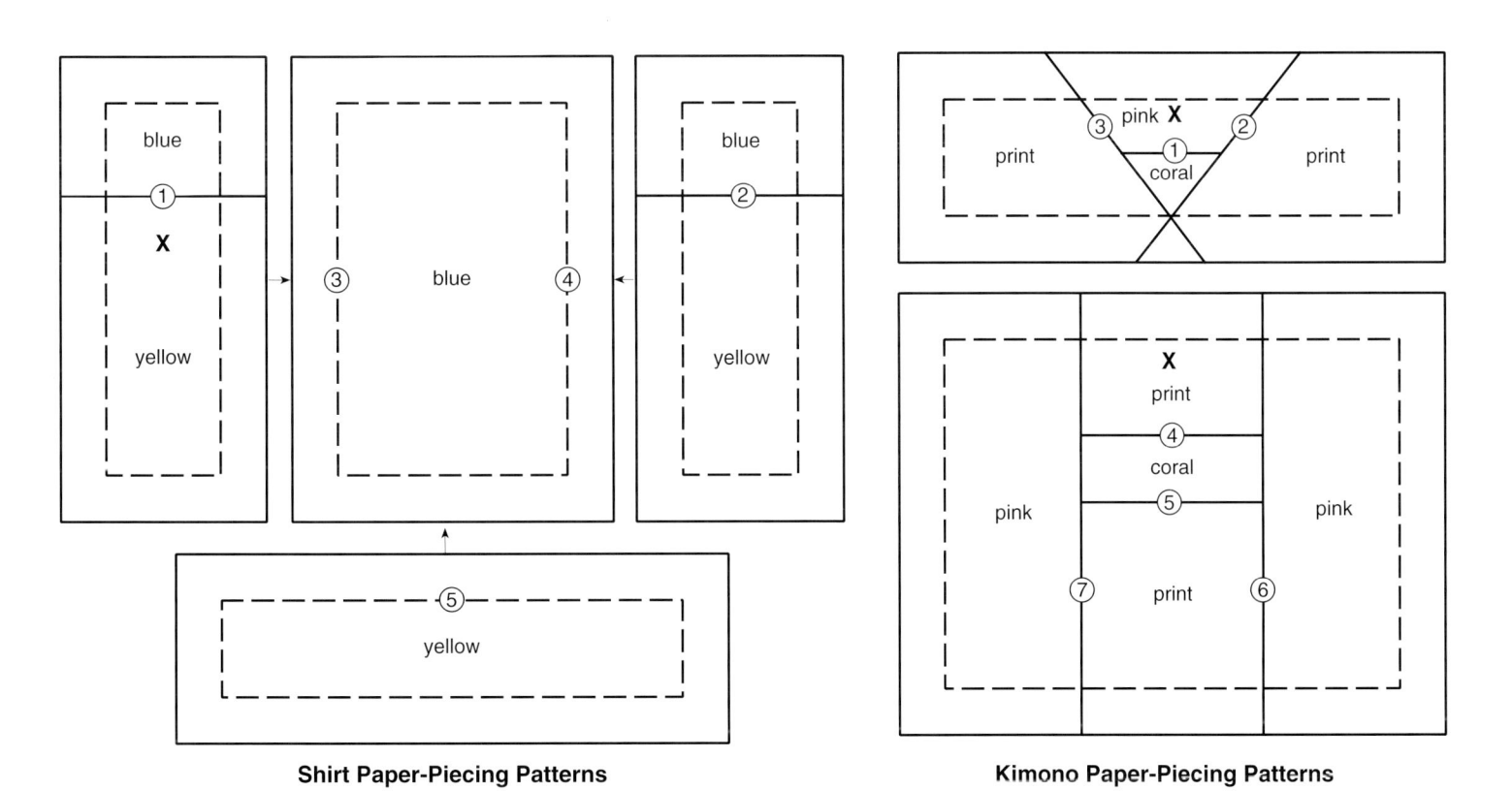

Shirt Paper-Piecing Patterns

Kimono Paper-Piecing Patterns

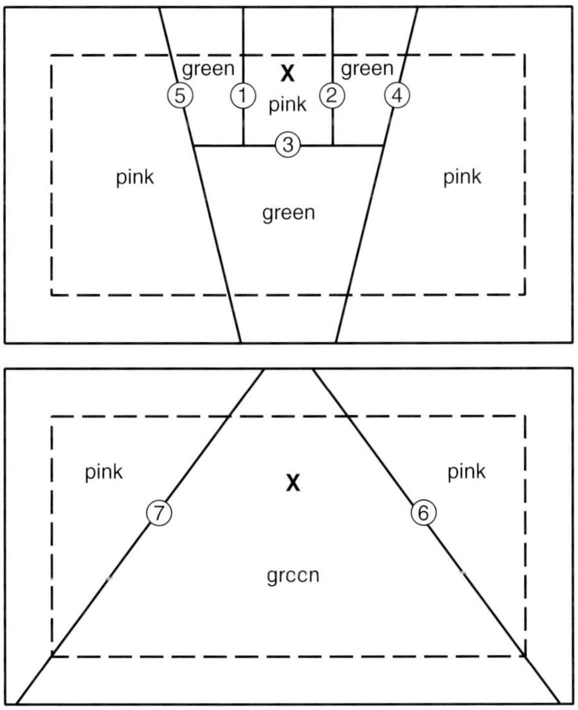

Dress Paper-Piecing Patterns

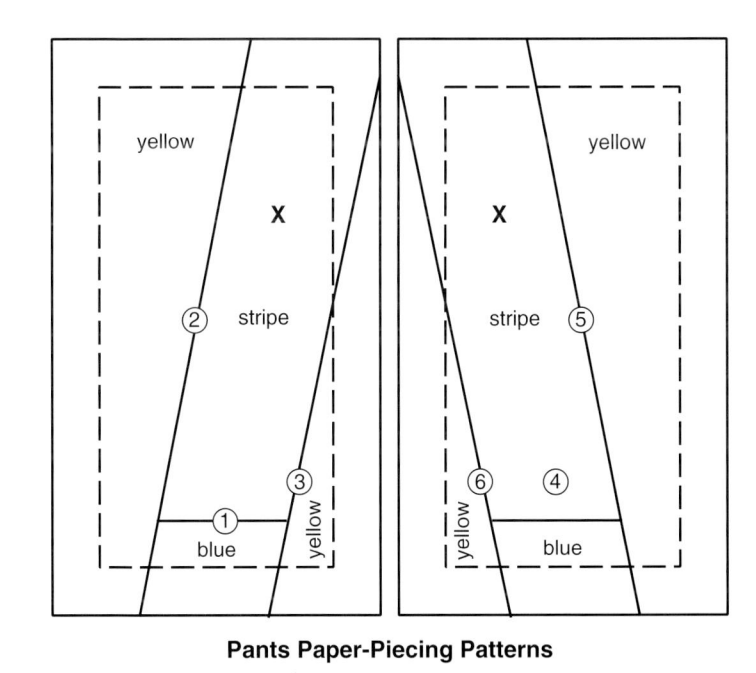

Pants Paper-Piecing Patterns

Illustrated Guide to Scrap Miniature Magic **93**

Country Folk

Combine stenciling with simple appliqué and embroidery to make this tiny quilt with a primitive look.

PROJECT SPECIFICATIONS
Skill Level: All levels
Quilt Size: 15" x 15"
Block Size: 3½" x 3½"
Number of Blocks: 4
Techniques: Diagonal block setting, quick-cut triangle, border with cornerstones, stenciling, floss embroidery work

Country Folk
3 1/2" x 3 1/2" Block

MATERIALS
- ½ fat quarter beige solid
- 2" x 2" D squares of 4 assorted plaids or checks for dresses
- 13" x 13" square brown print border fabric
- 8" x 8" square dark green solid
- ⅛ yard cream-with-brown stripe for binding
- 17" x 17" lightweight batting
- 18" x 18" backing
- Neutral color all-purpose thread
- Tan quilting thread
- Rust, tan, gold and green 6-strand embroidery floss
- 4 (½") tan buttons
- 4 (⅜") brown buttons
- Freezer paper
- Fabric glue
- Stencil Magic navy blue stencil cream
- Small stencil brush
- Basic sewing tools and supplies, small, sharp-point paper scissors, large-eye, sharp needle, removable fabric marker, ¼"-gridded plastic template material and marker

CUTTING
Step 1. Cut five 4" x 4" A squares, one 6¼" x 6¼" B square and two 3⅜" x 3⅜" C squares beige solid.

Step 2. Cut four 2¾" x 10½" E strips brown print.

Step 3. Cut four 2¾" x 2¾" F squares dark green solid.

Step 4. Cut 1"-wide strips cream-with-brown stripe to create a 68" binding strip referring to Binding Your Quilt on page 36.

MAKING BLOCKS
Note: Use a ¼" seam allowance; press seams before trimming. Press all seams in the direction of small arrows shown on figure drawings.

Step 1. Fold each A square to find diagonal centers; crease.

Step 2. Trace body stencil design on dull side of freezer paper; cut out head, arms and legs, leaving the paper whole and removing shapes referring to Figure 1.

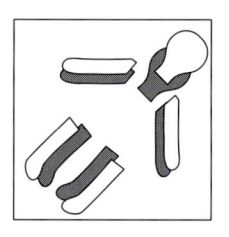

Figure 1
Cut head, arms and legs away from freezer-paper square.

Step 3. With a dry iron set on medium, center and iron the waxy side of cut-out freezer-paper shape to the right side of an A square.

Step 4. Gently stencil open areas using the stencil cream and brush and a circular motion; let dry a little. Gently peel off freezer paper; repeat on four A squares. Let dry overnight.

Step 5. Fold under two opposite sides of each D square ¼"; press. Using 2 strands of gold embroidery floss and a knotted running stitch, stitch up each side to the end; knot floss. Fold under one remaining edge for dress top; press.

Step 6. Knotting one end of the floss and keeping the knot on the wrong side, stitch across top edge, stopping in the center; trim floss to 8". Repeat on opposite top edge as shown in Figure 2. Pull both ends to gather; tie ends in a bow. Leave bottom edge raw.

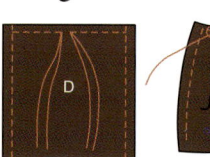

Figure 2
Stitch edge of D to the center; trim floss to 8" length. Repeat on opposite side to the center. Pull floss ends to gather top edge.

94 *Master Quilter's Workshop*

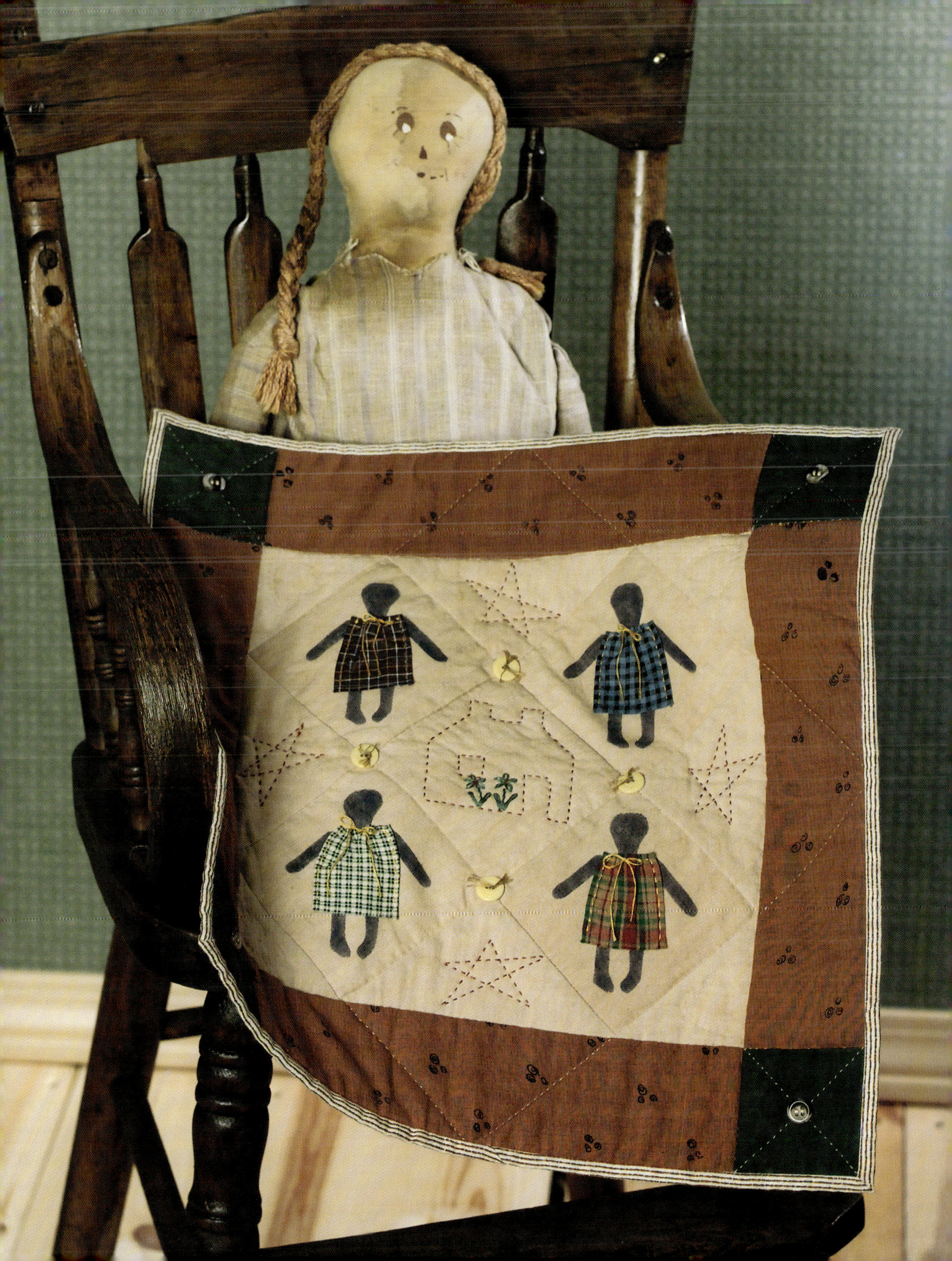

Step 7. Place a D piece on an A square to cover body area as shown in Figure 3; pin in place. Secure D pieces in place at edges using fabric glue to complete one block; repeat for four blocks.

Figure 3
Place the stitched D piece on the stenciled doll shape.

PIECING THE TOP

Step 1. Cut the B square in half on both diagonals to make four B triangles. Cut each C square in half on one diagonal to make four C triangles.

Step 2. Arrange the appliquéd blocks with the A square and B and C triangles in diagonal rows as shown in Figure 4; join in rows. Join the rows and add C triangles to corners to complete the pieced center, again referring to Figure 4.

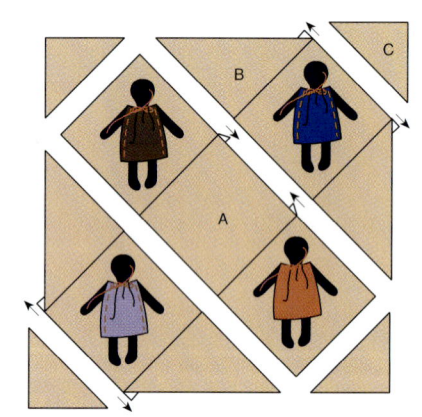

Figure 4
Arrange and stitch the appliquéd blocks with the A square and B triangles in diagonal rows; add C.

Step 3. Sew an E piece to opposite sides of the pieced center; press seams toward E.

Step 4. Sew F to each end of each remaining E piece;

Country Folk
Placement Diagram
15" x 15"

press seams toward E. Sew an E/F unit to the top and bottom of the pieced center; press seams toward E/F.

FINISHING

Step 1. Press quilt top on both sides; check for proper seam pressing and trim all loose threads.

Step 2. Mark the house design in the center of A, a star design in the center of each B triangle and a heart design in the center of each C triangle using the removable fabric markers and referring to the Placement Diagram for positioning. *Note: The quilt shown was hand-quilted in blocks using designs given using 2 strands rust embroidery floss, and in X design in F squares, heart shapes in the C triangles and in the ditch of seams and a continuation of triangles to make squares in borders using tan quilting thread.*

Step 3. Using 2 strands green embroidery floss, make Lazy-Daisy stitches for flower leaves and petals and a

Helpful Hints for Miniature Quiltmaking

- As you sew and press, constantly measure your work with a C-Thru ruler, available at any office supply store. Be prepared to rip when necessary.

- Blocks must be consistent in size. They can either be all slightly smaller or all slightly larger in size than the quilt plan, but mathematical adjustments must be made accordingly for remainder of pattern pieces.

- If one block is way off in size, it is usually more practical and accurate to make a new block than to rip and resew the off-size one.

- Gently press pieces with the tip of the iron as you sew—no finger pressing, except when foundation piecing.

- Avoid heavy-handed ironing, which can distort small pieces.

- If marking top with quilting template before layering, draw finished quilt to size on gridded graph paper. Pencil in template designs to your liking; replicate their placement on the quilt top with removable markers.

House Quilting Design

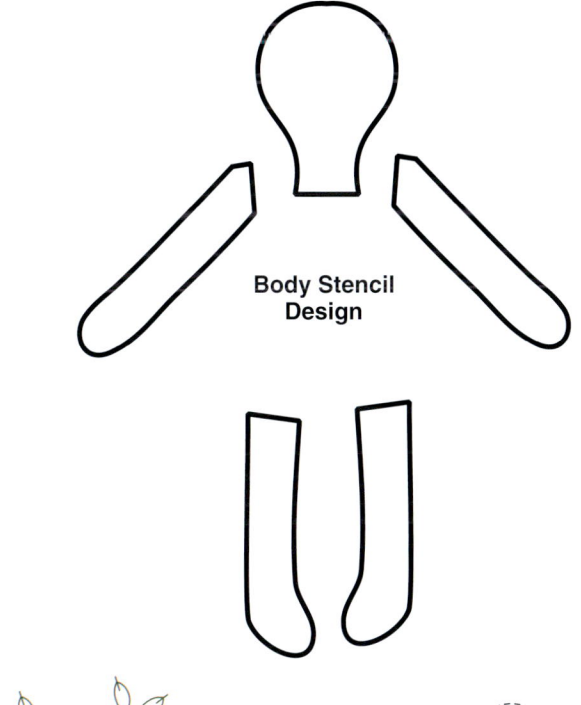

stem stitch for stem. Use 2 strands rust embroidery floss to make French knots in the center of each flower referring to Embroidery Stitches on page 40.

Step 4. Sandwich batting between the stitched top and the backing piece; pin or baste layers together to hold. Quilt as desired by hand or machine.

Step 5. When quilting is complete, trim batting and backing fabric even with raw edges of quilt top.

Step 6. Bind edges with 1"-wide cream-with-brown stripe prepared binding strip referring to Binding Your Quilt on page 36.

Step 7. Sew a tan button at the intersection of A seams and brown buttons in the center of F squares to finish. ❖

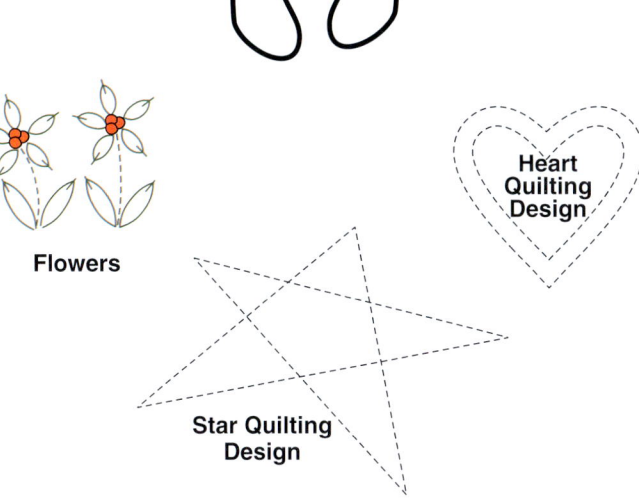

Body Stencil Design

Flowers

Heart Quilting Design

Star Quilting Design

Illustrated Guide to Scrap Miniature Magic **97**

Fanciful Daisies

Vintage-fabric appliquéd daisy petals and yo-yo flower centers make a perfect mood-setting little quilt.

PROJECT SPECIFICATIONS
Skill Level: Beginner
Quilt Size: 18¼" x 18¼"
Block Size: 5½" x 5½"
Number of Blocks: 4
Techniques: Strip-pieced sashing border with cornerstones, iron-on petals and stem and yo-yos

Daisy
5 1/2" x 5 1/2" Block

MATERIALS
- 32 assorted scraps 2" x 3½"
- 3" x 3" square dark green solid
- 14" x 14" square muslin
- 12" x 14" rectangle pink solid
- ½ fat quarter orange solid
- 14" x 16" rectangle green print
- 7" x 7" square peach print
- ⅛ yard green solid for binding
- 20" x 20" lightweight batting
- 21" x 21" backing
- Neutral color all-purpose thread
- Cream quilting thread
- ½ yard HeatnBond Lite iron-on adhesive
- Basic sewing tools and supplies, white paper, paper scissors, removable fabric marker

CUTTING

Step 1. Prepare template for the A petal using the full-size pattern given; reverse template and trace 32 A pieces on the paper side of the iron-on adhesive. Cut out shapes, leaving a margin around each one. Fuse shapes to the wrong side of the 2" x 3½" assorted scrap pieces.

Step 2. Cut out A shapes on traced lines; remove paper backing.

Step 3. Cut a 3" x 3" square iron-on adhesive; fuse to the wrong side of the 3" x 3" square green solid. Trace and cut four B stem pieces on the paper side of the fused square; cut out B on the traced lines. Remove paper backing.

Step 4. Cut four 6" x 6" C squares muslin.

Step 5. Cut six 1¼" x 6" D strips and two 5" x 6" E strips pink solid.

Step 6. Cut three 1¼" x 5" F strips and four G circles orange solid.

Step 7. Cut four 2¾" x 13¾" H strips green print.

Step 8. Cut four 2¾" x 2¾" I squares peach print.

Step 9. Cut 1"-wide strips green solid and join to create an 81" binding strip referring to Binding Your Quilt on page 36.

APPLIQUÉING BLOCKS

Note: Use a ¼" seam allowance; press seams before trimming. Press all seams in the direction of small arrows shown on figure drawings.

Step 1. Trace the full-size pattern onto a piece of paper.

Step 2. Fold and crease C squares to find the center as shown in Figure 1.

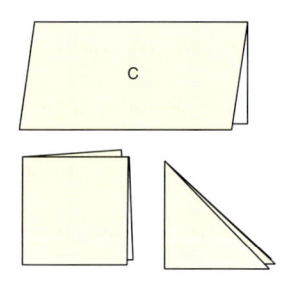

Figure 1
Fold and crease C squares to find the center.

Step 3. Center a C square on the traced paper pattern; transfer design to fabric using a removable fabric marker.

Step 4. Place one B stem piece on a C square on the marked lines for B as shown in Figure 2; fuse in place.

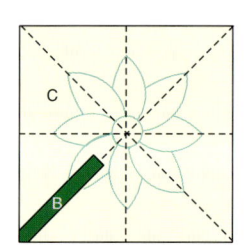

Figure 2
Place 1 B stem piece on a C square on the marked lines for B.

Step 5. Arrange A shapes in place, beginning with four A pieces at each diagonal crease line as shown in Figure 3.

98   Master Quilter's Workshop

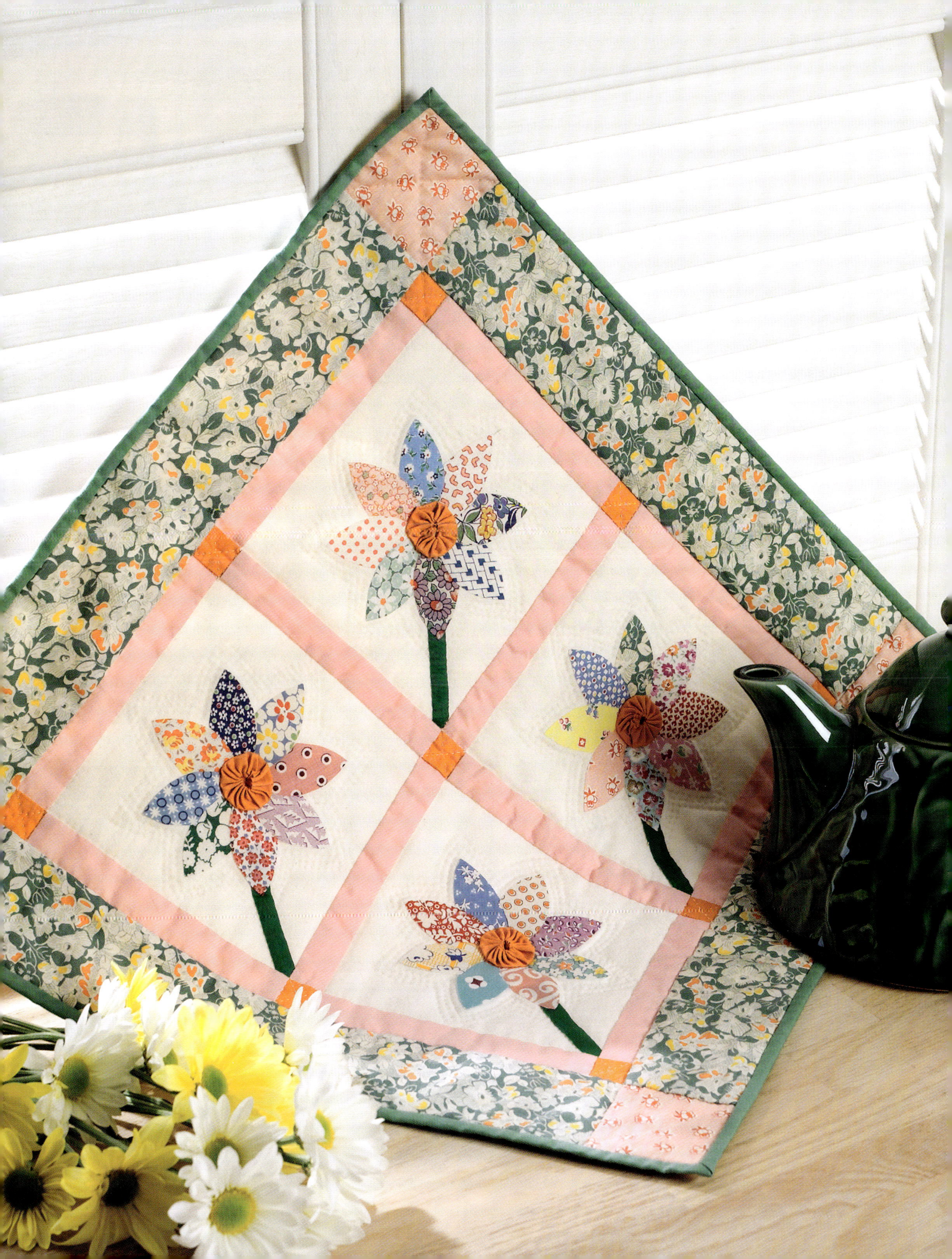

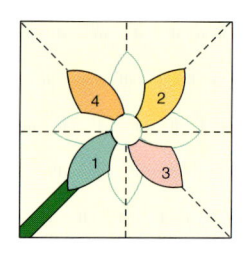

Figure 3
Arrange petal shapes in place, beginning with 4 petals at each diagonal crease line.

Figure 4
Press remaining petal shapes in place, matching their points with folds in C square.

Step 6. Arrange remaining A shapes in place, matching their points with folds in C square as shown in Figure 4; when satisfied with positioning, fuse in place. Repeat for four block units. *Note: When pressing petal shapes in place, always match bottom curved edge of each one with circle edge.*

Step 7. Make yo-yos using G pieces referring to Making Yo-Yos on page 38. Center a G yo-yo on a block unit; hand-stitch in place to complete a block; repeat for four blocks.

PIECING THE TOP
Step 1. Join two blocks with three D strips to make a block row as shown in Figure 5; repeat for two block rows.

Figure 5
Join 2 blocks with 3 D strips to make a block row.

Step 2. Join three F and two E strips with right sides together along length referring to Figure 6 for positioning of strips; press. Subcut strip set into three $1^{1}/_{4}$" segments, again referring to Figure 6.

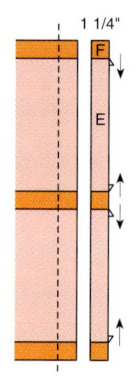

Figure 6
Join 3 F and 2 E strips with right sides together along length; press. Subcut strip set into three 1 1/4" segments.

Fanciful Daisies
Placement Diagram
18 1/4" x 18 1/4"

Step 3. Join the block rows with the E-F segments as shown in Figure 7; press.

Figure 7
Join the block rows with the E-F segments.

Step 4. Sew an H strip to two opposite sides of the pieced center; press seams toward strips.

Step 5. Sew an I square to each end of each remaining H strip; press seams toward I. Sew the H-I strips to the remaining sides of the pieced center to complete the top; press seams toward strips.

FINISHING
Step 1. Press quilt top on both sides; check for proper seam pressing and trim all loose threads.

Step 2. Mark top for quilting. *Note: The quilt shown was hand-quilted in an echo design around flower motifs, in*

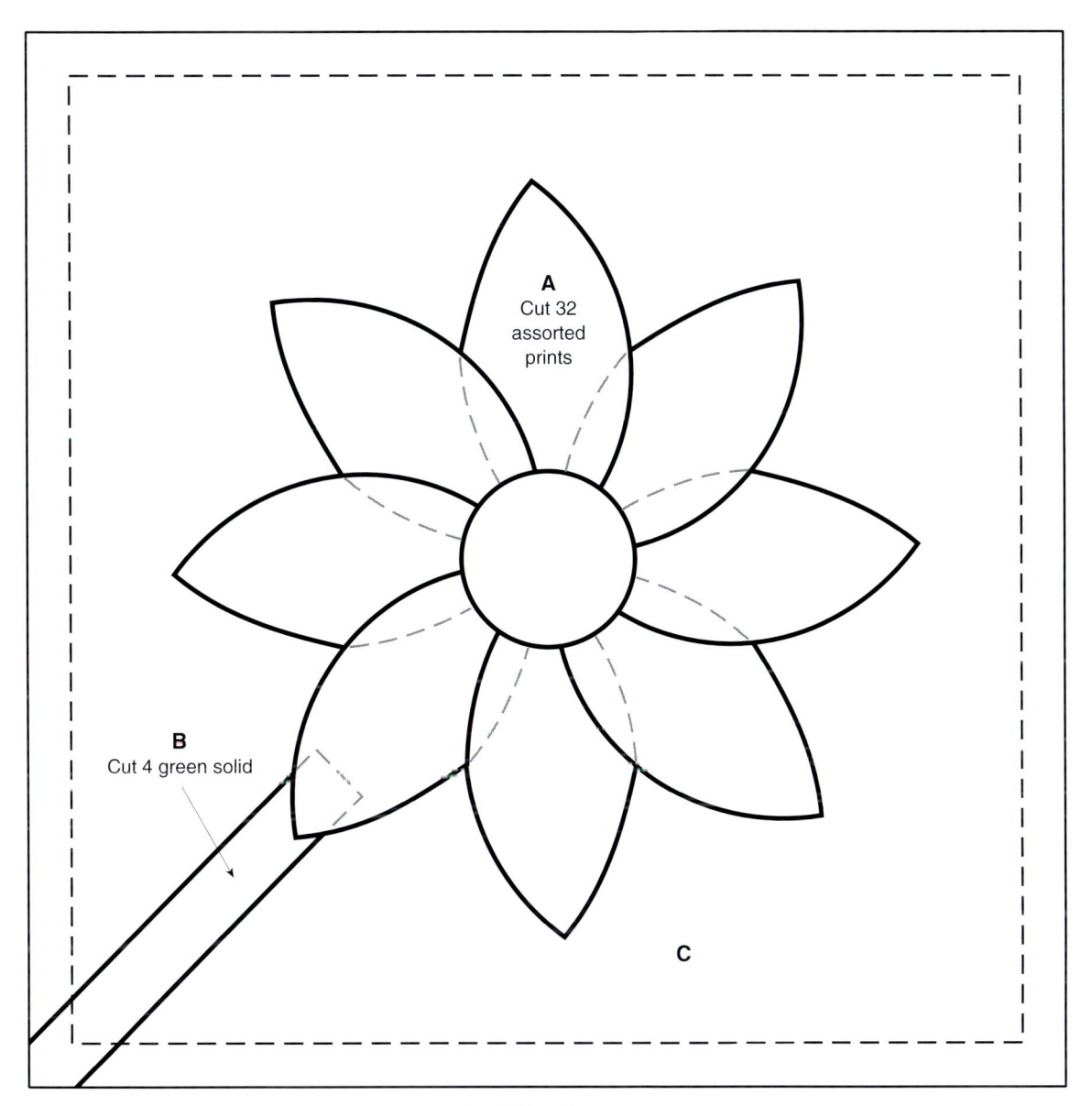

Full-Size Pattern
Trace on paper

A
Cut 32 assorted prints

B
Cut 4 green solid

C

G
Cut 4 orange solid

the ditch of seams and in an X pattern in the F squares using cream quilting thread.

Step 3. Sandwich batting between the stitched top and the backing piece; pin or baste layers together to hold. Quilt as desired by hand or machine.

Step 4. When quilting is complete, trim batting and backing fabric even with raw edges of quilt top.

Step 5. Bind edges with 1"-wide green solid prepared binding strips referring to Binding Your Quilt on page 36. ❖

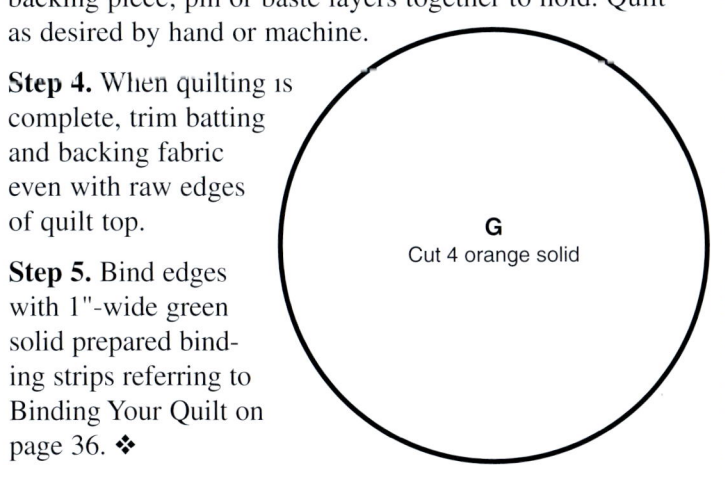

Illustrated Guide to Scrap Miniature Magic **101**

Fans

The flip-and-sew method was used to make the angled fan sections on the tiny fan blocks.

PROJECT SPECIFICATIONS

Skill Level: All levels
Quilt Size: 14" x 18¼"
Block Size: 3" x 3"
Number of Blocks: 6
Techniques: Flip-and-sew, quick-cut triangle, diagonal block setting and borders with cornerstones

Fan
3" x 3" Block

MATERIALS

- 8" x 10" rectangle each 6 different fabrics for pieces A–F
- 4" x 9" rectangle purple print
- 8" x 8" square floral print
- 12" x 14" rectangle mauve print
- 14" x 15" rectangle red print
- ⅛ yard pink solid for binding
- 16" x 20½" lightweight batting
- 17" x 21½" backing
- Neutral color all-purpose thread
- White quilting thread
- Basic sewing tools and supplies

CUTTING

Step 1. Cut three 2⅜" x 2⅜" purple print G squares. Cut each square in half on one diagonal to make G triangles as shown in Figure 1.

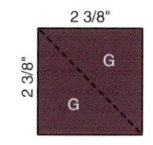

Figure 1
Cut each square in half on 1 diagonal to make G triangles.

Step 2. Cut two 5½" x 5½" H squares, two 3½" x 3½" I squares and two 3" x 3" J squares mauve print. Cut each H square in half on both diagonals to make H triangles as shown in Figure 2. Cut each J square in half on one diagonal to make J triangles as shown in Figure 3.

Step 3. Cut two 3" x 13¼" K strips and two 3" x 9" L strips red print.

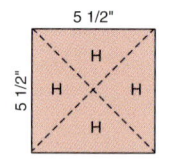

Figure 2
Cut each H square in half on both diagonals to make H triangles.

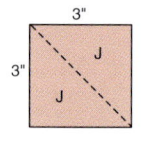

Figure 3
Cut each J square in half on 1 diagonal to make J triangles.

Step 4. Cut four 3" x 3" M floral print squares.

Step 5. Cut 1"-wide strips pink solid and join to create a 73" binding strip referring to Binding Your Quilt on page 36.

PIECING BLOCKS

Note: Use a ¼" seam allowance; press seams before trimming. Press all seams in the direction of small arrows shown on figure drawings.

Step 1. Make six copies of the paper-piecing pattern. Prepare fabric pieces and complete six Fan blocks referring to Machine Paper-Foundation Piecing on page 38.

Step 2. Stitch a G triangle to the corner of each pieced section as shown in Figure 4.; trim excess layers away from underneath G to complete the Fan blocks.

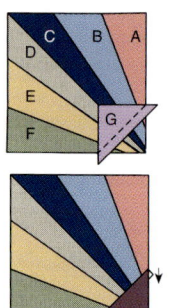

Figure 4
Stitch a G triangle to the corner of a pieced section.

102 *Master Quilter's Workshop*

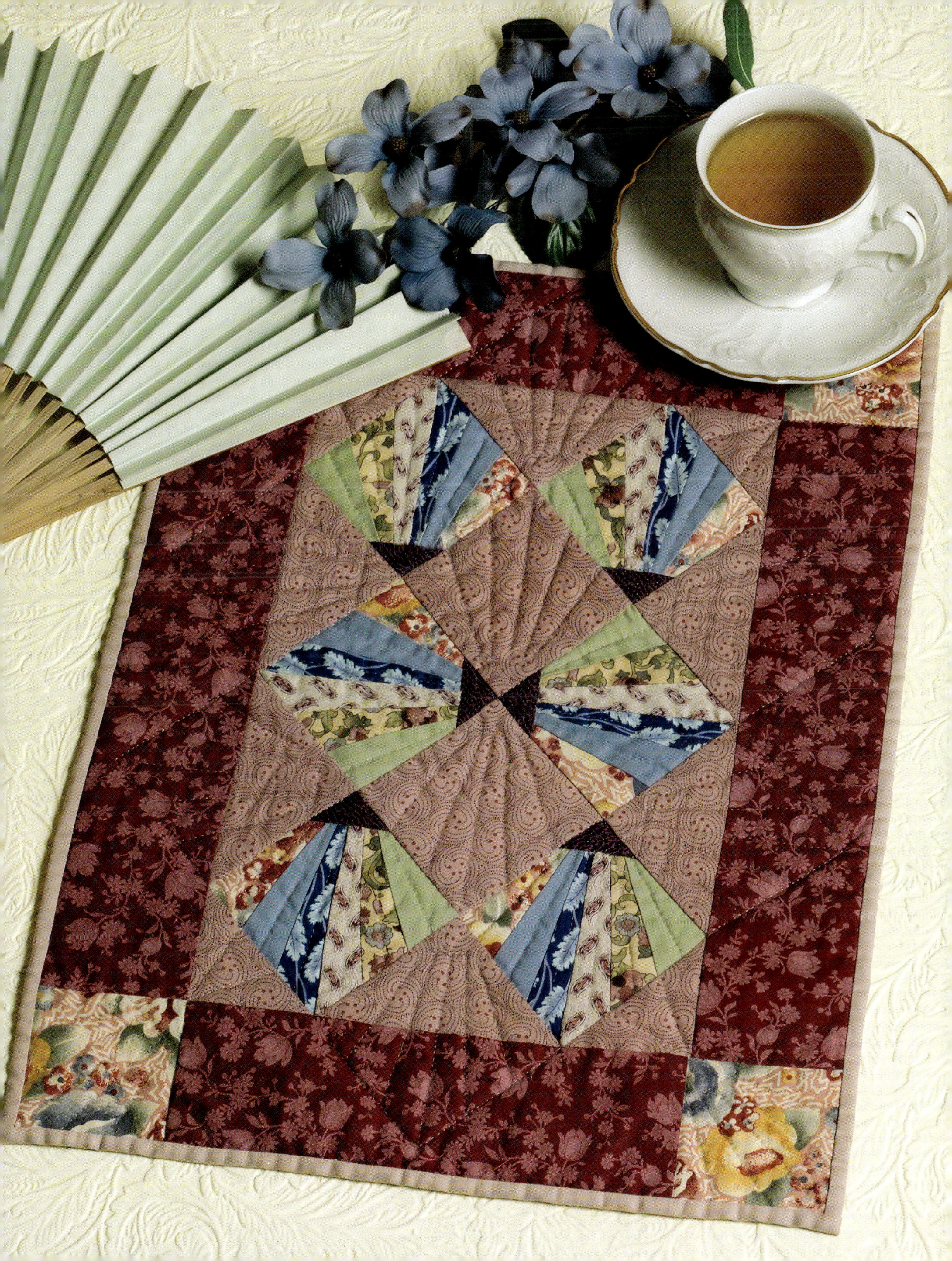

PIECING THE TOP

Step 1. Arrange the Fan blocks with H, I and J as shown in Figure 5; join in diagonal rows. Join rows and add J to corners, again referring to Figure 5 for positioning; press seams in one direction. Remove paper backing from blocks.

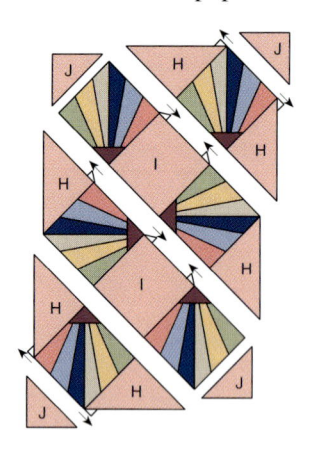

Figure 5
Arrange the Fan Blocks with H, I and J.

Step 2. Sew L to the top and bottom of the pieced center; press seams toward L.

Step 3. Sew an M square to each end of each K strip; press seams toward M. Sew a K/M strip to opposite long sides of the pieced center; press seams toward K/M.

FINISHING

Step 1. Press quilt top on both sides; check for proper seam pressing and trim all loose threads.

Step 2. Mark top for quilting. *Note: The quilt shown was hand-quilted through the center of each fan piece, in the ditch of seams and in an echo of the fan block in the setting pieces and borders using white quilting thread.*

Step 3. Sandwich batting between the stitched top and the backing piece; pin or baste layers together to hold. Quilt as desired by hand or machine.

Step 4. When quilting is complete, trim batting and backing fabric even with raw edges of quilt top.

Step 5. Bind edges with 1"-wide pink solid prepared binding strips referring to Binding Your Quilt on page 36. ❖

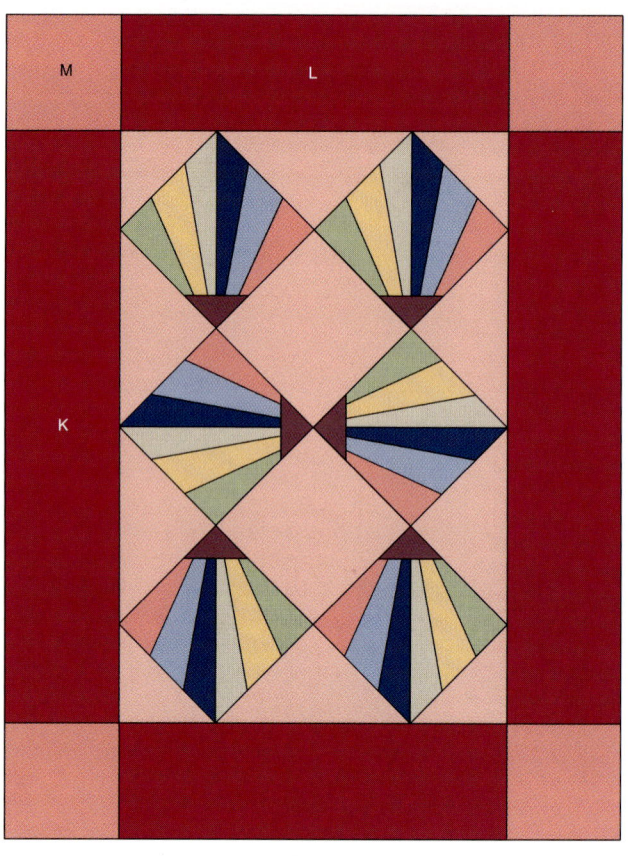

Fans
Placement Diagram
14" x 18 1/4"

Helpful Hints for Miniature Quiltmaking

- Use a fine thread for hand quilting and strive for evenly spaced, small stitches.
- Cut binding strips 1" wide; 1 1/16" wide for woven fabric, such as homespun.
- For pucker-free binding, use a sewing machine with an even-feed, walking foot.
- Turn under one long edge of the binding 1/4" and press. Sew binding to quilt top with right sides together, turn to the backside and hand-stitch in place.
- Choose to bind each edge separately or in one continuous seam.
- Use lightweight batting. Try 80 percent cotton/20 percent polyester mix or 100 percent cotton for a traditional look. Use of polyester batting results in a puffier look.
- Sign and date the quilt. Keep away from sunlight. Shake to remove dust. If necessary, wash with Orvus paste in cold water.

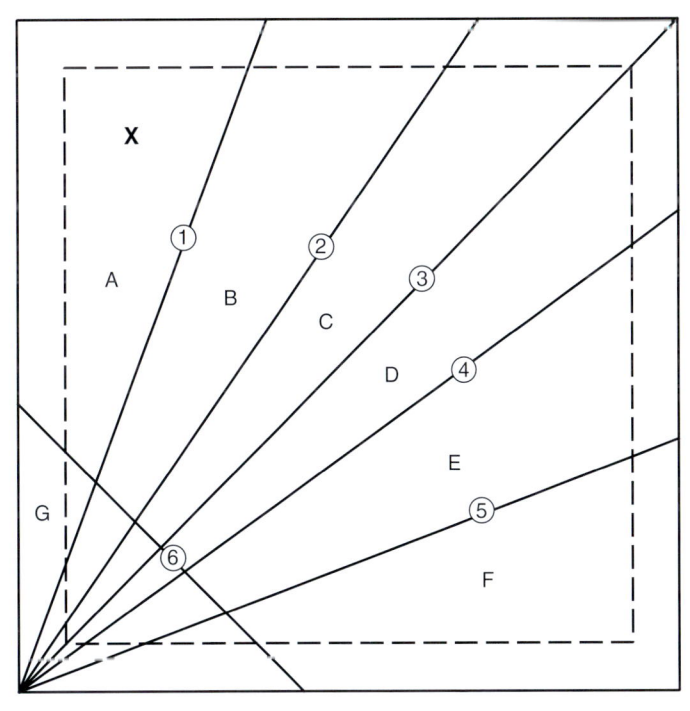

Fan Paper-Piecing Pattern
Make 6 copies

Illustrated Guide to Scrap Miniature Magic **105**

3-D Sunbonnet Sue

Combine paper piecing, appliqué, stenciling and yo-yos to make this adorable wall quilt for someone special.

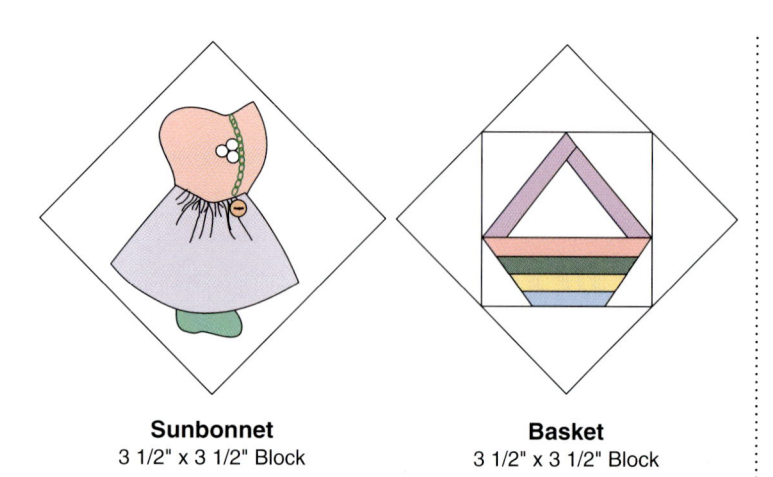

Sunbonnet
3 1/2" x 3 1/2" Block

Basket
3 1/2" x 3 1/2" Block

PROJECT SPECIFICATIONS
Skill Level: Intermediate
Quilt Size: 15 1/2" x 20 1/2"
Block Size: 3 1/2" x 3 1/2"
Number of Blocks: 8
Techniques: Stenciling, paper-foundation piecing, diagonal block setting, folded sashing, straight border with cornerstones and yo-yos

MATERIALS
- Scraps blue, yellow, green, pink and lilac prints for basket pieces
- 6 (2" x 2") squares pastel prints for yo-yos
- 6 (1 3/4" x 3 1/2") rectangles assorted white prints for dresses
- 6" x 18" rectangle pink print
- 13" x 18" rectangle green print
- 7" x 7" square green floral
- Fat quarter white solid
- 1/8 yard yellow print for binding
- Backing 18" x 23"
- Batting 17" x 22"
- Neutral color all-purpose thread
- Cream quilting thread
- 2 (4" x 4") squares wax-coated freezer paper
- Pink and green Stencil Magic paint
- 2 small stencil brushes
- Pink, yellow and green 6-strand embroidery floss
- Fabric glue stick
- 6 assorted 1/4" buttons
- 7 matching 1/2" buttons
- 18 (4mm) white pearls
- Basic sewing tools and supplies

CUTTING
Step 1. Cut six 4" x 4" A squares, four 2 5/8" x 2 5/8" B squares, two 6 3/4" x 6 3/4" C squares and two 3 7/8" x 3 7/8" D squares white solid.

Step 2. Referring to Figure 1, cut each B and D square in half on one diagonal to make triangles. Cut C squares on both diagonals to make triangles.

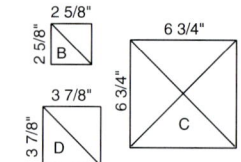

Figure 1
Cut B, C and D triangles as shown.

Step 3. Cut two 1" x 16" F strips and two 1" x 11" G strips pink print.

Step 4. Cut two 2 3/4" x 16" H strips and two 2 3/4" x 11" I strips green print.

Step 5. Cut four 2 3/4" x 2 3/4" J squares green floral.

Step 6. Cut 1"-wide strips yellow print and join to create an 80" binding strip referring to Binding Your Quilt on page 36.

PIECING THE BASKET BLOCKS
Note: Press seams before trimming.

Step 1. Using the paper-piecing pattern given for the basket and referring to Machine Paper-Foundation Piecing on page 38, make two Basket blocks, using B triangles on the corners as shown in Figure 2. Note that B is oversized and should be trimmed to the paper-foundation seams after stitching.

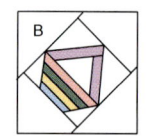

Figure 2
Sew oversize B triangles to the corners of the Basket block.

MAKING APPLIQUÉ BLOCKS
Step 1. Fold each A square to find diagonal centers; crease.

Step 2. Trace body stencil design on dull side of one freezer-paper square; reverse design and trace on second

106   *Master Quilter's Workshop*

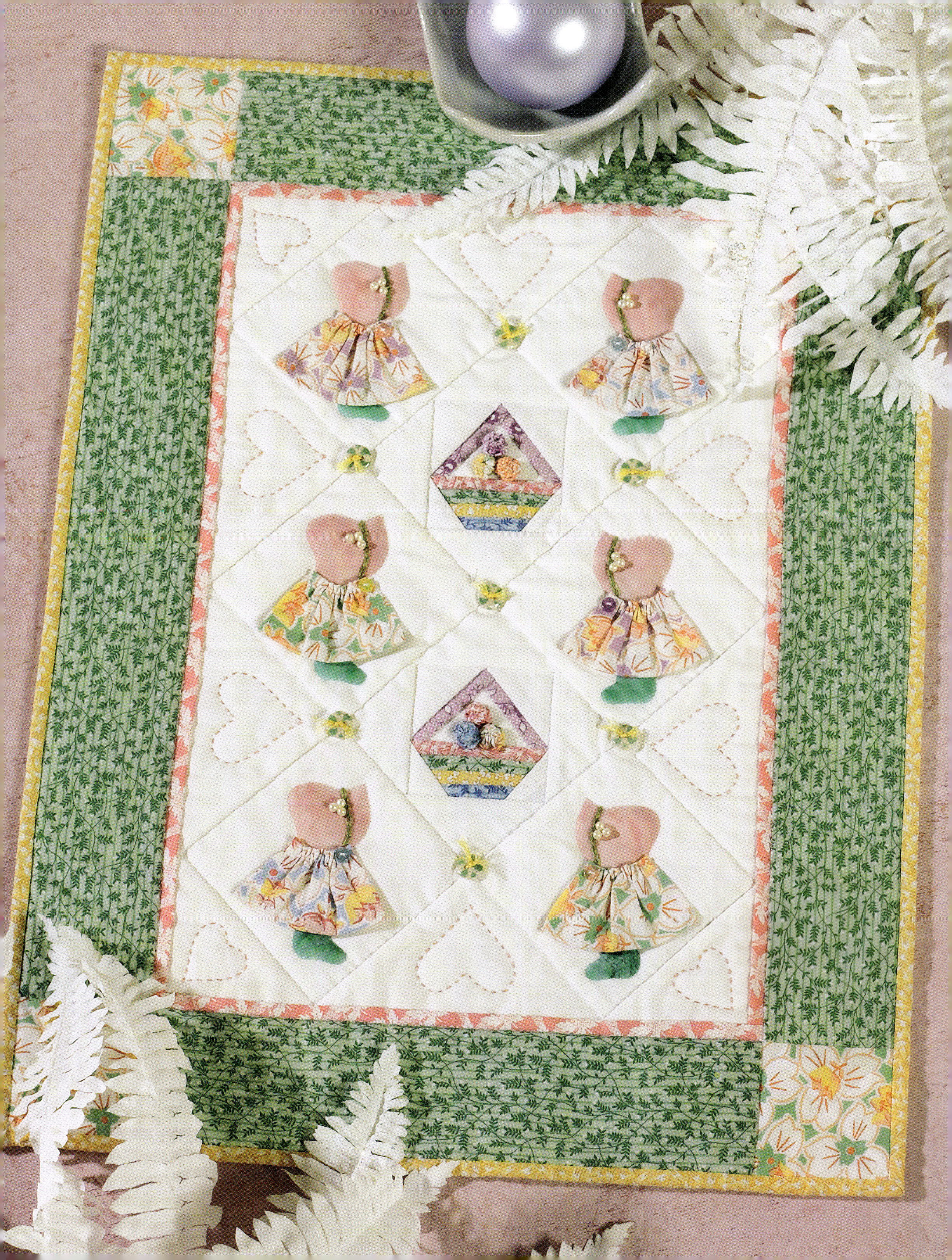

square. Cut out hat and foot, leaving the paper whole and removing shapes referring to Figure 3.

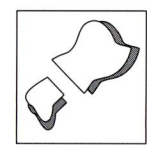

Step 3. With a dry iron set on medium, center and iron the waxy side of cut-out freezer-paper shape to the right side of an A square.

Figure 3
Cut foot and hat away from freezer-paper square.

Step 4. Gently stencil open areas using the stencil paint and brush in a circular motion using pink for hat and green for foot; let dry a little. Gently peel off freezer paper; repeat on six A squares using reversed motif for three. Let dry overnight.

PIECING THE TOP

Note: Use 1/4" seam allowance; press seams before trimming. Press all seams in the direction of small arrows shown on figure drawings.

Step 1. Arrange the stenciled A squares with the pieced Basket blocks and the C and D triangles in diagonal rows referring to Figure 4. *Note: The C and D triangles are oversized and will create extra background beyond the seams as shown in Figure 5.*

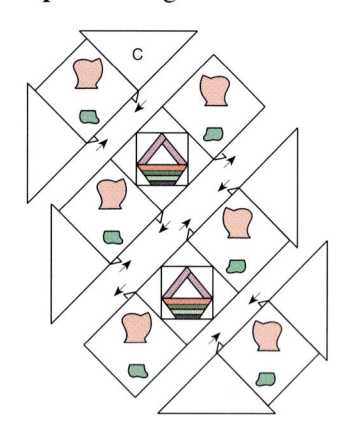

Figure 4
Arrange the stenciled A squares with the pieced Basket blocks and the C triangles in diagonal rows; join in rows.

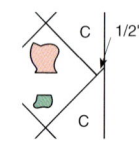

Figure 5
Oversize triangles result in this type of seam at the quilt edge.

Step 2. Join the blocks and triangles in rows, again referring to Figure 4; join the rows as shown in Figure 6.

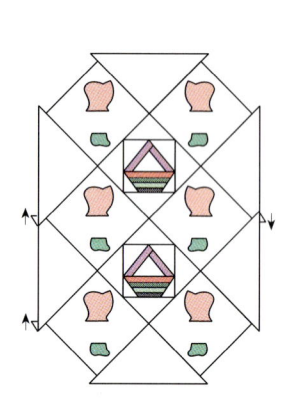

Figure 6
Join the rows as shown.

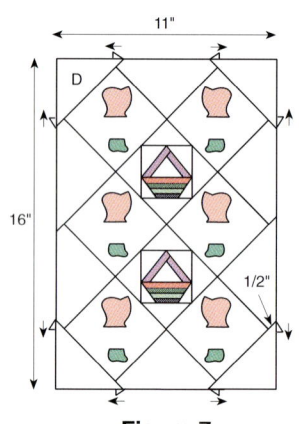

Figure 7
Sew D to each corner.

Step 3. Sew D to each corner as shown in Figure 7. Check quilt size; it should measure 11" x 16" including 1/2" beyond each block point.

Step 4. Fold each F and G strip in half along length with wrong sides together; press.

Step 5. Pin the F strips to opposite long sides of the quilt top with raw edges even. *Note: The folded edge of the strip will be toward the center of the quilt and will be left unattached on the folded edge on the finished quilt.* Stitch in place referring to Figure 8.

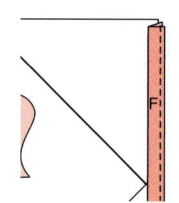

Figure 8
Stitch folded F piece to opposite sides of the quilt top.

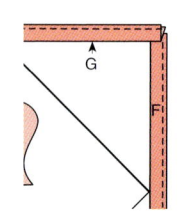

Figure 9
Pin and stitch the G strips to the top and bottom of the quilt top.

Step 6. Pin and stitch the G strips to the top and bottom of the quilt top referring to Figure 9.

Step 7. Sew H to opposite long sides of the quilt top; press seams toward H.

Step 8. Sew a J square to each end of each I strip as shown in Figure 10; sew a J/I strip to the top and bottom of the quilt center. Press seams toward J/I.

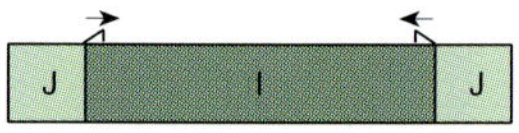

Figure 10
Sew a J square to each end of each I strip.

FINISHING

Step 1. Press quilt top on both sides; check for proper seam pressing and trim all loose threads.

Step 2. Mark top for quilting using heart pattern design given. *Note: The quilt shown was hand-quilted with the small heart design in D and the large heart design in C using 2 strands of pink embroidery floss and in the ditch of seams and an X through the J squares using cream quilting thread.*

Step 3. Fold under each 1 3/4" side of each dress rectangle 1/8"; hand-stitch in place. Repeat on one remaining side for hem edges. At the neck edge, turn under 1/8" and baste along edge; pull stitches to make a 1 1/4"-wide gathered top as shown in Figure 11.

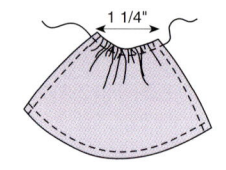

Figure 11
Pull stitches to make a 1 1/4"-wide gathered top.

Step 4. Hand-stitch dress pieces at the base of the stenciled hats. Using fabric glue, attach dress sides to the background, leaving bottom edge open.

108   Master Quilter's Workshop

Step 5. Using 2 strands of green embroidery floss, chain-stitch along detail line on each hat referring to block drawing for placement.

Step 6. Sandwich batting between the stitched top and the backing piece; pin or baste layers together to hold. Quilt as desired by hand or machine.

Step 7. When quilting is complete, trim batting and backing fabric even with raw edges of quilt top.

Step 8. Bind edges with 1"-wide yellow print prepared binding strips referring to Binding Your Quilt on page 36.

Step 9. Sew three 4mm white pearls in a cluster on each hat referring to the block drawing for placement.

Step 10. Sew a 1/4" button at each dress front neck edge.

Step 11. Sew a 1/2" button at block intersections using 6 strands yellow embroidery floss, tying a square knot on the top as shown in Figure 12. Trim floss ends to 1/2" after tying.

Step 12. Prepare template for yo-yo circle using pattern given; cut as directed on the piece.

Step 13. Make six yo-yos referring to Making Yo-Yos on page 38. Sew three yo-yos on each basket block referring to the Placement Diagram for positioning. ❖

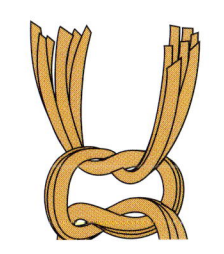

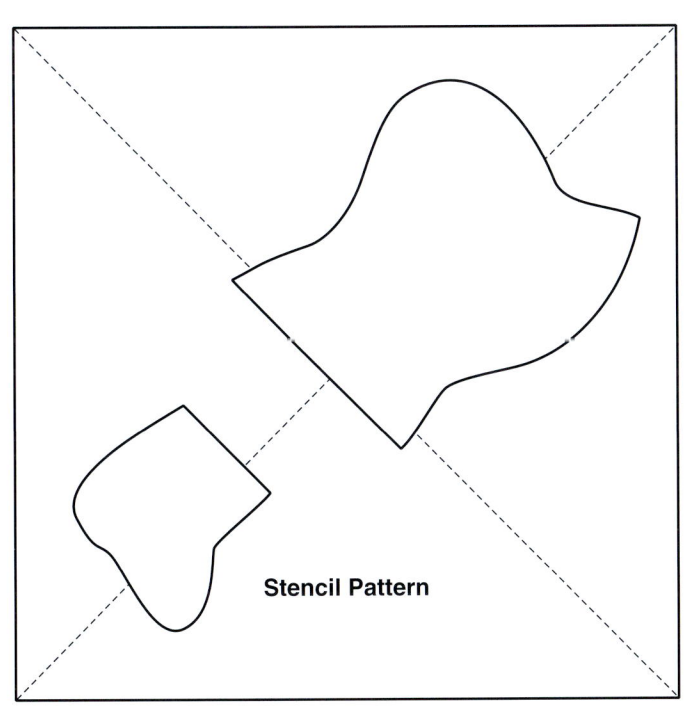

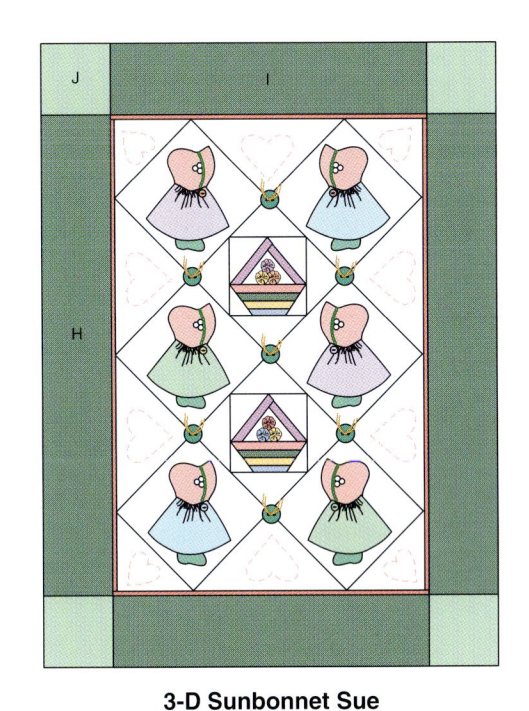

Figure 12
Tie a square knot using 6 strands of floss.

3-D Sunbonnet Sue
Placement Diagram
15 1/2" x 20 1/2"

Yo-Yo Circle
Cut 6 pastel prints

Small Heart

Large Heart

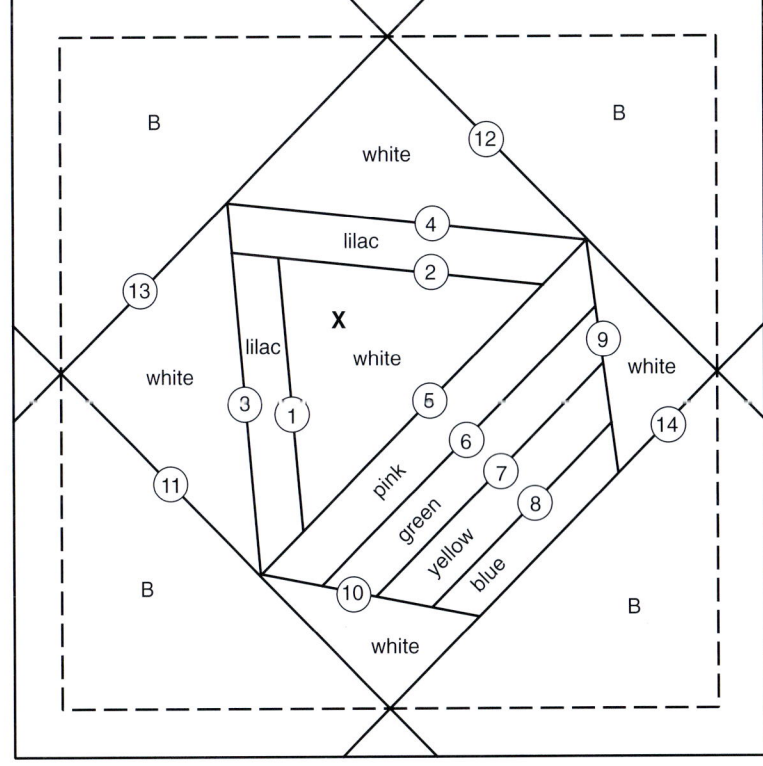

Stencil Pattern

Basket Pattern
Make 2 paper copies

Illustrated Guide to Scrap Miniature Magic

Nine-Patch Floral Garden

Made entirely with 1930s and 1940s vintage fabrics, this colorful quilt evokes thoughts of springtime.

PROJECT SPECIFICATIONS
Skill Level: Advanced
Quilt Size: 11¾" x 18½"
Block Size: 4½" x 4½"
Number of Blocks: 6
Techniques: Strip piecing, freezer-paper appliqué and yo-yos

Nine-Patch Floral
4 1/2" x 4 1/2" Block

MATERIALS
- 3" x 3" squares 6 assorted prints for yo-yos
- 3" x 9" rectangles of 4 assorted floral prints
- 4" x 12" rectangle dark green solid
- 7" x 10" rectangle violet solid
- 8" x 14" rectangle light green solid for G
- 12" x 17" rectangle peach solid
- ½ fat quarter rust solid
- Fat quarter blue solid
- ⅛ yard blue print for binding
- Backing 14" x 21"
- Batting 13" x 20"
- Neutral color all-purpose thread
- White quilting thread
- Pink and light green 6-strand embroidery floss
- 6 (⅜") orange buttons
- Freezer paper
- Basic sewing tools and supplies

CUTTING
Step 1. Cut one 1¼" x 9" A strip from each assorted floral print.

Step 2. Cut five 1¼" x 9" B strips, six 2¾" x 2¾" C squares and six 2¾" x 5" D rectangles blue solid.

Step 3. Cut two 1" x 12" E strips dark green solid.

Step 4. Cut six 2¾" x 2¾" F squares violet solid.

Step 5. Cut six 1¼" x 17" H strips and three 1¼" x 7" J strips peach solid.

Step 6. Cut three 1¼" x 17" I strips and three 1¼" x 7" K strips rust solid.

Step 7. Cut 1"-wide strips blue print and join to create a 69" binding strip referring to Binding Your Quilt on page 36.

PIECING & APPLIQUÉING BLOCKS
Note: Use a ¼" seam allowance; press all seams in the direction of small arrows shown on figure drawings.

Step 1. Sew one A strip between two B strips with right sides together along length as shown in Figure 1; repeat for two strip sets.

Step 2. Subcut each strip set into 1¼" segments, again referring to Figure 1; you will need 12 B/A/B segments.

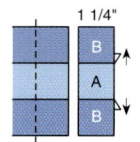

Figure 1
Sew 1 A strip between 2 B strips with right sides together along length; subcut each strip set into 1 1/4" segments.

Step 3. Referring to Figure 2, sew a B strip between two A strips with right sides together along length; subcut strip set into 1¼" A/B/A segments.

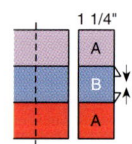

Figure 2
Sew a B strip between 2 A strips with right sides together along length; subcut strip set into 1 1/4" segments.

Step 4. Join two B/A/B segments with one A/B/A segment to make a Nine-Patch unit as shown in Figure 3; repeat for six Nine-Patch units.

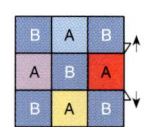

Figure 3
Join 2 B/A/B segments with 1 A/B/A segment to make a Nine-Patch unit.

Step 5. Sew C to a Nine-Patch unit and add D to make

110 *Master Quilter's Workshop*

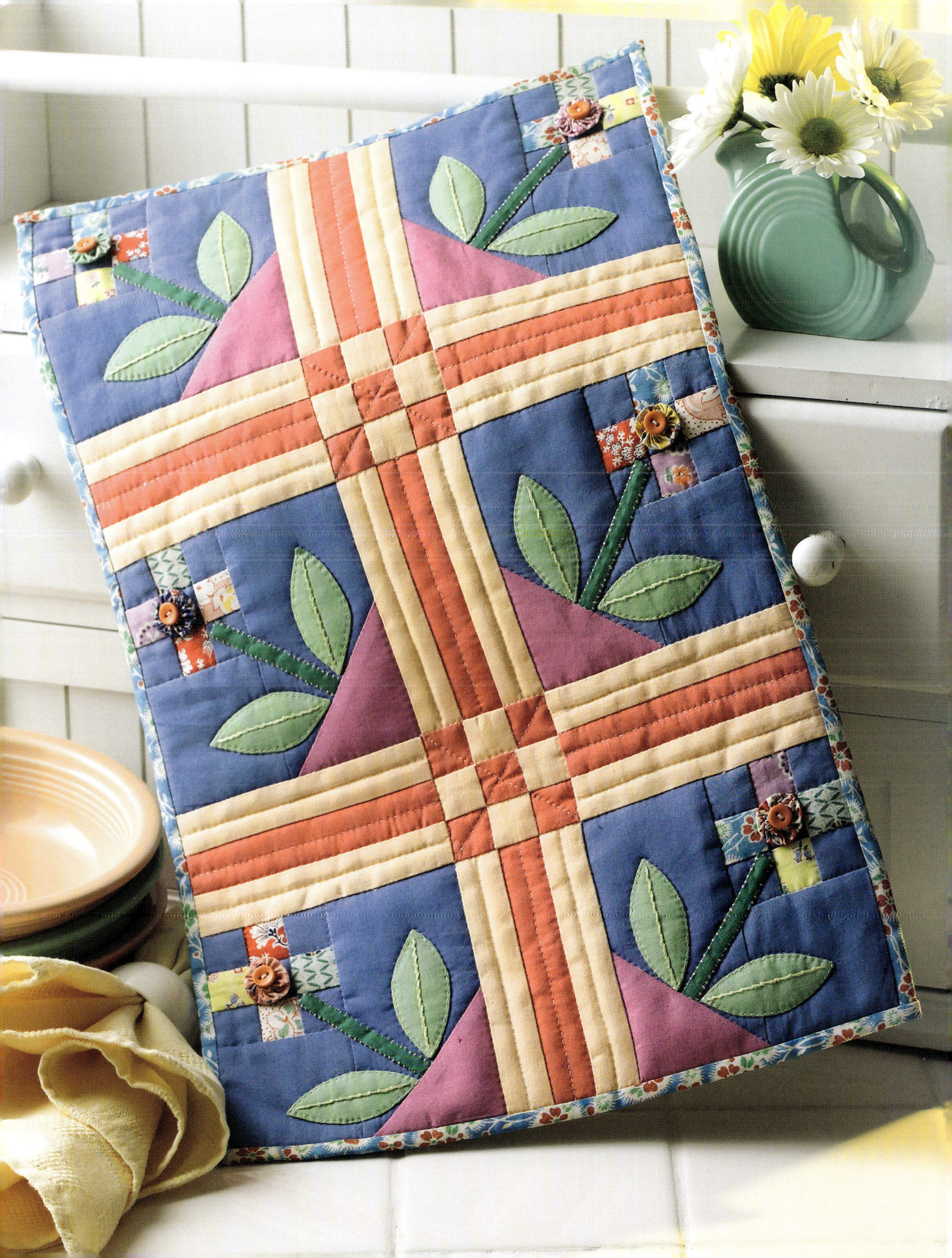

an X unit as shown in Figure 4; repeat for three X units. Repeat to make three Y units referring to Figure 5.

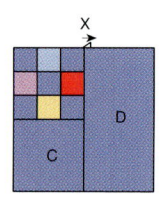

Figure 4
Sew C to a Nine-Patch unit and add D to make an X unit.

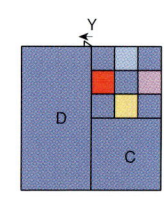

Figure 5
Make 3 Y units.

Step 6. Fold one E strip in half along length with wrong sides together; stitch with a scant 1/4" seam allowance to make a tube; repeat for two tubes. Trim seams to 1/8" as shown in Figure 6.

Figure 6
Stitch with a scant 1/4" seam allowance to make a tube; trim seams to 1/8".

Step 7. Referring to Figure 7, rotate seams to the center of each tube; press. Cut each tube into three 3 1/2" lengths for stems.

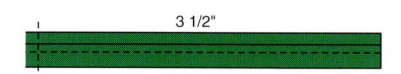

Figure 7
Rotate seams to the center of each tube; press. Cut each tube into three 3 1/2" lengths for stems.

Step 8. Trim one end of each tube to a point and fold it under as shown in Figure 8.

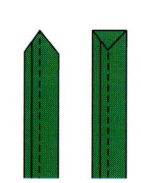

Figure 8
Trim 1 end of each tube to a point and fold it under.

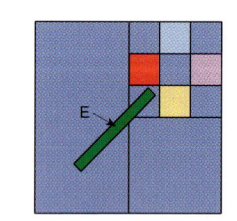

Figure 9
Center each E stem strip diagonally on each X and Y unit and into the first square of the Nine-Patch units.

Step 9. Center each E stem strip diagonally on each X and Y unit and into the first square of the Nine-Patch units as shown in Figure 9.

Step 10. Using 2 strands of pink embroidery floss, secure stem pieces in place with small, even overcast stitches as shown in Figure 10.

Step 11. Draw a diagonal line from corner to corner on the wrong side of each F triangle. Place a square right sides together on the corner of D of each Y block. Stitch on the marked line and trim seam allowance to 1/4" as shown in Figure 11; press F open. Repeat on the right corner of each X block referring to Figure 12.

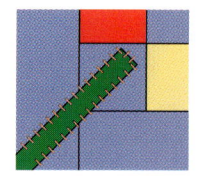

Figure 10
Secure stem pieces in place with small, even overcast stitches.

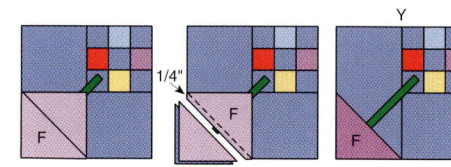

Figure 11
Sew F to the left corner of each Y block; trim excess layers.

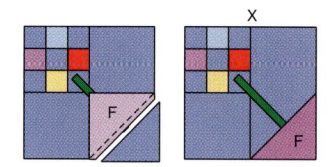

Figure 12
Sew F to the right corner of each X block; trim excess layers.

Step 12. Trace 12 leaf shapes on the paper side of the freezer paper using the pattern given. Iron the waxy side of the freezer paper to the wrong side of the light green solid G fabric.

Step 13. Cut out leaf shapes, leaving a 1/8" seam allowance all around when cutting.

Step 14. With paper side up and using the tip of the iron, press seam allowance on each leaf shape toward paper referring to Figure 13.

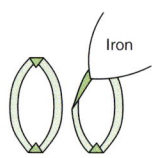

Figure 13
With paper side up and using the tip of the iron, press seam allowance on each leaf shape toward paper.

Step 15. Remove paper from each leaf shape. Pin or baste two leaves to each block referring to the block drawing for placement. Hand-stitch each shape in place using 2 strands of light green embroidery floss and a running stitch. Come up near the tip of each leaf and make one long stitch to the opposite tip; outline-stitch over the floss as shown in Figure 14 to complete blocks. *Note: Yo-yos and buttons are added after quilting.*

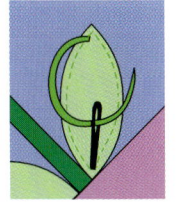

Figure 14
Come up near the tip of each leaf and make 1 long stitch to the opposite tip; outline-stitch over the floss.

PIECING THE TOP

Step 1. Referring to Figure 15, sew an I strip between two H strips with right sides together along length; repeat for three strip sets. Subcut strip sets into seven 5" segments.

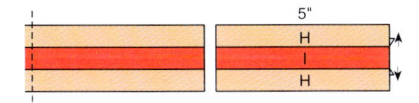

Figure 15
Sew an I strip between 2 H strips with right sides together along length; subcut strip sets into seven 5" segments.

Step 2. Referring to Figure 16, sew a J strip between two K strips with right sides together along length; subcut strip set into four 1 1/4" segments. Sew a K strip between two J strips; subcut strip set into two 1 1/4" segments, again referring to Figure 16.

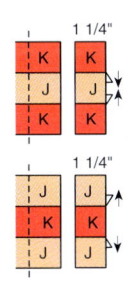

Figure 16
Join J and K strips to make strip sets; subcut into 1 1/4" segments.

Step 3. Sew a J/K/J segment between two K/J/K segments as shown in Figure 17; repeat.

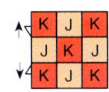

Figure 17
Sew a J/K/J segment between 2 K/J/K segments.

Nine-Patch Floral Garden
Placement Diagram
11 3/4" x 18 1/2"

Step 4. Join two H/I/H units with one J/K unit to make a sashing row as shown in Figure 18; repeat for two sashing rows.

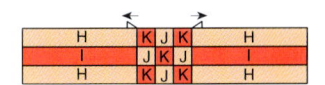

Figure 18
Join 2 H/I/H units with 1 J/K unit to make a sashing row.

Step 5. Join one each X and Y block with one H/I/H unit to make a block row as shown in Figure 19; repeat for three block rows.

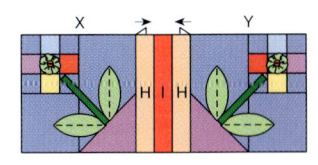

Figure 19
Join 1 each X and Y block with 1 H/I/H unit to make a block row.

Step 6. Join the block rows with the sashing rows to complete the pieced center referring to the Placement Diagram. Press seams toward sashing rows.

FINISHING

Step 1. Press quilt top on both sides; check for proper seam pressing and trim all loose threads.

Step 2. Mark top for quilting. *Note: The quilt shown was hand-quilted in the ditch of seams, through the center of the rust and peach solid strips and with an X through the center of the sashing Nine-Patch units using white quilting thread.*

Step 3. Sandwich batting between the stitched top and the backing piece; pin or baste layers together to hold. Quilt as desired by hand or machine.

Step 4. When quilting is complete, trim batting and backing fabric even with raw edges of quilt top.

Step 5. Bind edges with 1"-wide blue print prepared binding strips referring to Binding Your Quilt on page 36.

Step 6. Prepare six yo-yos using pattern given and referring to Making Yo-Yos on page 38.

Step 7. Center a yo-yo in each block Nine-Patch unit; hand-stitch in place. Sew a ³⁄₈" orange button in the center of each yo-yo to finish. ❖

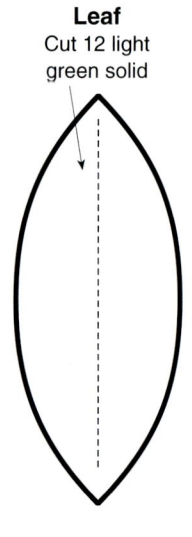

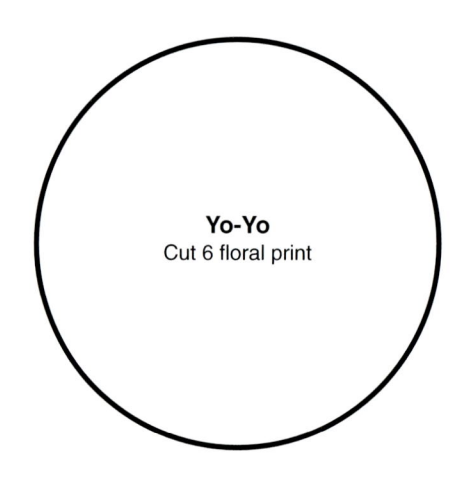

Leaf
Cut 12 light green solid

Yo-Yo
Cut 6 floral print

114   *Master Quilter's Workshop*

Kaleidoscope

The Kaleidoscope design can be made in planned color patterns or in a scrappy style like the one shown. Its versatility makes it a fun design for playing with fabrics.

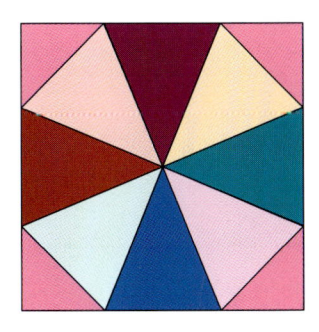

X Block
2 1/8" x 2 1/8" Block

Y Block
2 1/8" x 2 1/8" Block

PROJECT SPECIFICATIONS
Skill Level: All levels
Quilt Size: 13" x 15 1/8"
Block Size: 2 1/8" x 2 1/8"
Number of Blocks: 20
Techniques: Machine paper-foundation piecing and quick-cut triangles

MATERIALS
- 80 dark scrap 2 1/2" x 2 1/2" squares for D
- 80 light scrap 2 1/2" x 2 1/2" squares for L
- 1/2 fat quarter hot pink print
- 1/2 fat quarter turquoise print
- 1/8 yard blue print for binding
- 15" x 17" lightweight batting
- 16" x 18" backing
- Neutral color all-purpose thread
- Pink and blue quilting thread
- Basic sewing tools and supplies

CUTTING
Step 1. Cut 40 A squares 1 1/2" x 1 1/2" hot pink print. Cut each A square in half on one diagonal to make A triangles as shown in Figure 1; you will need 80 A triangles.

Step 2. Cut two 2 1/2" x 11 1/8" B strips and two 2 1/2" x 13" C strips turquoise print.

Step 3. Cut 1"-wide strips blue print and join to create a 64" binding strip referring to Binding Your Quilt on page 36.

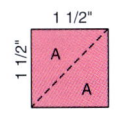

Figure 1
Cut each A square in half on 1 diagonal to make A triangles.

PIECING BLOCKS
Note: Use a 1/4" seam allowance; press seams before trimming. Press all seams in the direction of small arrows shown on figure drawings.

Step 1. Refer to Machine Paper-Foundation Piecing on page 38 for tracing and sewing instructions.

Step 2. Trace 20 copies each E and F sections using patterns given; complete each section using A triangles for corners and light (L) and dark (D) scraps as indicated on patterns.

Step 3. Join two E sections referring to Figure 2 to complete one X block; join two F sections to complete one Y block, again referring to Figure 2. Repeat for 10 blocks each X and Y.

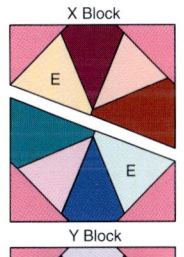

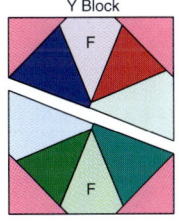

Figure 2
Join E and F sections to complete X and Y blocks.

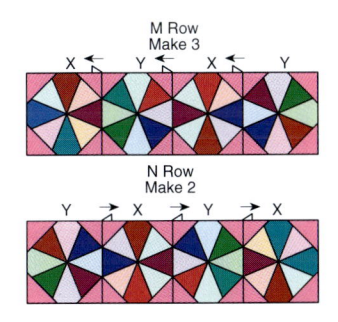

Figure 3
Make M and N rows as shown.

M Row Make 3

N Row Make 2

PIECING THE TOP
Step 1. Join four blocks to make a row, alternating X and Y blocks to make rows referring to Figure 3. Make three M and two N rows.

Step 2. Join the M and N rows, alternating rows as shown in Figure 4.

Step 3. Sew B strips to opposite sides of the pieced center; press seams toward B.

Step 4. Sew C strips to the top and bottom of the pieced center; press seams toward C. Remove paper patterns.

Illustrated Guide to Scrap Miniature Magic

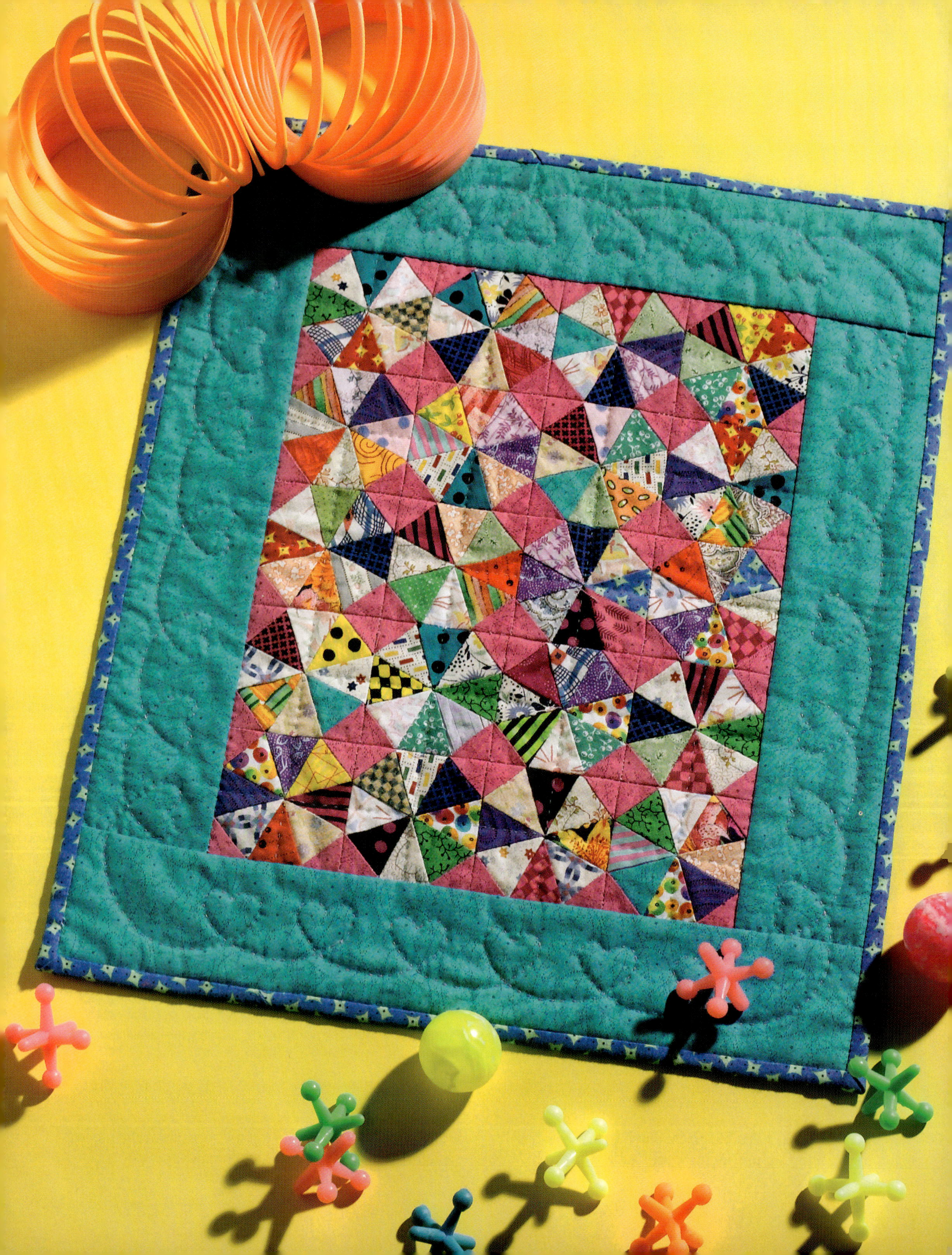

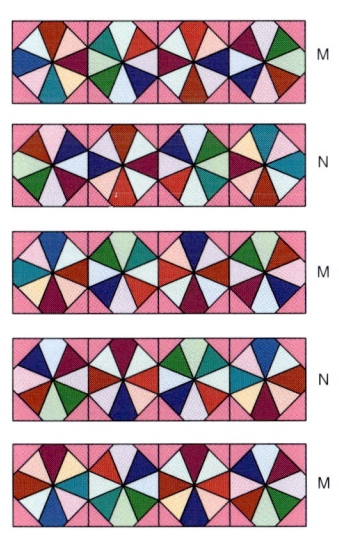

Figure 4
Join rows.

FINISHING

Step 1. Press quilt top on both sides; check for proper seam pressing and trim all loose threads.

Step 2. Mark top for quilting using border design given on B and C strips. *Note: The quilt shown was hand-quilted through the center of each block in vertical and horizontal rows using pink quilting thread and on the marked lines on B and C borders using blue quilting thread.*

Step 3. Sandwich batting between the stitched top and the backing piece; pin or baste layers together to hold. Quilt as desired by hand or machine.

Step 4. When quilting is complete, trim batting and backing fabric even with raw edges of quilt top.

Step 5. Bind edges with 1"-wide blue print prepared binding strips referring to Binding Your Quilt on page 36. ❖

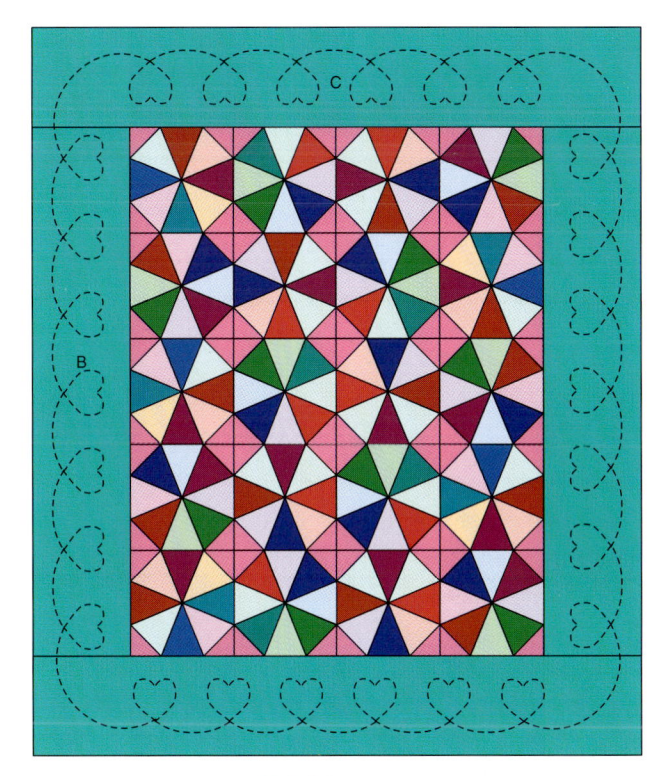

Kaleidoscope
Placement Diagram
13" x 15 1/8"

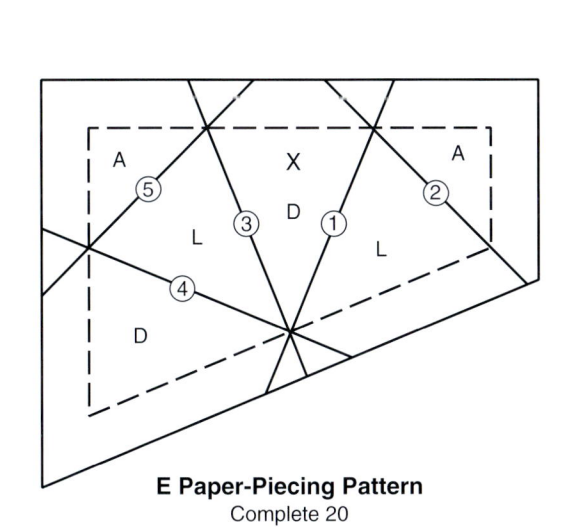

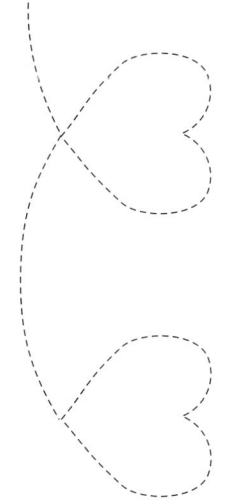

Border Quilting Design

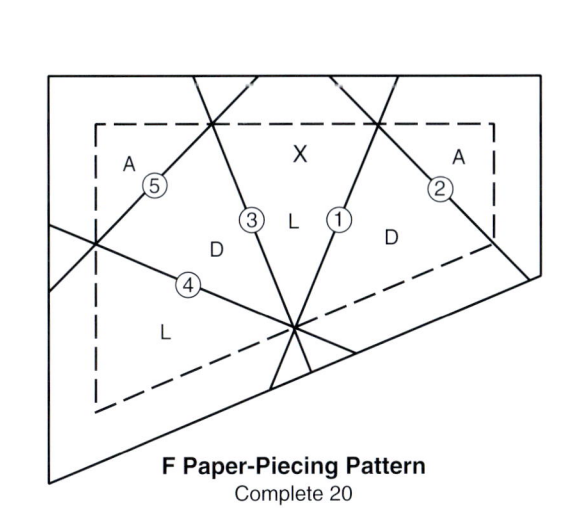

E Paper-Piecing Pattern
Complete 20

F Paper-Piecing Pattern
Complete 20

Illustrated Guide to Scrap Miniature Magic

Sunbonnet Sue & Sam

An old-fashioned look is perfect for Sunbonnet Sue and Sam appliqués, both old favorites of quilters.

PROJECT SPECIFICATIONS

Skill Level: All levels

Quilt Size: 13 3/4" x 15 1/2"

Techniques: Floss embroidery and straight borders

MATERIALS

- 1 rectangle each 4 3/8" x 5 1/4" yellow, blue, green and pink prints for A
- 2" x 2" square peach felt
- 6" x 12" rectangle gold print
- 13" x 16" rectangles pink-and-blue print
- 1/8 yard blue print for binding
- Backing 16 3/4" x 18 1/2"
- Batting 15 3/4" x 17 1/2"
- Neutral color all-purpose thread
- White quilting thread
- 4" x 14" piece HeatnBond Lite iron-on adhesive
- 1 rectangle each 4" x 5" red, green, blue and pink felt
- 1/8" x 3" piece blue satin ribbon
- Assorted colors 6-strand embroidery floss
- Fabric glue
- Basic sewing tools and supplies, large-eye sharp needle, dry iron and pencil

CUTTING

Step 1. Cut two 1" x 10" B strips and two 1" x 9 1/4" C strips gold print.

Step 2. Cut two 2 3/4" x 11" D strips and two 2 3/4" x 13 3/4" E strips pink-and-blue print.

Step 3. Cut 1"-wide strips blue print and join to create a 67" binding strip referring to Binding Your Quilt on page 36.

PIECING THE TOP

Note: Use a 1/4" seam allowance; press seams before trimming. Press all seams in the direction of small arrows shown on figure drawings.

Step 1. Join two A rectangles to make a row referring to Figure 1; repeat for two rows.

Step 2. Join the two rows to complete the pieced center, again referring to Figure 1.

Step 3. Sew B to opposite long sides and C to the top and bottom of the pieced center; press seams toward B and C.

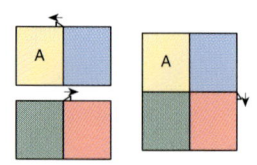

Figure 1
Join 2 A rectangles to make a row. Join the 2 rows to complete the pieced center.

Step 4. Sew D to opposite long sides and E to the top and bottom of the pieced center; press seams toward D and E.

APPLIQUÉ

Step 1. Place the iron-on adhesive on the patterns with paper side up; trace one of each on the iron-on adhesive.

Step 2. Turn iron-on adhesive over with paper side down; trace each design again for reverse pieces. Trace over these designs on the paper side of the iron-on adhesive. Cut out shapes, leaving a margin around each one.

Step 3. Fuse shapes to the felt rectangles as directed on patterns; cut out shapes on traced lines. Remove paper backing.

Step 4. Referring to Figure 2, make embroidered flowers on each Sunbonnet Sue referring to pattern for placement. Make three French knots and three lazy-daisy stitches using 2 strands of floss in your own color choices for each motif.

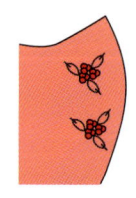

Figure 2
Make embroidered flowers on each Sunbonnet Sue.

Step 5. Place a little fabric glue on the 1/8" x 3" blue satin ribbon and place on the green Sam motif referring to pattern for placement; turn ends to the backside of the motif; glue in place.

Step 6. Make a chain stitch along placement line on the red Sam using 2 strands of floss in your own color choices and referring to Figure 3.

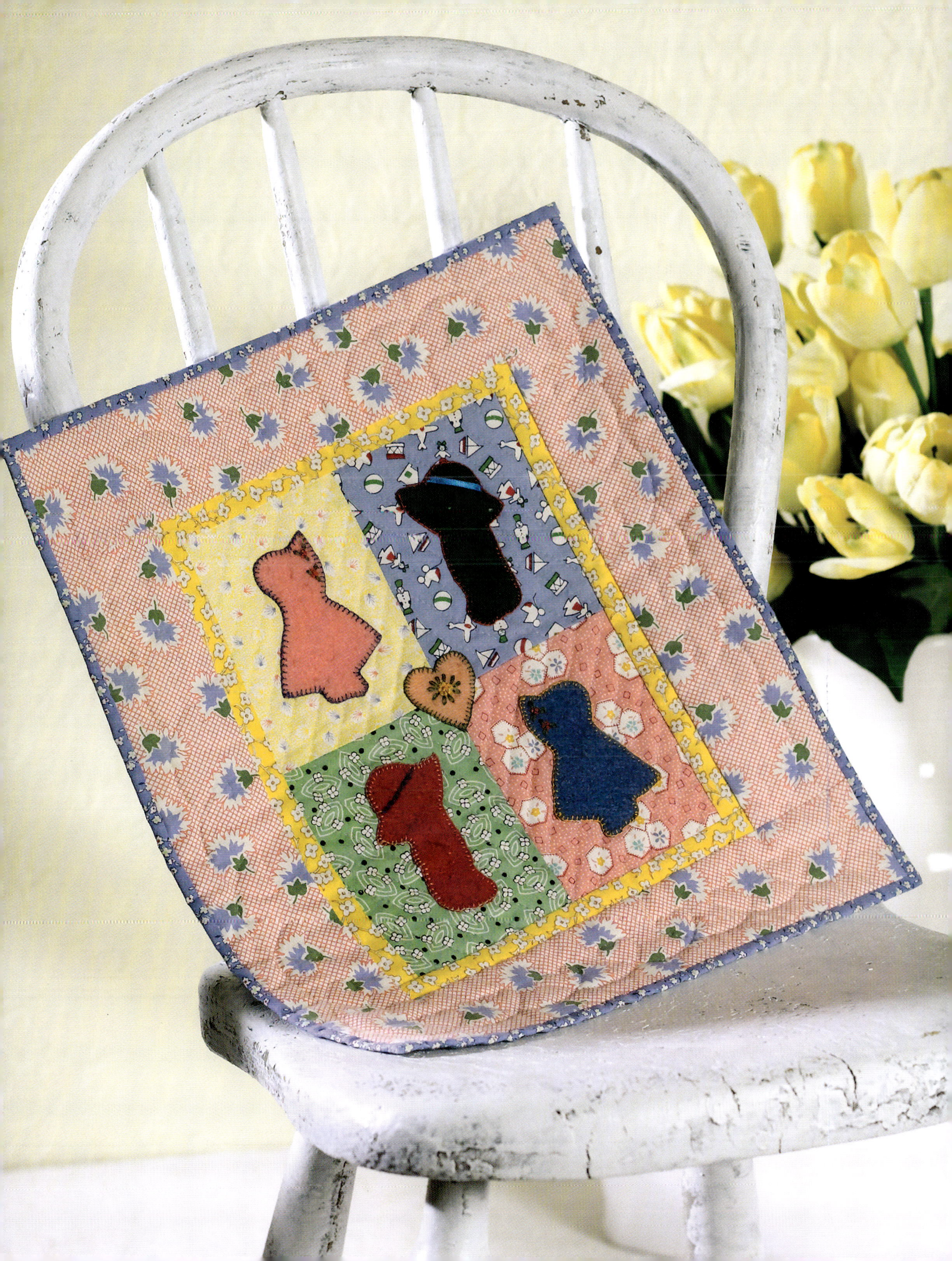

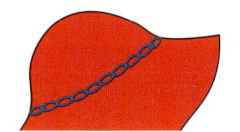

Figure 3
Make a chain stitch along placement line on the red Sam using 2 strands of floss.

Step 7. Trace the heart motif on the paper side of the iron-on adhesive; bond to the peach felt. Cut out shape on traced line; remove paper backing.

Step 8. Make lazy-daisy stitches for petals and fill the center with French knots using 2 strands of embroidery floss in your own color choices referring to the pattern for placement.

Step 9. Center and fuse the heart shape on the quilt center and the Sue and Sam motifs to the A rectangles referring to the Placement Diagram for positioning.

Step 10. Make hand-stitched buttonhole stitches all around each motif using 2 strands of embroidery floss. *Note: On the sample, the pink Sue is stitched with blue, the blue Sue with yellow, the green Sam with red and the red Sam with pink embroidery floss.*

FINISHING

Step 1. Press quilt top on both sides; check for proper seam pressing and trim all loose threads.

Step 2. Mark top for quilting, if using patterned design. *Note: The quilt shown was hand-quilted in diagonal lines spaced 1/2" apart in block backgrounds in alternate directions as shown in Figure 4, in the ditch of seams and using the heart quilting design given with Kaleidoscope on page 117 using white quilting thread.*

Figure 4
Mark blocks with 1/2" spaced diagonal lines.

Step 3. Sandwich batting between the stitched top and the backing piece; pin or baste layers together to hold. Quilt as desired by hand or machine.

Step 4. When quilting is complete, trim batting and backing fabric even with raw edges of quilt top.

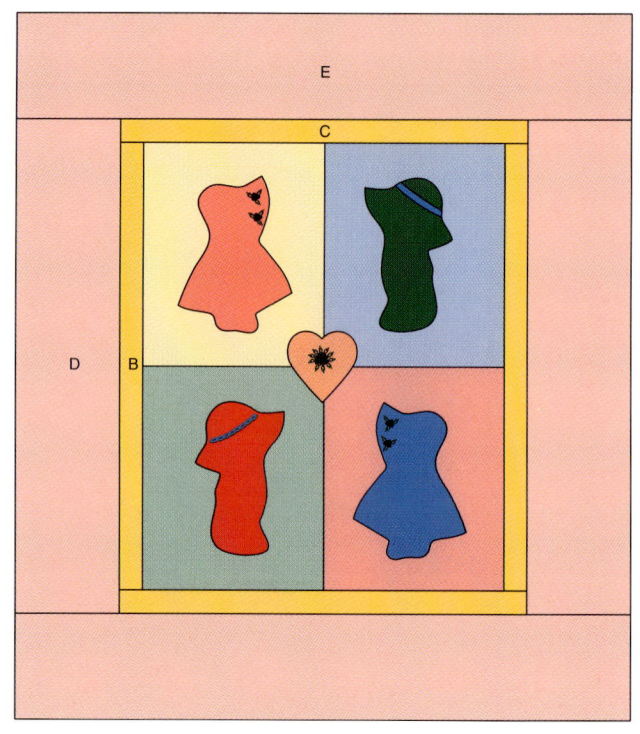

Sunbonnet Sue & Sam
Placement Diagram
13 3/4" x 15 1/2"

Step 5. Bind edges with 1"-wide blue print prepared binding strips referring to Binding Your Quilt on page 36. ❖

Sam
Cut 1 red felt;
reverse & cut 1
green felt

Heart
Cut 1
peach
felt

Sue
Cut 1 pink felt; reverse & cut 1 blue felt

Illustrated Guide to Scrap Miniature Magic

Log Cabin Pine Trees

Liven up simple Pine Tree blocks with Log Cabin strips and finish off with an interesting directional border.

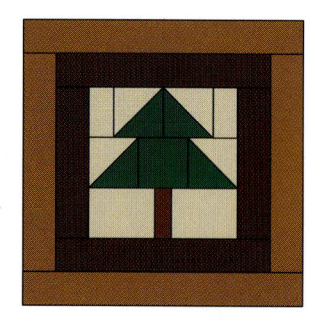

Log Cabin Pine Tree
4 1/4" x 4 1/4" Block

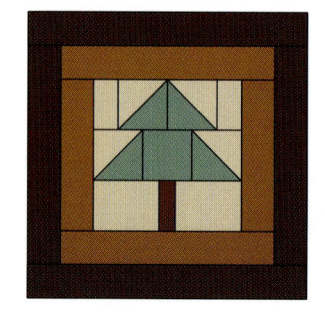

Center Log Cabin Pine Tree
4 1/4" x 4 1/4" Block

PROJECT SPECIFICATIONS

Skill Level: Beginner

Quilt Size: 8¾" x 17¼"

Block Size: 4¼" x 4¼"

Number of Blocks: 3

Techniques: Quick-cut triangles, strip piecing, straight-block setting and one straight border

MATERIALS

- 6" x 12" rectangle tan solid
- 5" x 5" square each 3 different green prints
- 1½" x 5" strip medium brown print
- 8" x 12" rectangle dark brown print
- 8" x 12" rectangle green-and-gold plaid
- 12" x 15" rectangle rust/black border print
- ⅛ yard black print for binding
- 11" x 19" lightweight batting
- 12" x 20" backing
- Neutral color all-purpose thread
- Tan quilting thread
- Basic sewing tools and supplies

CUTTING

Step 1. Cut one 1¼" x 7" A strip tan solid; subcut into six ⅞" A segments as shown in Figure 1.

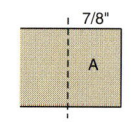

Figure 1
Cut the A strip into six ⅞"-wide pieces.

Step 2. Cut six 1⅝" x 1⅝" B squares tan solid and two 1½" x 5" C pieces.

Step 3. Cut two 1⅝" x 1⅝" D squares and one 1¼" x 1¼" E square from each of the 5" x 5" green print squares.

Step 4. Cut one ¾" x 5" F strip from medium brown print strip.

Step 5. Cut four 1" x 2¾" G strips, four 1" x 3¾" H strips, two 1" x 3¾" M strips and two 1" x 4¾" N strips dark brown print.

Step 6. Cut two 1" x 2¾" K strips, two 1" x 3¾" L strips, four 1" x 3¾" I strips and four 1" x 4¾" J strips green-and-gold plaid.

Step 7. Cut two 2½" x 13¼" O strips and two 2½" x 8¾" P strips rust/black border print.

Step 8. Cut 1"-wide strips black print and join to create a 60" binding strip referring to Binding Your Quilt on page 36.

PIECING BLOCKS

Note: Use a ¼" seam allowance; press seams before trimming. Press all seams in the direction of small arrows shown on figure drawings.

Step 1. Cut B and D squares in half from corner to corner to make B and D triangles as shown in Figure 2.

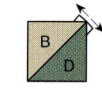

Figure 2
Cut B and D squares in half from corner to corner.

Figure 3
Sew B to D.

Step 2. Sew B to D as shown in Figure 3; repeat for three sets of four matching units.

Step 3. Join two matching B/D units with two A pieces matching center seams as shown in Figure 4; repeat for three matching sets.

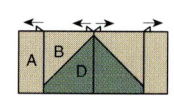

Figure 4
Join 2 matching B/D units with 2 A pieces.

122   *Master Quilter's Workshop*

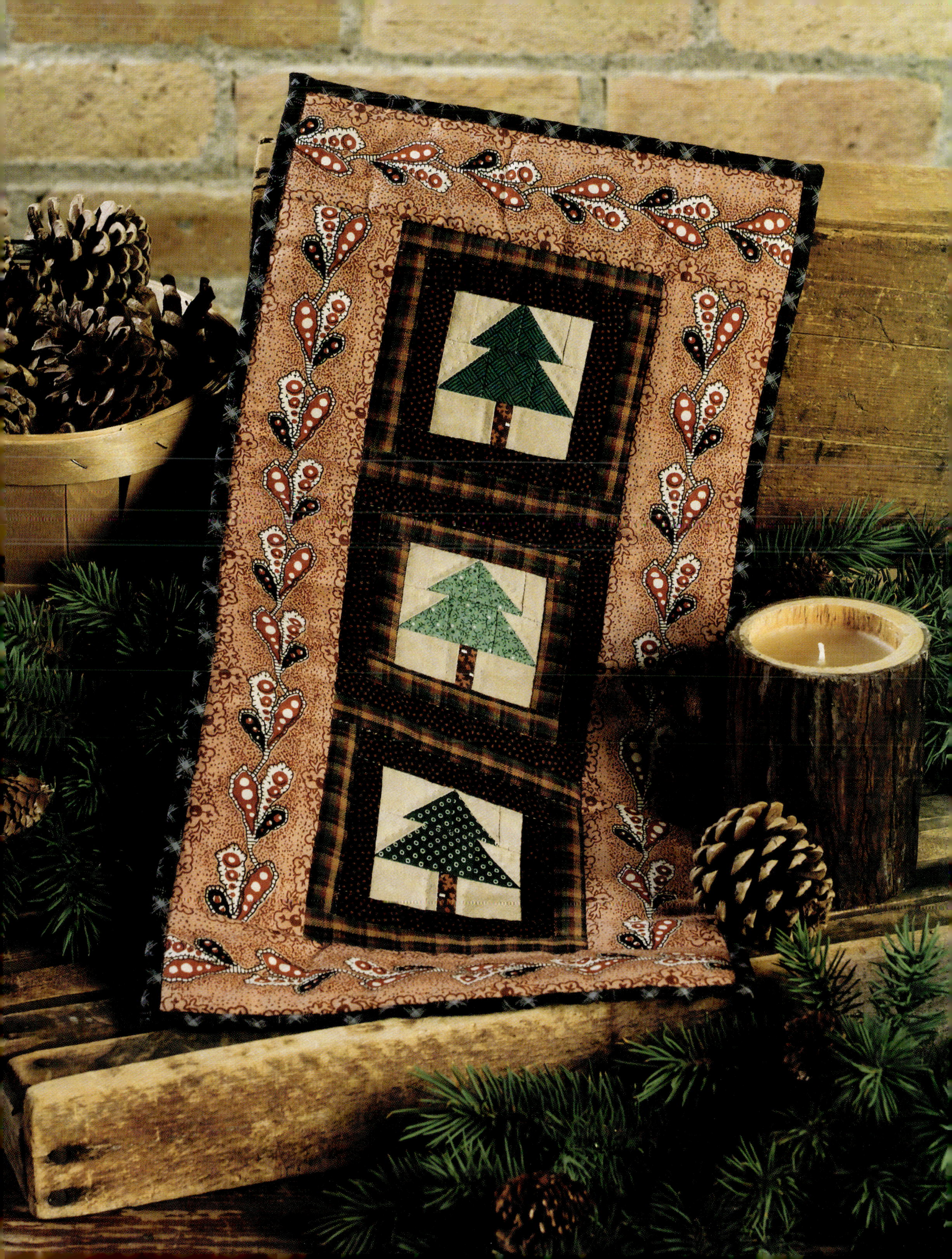

Step 4. Sew two matching B/D units to E as shown in Figure 5.

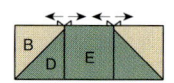

Figure 5
Sew 2 matching B/D units to E.

Step 5. Sew the F strip between two C strips with right sides together along length; subcut into three 1¼"-wide segments as shown in Figure 6.

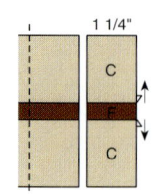

Figure 6
Subcut into three 1 1/4"-wide segments.

Step 6. Join the pieced segments as shown in Figure 7 to complete one Pine Tree center; repeat for three Pine Tree centers.

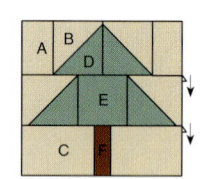

Figure 7
Join the pieced segments to complete 1 Pine Tree center.

Step 7. Sew G, H, I and J strips around two Pine Tree centers and K, L, M and N strips around the remaining Pine Tree center to complete the blocks as shown in Figure 8; press all seams away from block centers.

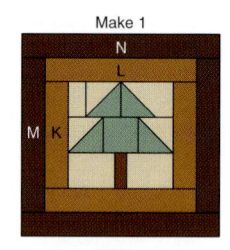

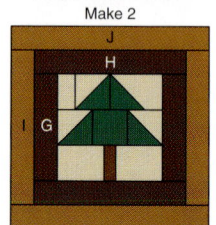

Figure 8
Sew strips to block centers to complete the blocks.

124   *Master Quilter's Workshop*

Log Cabin Pine Trees
Placement Diagram
8 3/4" x 17 1/4"

PIECING THE TOP

Step 1. Join the blocks in one vertical row referring to the Placement Diagram for positioning; press seams in one direction.

Step 2. Sew O strips to opposite long sides and P strips to the top and bottom of the row; press seams toward strips.

FINISHING

Step 1. Press quilt top on both sides; check for proper seam pressing and trim all loose threads.

Step 2. Mark top for quilting. *Note: The quilt shown was hand-quilted in the ditch of seams around blocks and between border strips and ⅛" from tree motifs using cream quilting thread.*

Step 3. Sandwich batting between the stitched top and the backing piece; pin or baste layers together to hold. Quilt as desired by hand or machine.

Step 4. When quilting is complete, trim batting and backing fabric even with raw edges of quilt top.

Step 5. Bind edges with 1"-wide black print prepared binding strip referring to Binding Your Quilt on page 36. ❖

Log Cabin Baby Dolls

Border a simple pieced center with Log Cabin strips and add faces to make the blocks for this cute kid's quilt.

Baby Doll
3 1/2" x 3 1/2" Block

Basket
3 1/2" x 3 1/2" Block

PROJECT SPECIFICATIONS
Skill Level: Intermediate
Quilt Size: 14 1/2" x 14 1/2"
Block Size: 3 1/2" x 3 1/2"
Number of Blocks: 5
Techniques: Strip piecing, quick-cut triangles, diagonal block setting, fusible ironing and straight border with cornerstone

MATERIALS
- 2 (3" x 3") squares pastel prints for yo-yos
- 5" x 8" rectangle tan solid
- 1/2 fat quarter white-on-white print
- 3" x 9" rectangle yellow print
- 32 assorted 7/8" x 4" print strips for logs
- 12" x 14" rectangle red plaid
- 4" x 12" rectangle dark blue print
- 4" x 4" square dark brown print
- 1/8 yard maroon print for binding
- Backing 17 1/2" x 17 1/2"
- Batting 16 1/2" x 16 1/2"
- Neutral color all-purpose thread
- Cream quilting thread
- Green and yellow 6-strand embroidery floss
- 4" x 4" square fusible transfer web
- 4" x 4" square blue felt
- Curly Hair
- Fabric glue
- 2 (1/4") purple buttons
- 4 (1/2") assorted color buttons
- Red and black Pigma fine-point pens
- 1/2 yard (1/8"-wide) pink satin ribbon
- Basic sewing tools and supplies, removable fabric marker and large-eye, sharp embroidery needle

CUTTING
Step 1. Cut one 1 1/4" x 6" A strip and two 3/4" x 6" B strips tan solid.

Step 2. Cut two 3/4" x 6" C and two 1 1/4" x 6" D strips, one 4" x 4" J square, one 6 1/4" x 6 1/4" K square and two 3 3/8" x 3 3/8" L squares white-on-white print.

Step 3. Cut four 1 3/4" x 1 3/4" E squares yellow print.

Step 4. Cut the following sizes from the 32 assorted scrap log pieces: four each 7/8" x 2 1/2" for F and 7/8" x 4" for J, and eight each 7/8" x 2 7/8" for G, 7/8" x 3 1/4" for H and 7/8" x 3 5/8" for I.

Step 5. Cut four 2 1/2" x 10 1/2" M strips red plaid.

Step 6. Cut four 2 1/2" x 2 1/2" N squares dark blue print.

Step 7. Cut 1"-wide strips maroon print and join to create a 66" binding strip referring to Binding Your Quilt on page 36.

PIECING LOG CABIN BABY DOLL BLOCKS
Note: Use a 1/4" seam allowance; press all seams in the direction of small arrows shown on figure drawings.

Step 1. To piece one block, join one each C, B and D strips with right sides together along length; subcut into 1 1/4" segments referring to Figure 1.

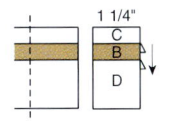

Figure 1
Join 1 each C, B and D strips with right sides together along length; subcut into 1 1/4" segments.

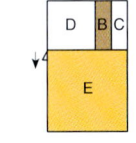

Figure 2
Sew a C/B/D segment to E.

Step 2. Sew a C/B/D segment to E as shown in Figure 2.

Step 3. Referring to Figure 3, join one each A, C, B and D strips with right sides together along length; subcut into 1 1/4" segments.

Illustrated Guide to Scrap Miniature Magic **125**

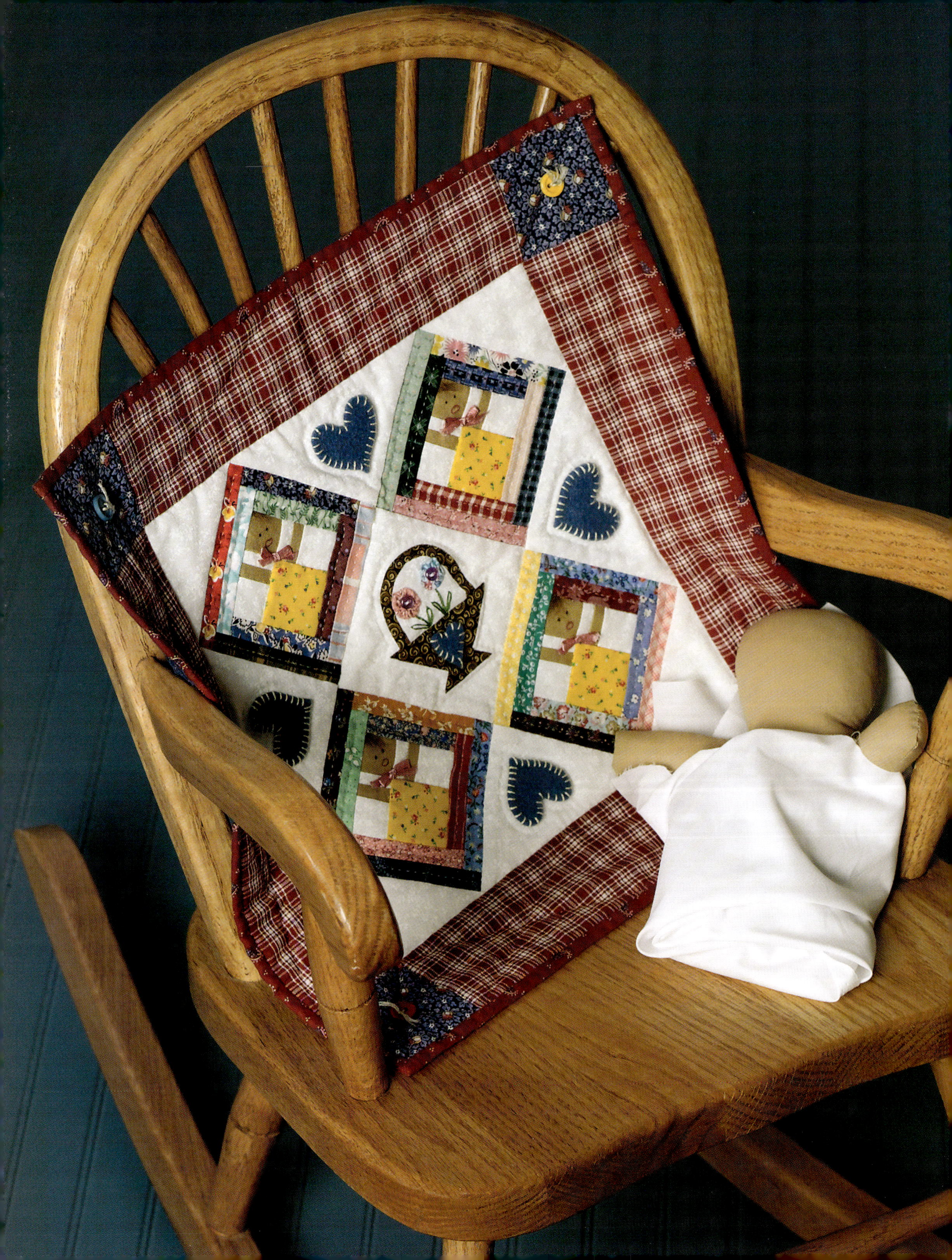

Figure 3
Join 1 each A, C, B and D strips with right sides together along length; subcut into 1 1/4" segments.

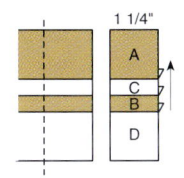

Step 4. Sew an A/C/B/D segment to the C/B/D/E unit as shown in Figure 4.

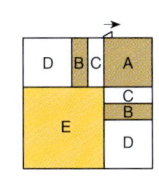

Figure 4
Sew an A/C/B/D segment to the C/B/D/E unit.

Step 5. Cut a short length of Curly Hair and glue to the A corner of the block as shown in Figure 5.

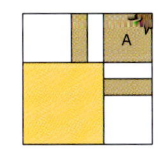

Figure 5
Cut a short length of Curly Hair and glue to the A corner of the block.

Step 6. Sew an F strip to one side of the pieced unit as shown in Figure 6. Sew G to the adjacent side of the pieced unit as shown in Figure 7. Continue to add strips around the pieced unit in alphabetical order to complete one block as shown in Figure 8; press seams toward strips after each addition. Repeat for four Log Cabin Baby Doll blocks.

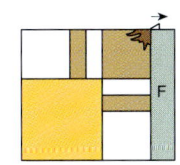

Figure 6
Sew F to 1 side of the pieced unit.

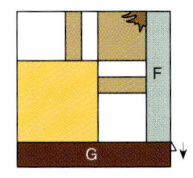

Figure 7
Sew G to the adjacent side of the pieced unit.

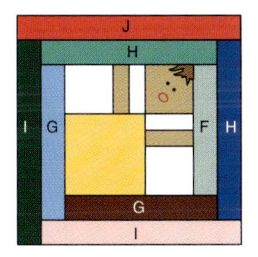

Figure 8
Continue to add strips around center in alphabetical order to complete 1 block.

Step 7. Transfer face patterns to A pieces using pattern given. Draw eyes using the black fine-point permanent fabric pen and the mouths with red fine-point permanent fabric pen referring to the block drawing for positioning.

APPLIQUÉING THE BASKET BLOCK

Step 1. Trace the basket pattern given on the paper side of the fusible transfer web; fuse to the wrong side of the wrong side of the 4" x 4" dark brown print square following manufacturer's instructions.

Step 2. Cut out shape on traced lines; remove paper backing.

Step 3. Center the shape on the diagonal of the J square; fuse in place.

PIECING THE TOP

Step 1. Referring to Figure 9, cut the K square in half on both diagonals to make four K triangles. Cut each L square in half on one diagonal to make a total of four L triangles.

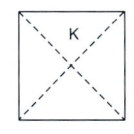

Figure 9
Cut K and L squares as shown.

Step 2. Arrange and join the pieced blocks with the appliquéd block and K in diagonal rows as shown in Figure 10.

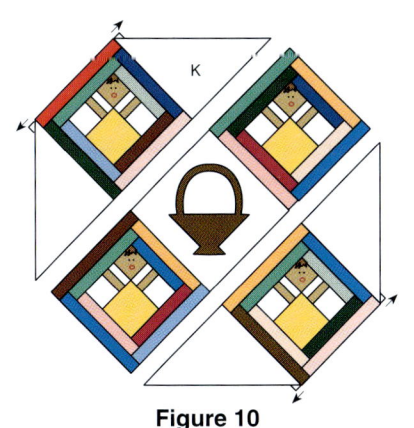

Figure 10
Arrange and join the pieced blocks with the appliquéd block and K in diagonal rows.

Illustrated Guide to Scrap Miniature Magic **127**

Step 3. Join the rows and add L to corners as shown in Figure 11 to complete the pieced center.

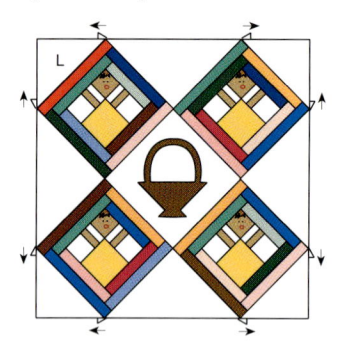

Figure 11
Join the rows and add L to corners.

Step 4. Sew M to opposite sides of the pieced center; press seams toward M.

Step 5. Sew an N square to each end of each remaining M strip as shown in Figure 12; sew an N/M strip to the remaining sides of the pieced center. Press seams toward N/M strips.

Figure 12
Sew an N square to each end of each remaining M strip.

FINISHING

Step 1. Press quilt top on both sides; check for proper seam pressing and trim all loose threads.

Step 2. Mark top for quilting if using patterned design. *Note: The quilt shown was hand-quilted through the center of each Log Cabin strip, 1/4" from seams in K triangles, outline around each large heart and the basket shape, with an X through the center of each N square and in a large double X meeting in the center of each M strip using cream quilting thread.*

Step 3. Prepare templates for large heart and small heart using patterns given; cut as directed on each piece.

Step 4. Using fabric glue, glue a large heart in the center of each K triangle and the small heart in the center of the basket base.

Step 5. Using 2 strands yellow embroidery floss, stitch an edging stitch around each heart shape referring to Figure 13.

Figure 13
Edge-stitch around each heart shape.

Step 6. Using 2 strands green embroidery floss, add lazy-daisy stitches for flower leaves and stem stitches for the flower stems referring to Embroidery Stitches on page 40.

Step 7. Prepare a template for the yo-yo circle using pattern given; cut as directed on template. Prepare two yo-yos referring to Making Yo-Yos on page 38.

Step 8. Stitch a yo-yo at the top of each stem in the Basket block. Sew a 1/4" purple button in the center of each yo-yo.

Step 9. Cut the 1/8"-wide pink satin ribbon in four 5" lengths. Tie a bow with each length; glue in place at the intersection of the A and E pieces. Trim bow ends.

Step 10. Sandwich batting between the stitched top and the backing piece; pin or baste layers together to hold. Quilt as desired by hand or machine.

Step 11. When quilting is complete, trim batting and backing fabric even with raw edges of quilt top.

Step 12. Bind edges with 1"-wide maroon print prepared binding strips referring to Binding Your Quilt on page 36.

Step 13. Stitch a 1/2" button in the center of each N square to finish. ❖

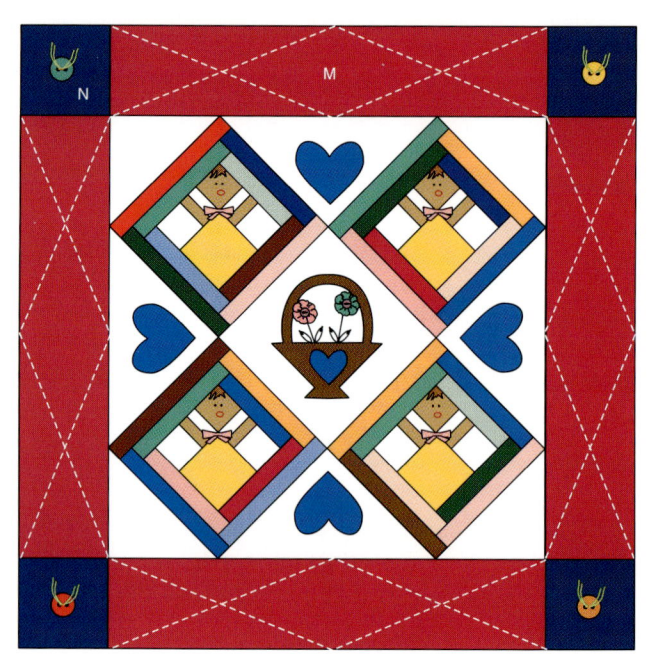

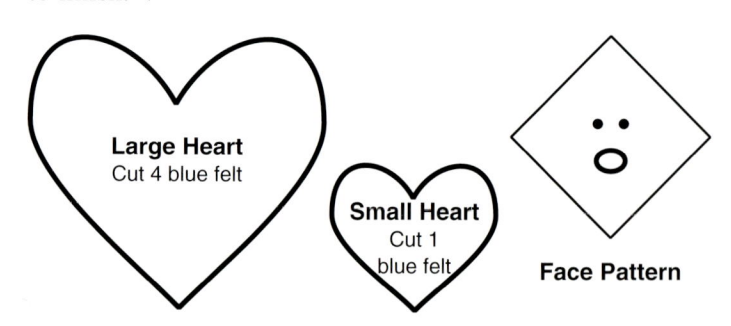

Log Cabin Baby Dolls
Placement Diagram
14 1/2" x 14 1/2"

Large Heart
Cut 4 blue felt

Small Heart
Cut 1 blue felt

Face Pattern

128 Master Quilter's Workshop

Basket
Cut 1 dark brown print

Circle
Cut 2 pastel prints

Illustrated Guide to Scrap Miniature Magic

Metric Conversion Charts

Metric Conversions

U.S. Measurement		Multiplied by		Metric Measurement
yards	x	.9144	=	meters (m)
yards	x	91.44	=	centimeters (cm)
inches	x	2.54	=	centimeters (cm)
inches	x	25.40	=	millimeters (mm)
inches	x	.0254	=	meters (m)

Metric Measurement		Multiplied by		U.S. Measurement
centimeters	x	.3937	=	inches
meters	x	1.0936	=	yards

Standard Equivalents

U.S. Measurement		Metric Measurement		
1/8 inch	=	3.20 mm	=	0.32 cm
1/4 inch	=	6.35 mm	=	0.635 cm
3/8 inch	=	9.50 mm	=	0.95 cm
1/2 inch	=	12.70 mm	=	1.27 cm
5/8 inch	=	15.90 mm	=	1.59 cm
3/4 inch	=	19.10 mm	=	1.91 cm
7/8 inch	=	22.20 mm	=	2.22 cm
1 inch	=	25.40 mm	=	2.54 cm
1/8 yard	=	11.43 cm	=	0.11 m
1/4 yard	=	22.86 cm	=	0.23 m
3/8 yard	=	34.29 cm	=	0.34 m
1/2 yard	=	45.72 cm	=	0.46 m
5/8 yard	=	57.15 cm	=	0.57 m
3/4 yard	=	68.58 cm	=	0.69 m
7/8 yard	=	80.00 cm	=	0.80 m
1 yard	=	91.44 cm	=	0.91 m

U.S. Measurement		Metric Measurement		
1 1/8 yard	=	102.87 cm	=	1.03 m
1 1/4 yard	=	114.30 cm	=	1.14 m
1 3/8 yard	=	125.73 cm	=	1.26 m
1 1/2 yard	=	137.16 cm	=	1.37 m
1 5/8 yard	=	148.59 cm	=	1.49 m
1 3/4 yard	=	160.02 cm	=	1.60 m
1 7/8 yard	=	171.44 cm	=	1.71 m
2 yards	=	182.88 cm	=	1.83 m
2 1/8 yards	=	194.31 cm	=	1.94 m
2 1/4 yards	=	205.74 cm	=	2.06 m
2 3/8 yards	=	217.17 cm	=	2.17 m
2 1/2 yards	=	228.60 cm	=	2.29 m
2 5/8 yards	=	240.03 cm	=	2.40 m
2 3/4 yards	=	251.46 cm	=	2.51 m
2 7/8 yards	=	262.88 cm	=	2.63 m
3 yards	=	274.32 cm	=	2.74 m
3 1/8 yards	=	285.75 cm	=	2.86 m
3 1/4 yards	=	297.18 cm	=	2.97 m
3 3/8 yards	=	308.61 cm	=	3.09 m
3 1/2 yards	=	320.04 cm	=	3.20 m
3 5/8 yards	=	331.47 cm	=	3.31 m
3 3/4 yards	=	342.90 cm	=	3.43 m
3 7/8 yards	=	354.32 cm	=	3.54 m
4 yards	=	365.76 cm	=	3.66 m
4 1/8 yards	=	377.19 cm	=	3.77 m
4 1/4 yards	=	388.62 cm	=	3.89 m
4 3/8 yards	=	400.05 cm	=	4.00 m
4 1/2 yards	=	411.48 cm	=	4.11 m
4 5/8 yards	=	422.91 cm	=	4.23 m
4 3/4 yards	=	434.34 cm	=	4.34 m
4 7/8 yards	=	445.76 cm	=	4.46 m
5 yards	=	457.20 cm	=	4.57 m